UNDER THE FLAG OF THE NATION

UNDER THE FLAG
OF THE NATION

Diaries and Letters of Owen Johnston Hopkins,
a Yankee Volunteer in the Civil War

EDITED BY OTTO F. BOND

OHIO STATE UNIVERSITY PRESS
Columbus

Frontispiece: Photograph of Lieutenant Owen Johnston Hopkins taken in October 1864, when he was twenty years old.

Library of Congress Cataloging-in-Publication Data

Hopkins, Owen Johnston, 1844–1902.
Under the flag of the nation : diaries and letters of
Owen Johnston Hopkins, a Yankee volunteer in the Civil War
/ edited by Otto F. Bond.   p. cm.
Originally published: Columbus : Ohio State University Press for
the Ohio Historical Society, 1961, in series: Publications of the Ohio
Civil War Centennial Commission, no. 1.
Includes bibliographical references.
ISBN 0-8142-0743-X (pbk. : alk. paper)
1. Hopkins, Owen Johnston, 1844–1902—Diaries.   2. Hopkins, Owen
Johnston, 1844–1902—Correspondence.   3. United States. Army. Ohio
Infantry Regiment, 42nd (1861–1864)   4. United States. Army. Ohio
Infantry Regiment, 182nd (1864–1865)   5. Ohio—History—Civil War,
1861–1865—Personal narratives.   6. United States—History—Civil War,
1861–1865—Personal narratives.   7. Ohio—History—Civil War,
1861–1865—Regimental histories.   8. United States—History—Civil War,
1861–1865—Regimental histories.   9. Soldiers—Ohio—Biography.
I. Bond, Otto Ferdinand, 1885–   . II. Title.
E525.5 42nd.H66   1998
973.7'471—dc21   98–12833
CIP

Cover design by Gore Studio, Inc.

The paper used in this publication meets the minimum requirements
of the American National Standards for Information Sciences—
Permanence of Paper for Printed Library Materials.
ANSI Z39.48–1992.

9 8 7 6 5 4 3 2 1

ACKNOWLEDGMENT

The editor acknowledges his indebtedness to his wife, Julia Hopkins Bond, for the use of her family archives, the factual data relating to her parents and their ancestry, and the identification of many of the personal references in her father's diaries and letters. Her research and encouragement have made this work possible and pleasant.

OTTO F. BOND

CONTENTS

UNDER THE FLAG OF THE NATION

INTRODUCTION

From these diaries and letters of a young soldier in the Union Army emerges a clear and unmistakable portrait of their author, a portrait as unique and revealing as a daguerreotype, as personal and intimate as a confession. It is in their revelation of an engaging and rare personality caught up in a life and death struggle of national import, as well as in their narration of the sequence and execution of military maneuvers, that these lines written one hundred years ago hold their present interest.

Indeed, Private Owen Johnston Hopkins still lives in that his unquenchable pride and patriotism, his defiant good humor, his deep-seated loyalty and attachment to family, friends, and comrades, and his unflagging zest for adventure and new experiences, are characteristic of his fellow soldiers of the twentieth century. They, too, have known the choking dust and drenching rains, the scorching heat and numbing cold, the aching muscles and utter weariness of unending maneuvers. With him they have felt the dread loneliness of the night watch, the *élan* of victory, the bitterness of defeat. They have shared the feeling of being isolated from one's own world, and have hoped for letters that did not come, or that coming brought no relief. And, like Private Hopkins, they have longed for an end to it all.

Again, in these pages, companies form for inspection or dress parade, entrain or embark for unrevealed destinations, break the monotony of camp life by lining up for the paymaster or to receive mail. Here are the old familiar work details under the same old sergeants. Men get promoted or reduced to the ranks, smuggle in contraband, scrounge, go out on the town, hold bull sessions, swap rumors, gripe, write to their girls left behind. And always, everywhere, in the back of their minds, surge the remorseless memories of carnage and destruction.

The setting and the cast of Hopkins' diaries are different from those familiar to the veterans of today, but the play is the same. The actors are our grandfathers in the blue uniform of the Union Army, serving under Garfield, Sherman, and Grant. The setting is the mid-continent along the Ohio and Mississippi valleys from the Cumberland Gap in Tennessee to New Orleans. On this vast stage of waterways, wilderness, and plantations, moves a confusing array of side-wheelers, ironclads, mule trains, troops of cavalry, armies of men marching and countermarching, guerrilla bands, terror-stricken fugitives, and Negro slaves—a constantly shifting backdrop of war. Seemingly, it is movement without plan.

The Civil War in these pages is Hopkins' war, as he saw it day by day; it is a savage, vindictive conflict fought with canister, "minnie balls," grapeshot, the Enfield rifle, and the bayonet. He was a foot soldier, and was, therefore, a witness on the ground level. What he saw both thrilled and saddened him, aged him beyond his years, and left its imprint upon him for his lifetime.

Why did this seventeen-year-old country boy, still in school, against the wishes of family and friends, volunteer his services for three years in an unpremeditated and bitter war for an idealistic cause? "When the call for troops came after the battle of Bull Run," he writes simply in his notebook, "I felt it my duty to enlist under the flag of the Nation . . . and I enlisted as private in Captain Gardner's company." "Duty," "the flag of the Nation"—were these shibboleths, or do they express a personal moral obligation?

These were not mere words. Duty to the nation had been built into Hopkins' moral fibre by a hundred years of intrepid and patriotic forebears, pioneer men and women inured to hardships and self-denial, who were inordinately proud of their national heritage. He could not have acted otherwise that June day in 1861.

His mother, Sarah Carter, was the granddaughter of Stephen Carter, a ranger on the frontier during the American

Revolution. Carter had come to Pennsylvania from New Jersey with a group of Presbyterians, and had married Elizabeth Gerrard of the Maryland and New Jersey family that produced John Gerrard, the founder of Gerrardstown in the Shenandoah Valley, and James Garrard, the second governor of Kentucky. It was John's sons who established, in 1790, near the present site of Cincinnati, Gerard's Station, for many years an outpost refuge for early Ohio settlers in the Miami Valley.

At the close of the Revolutionary War, Stephen Carter moved down the Ohio River with his family, and in 1792, he bought land near present-day Cincinnati. Four years later, he was killed by Indians. His widow Elizabeth subsequently married Daniel Cox. When he, too, was killed, she took shelter in the family's station. Eventually, she married again; this time to Joseph Coe, son of the founder of the Old Redstone Presbyterian Church in Pennsylvania. As settlements pushed further north, members of these families moved on into Shelby County.

Sarah Carter's mother, Jemima Hathaway, was the daughter of Abraham and Sarah (Goble) Hathaway, who were early settlers in the Miami Valley. Hathaways and Gobles had left New Jersey to settle lands in western Pennsylvania; they, too, had been members of the Old Redstone Presbyterian Church and rangers on the frontier. Abraham is described in county histories as "a great Indian fighter" whose life spanned a hundred years.

Owen J. Hopkins' father, Daniel, was born in Vermont in 1800. With six other children he was brought by his parents, Joseph and Olivia (Howard) Hopkins, to the vicinity of what is now Maumee and Perrysburg on the Maumee River in Ohio, in 1810. Either Joseph or his father had been a Revolutionary soldier, as had the father of Olivia Howard.

The Joseph Hopkins family was one of many which followed in the wake of their former neighbor and friend, Amos Spafford, then collector of the Port of Miami, at Fort Miami on the lower Maumee River. It was the intention of these families to become homesteaders; and without waiting for the government to place on sale the rich river-bottom lands recently acquired by treaty with the Indians, they proceeded at once to plow and plant, to raise corn and vegetables, and to erect a church and a school.[1]

After Hull's surrender of Detroit in the War of 1812, the little group of settlers were forced to flee inland before the onrush of the hostile Indians. Most of them found refuge at Urbana, in Champaign County, not far from the present town of Bellefontaine. Among them were Joseph Hopkins and his family.

It is said that in the wave of enthusiasm that swept the young state at this time, all the men old enough to bear arms volunteered for service in the war. Joseph, serving as cavalryman with General Tupper's forces, went back to the river in the fall of 1812 in order to harvest for the army the corn planted by the settlers near the site where Fort Meigs was built in January of the following year. As he was gathering the crop of his own land, he was scalped by the Indians, according to the testimony of the famous scout, Christopher Wood, and the constable of Urbana, John Davis, both of whom were there with the expedition.

After his father's death, the twelve-year-old Daniel was taken by a family friend either to Detroit or Cincinnati and given an excellent schooling. At the age of eighteen he was appointed clerk of the Shelby County commissioners. In 1824, he met and married Sarah Carter. The following year he became a surveyor and clerk of the county trustees. He surveyed the road leading from Sidney to Bellefontaine, moved his family to the latter place about 1832, and invested heavily in land. He also did some teaching; for Perrin and Battle, in discussing the early schools in Bellefontaine, state that "the people applied themselves to procuring good teachers for their children," list a few of "the new class of teachers," and add that "Daniel Hopkins was another select school teacher."[2]

Daniel and Sarah had fifteen children. Being ardent and ac-

---

[1] Charles Slocum, *History of the Maumee River Basin* (Indianapolis and Toledo: Bowen & Slocum, 1905), p. 512. In addition, Slocum states that at the outbreak of the War of 1812, there were sixty-seven families of Caucasian blood established at, or tributary to, the little village of Miami.

[2] William H. Perrin and J. H. Battle, *History of Logan County, Ohio* (Chicago: Baskin & Co., 1880), p. 342.

tive Methodists, they named several of them after Methodist ministers, such as Owen Johnston and Livingston Yourtee. Owen Johnston Hopkins was born in June, 1844.

Shortly after the death of her husband in 1849, Sarah took her seven surviving and unmarried children and moved to a farm near Bellefontaine. The family remained there until she married Judge Silas McClish, of Putnam County. Widowed a second time, she moved to Toledo to be near her eldest son Almon.

Because of these family changes, Owen Johnston and his younger brother Livingston Yourtee received their education piecemeal, first in the Bellefontaine schools, then in Kalida in Putnam County, and finally in Toledo. In 1864, Hopkins wrote: "Early in March, 1861, I went to Toledo, Ohio, and entered School, where I 'distinguished' myself for hard study and aptness in learning mischief, remaining at school until June following, when I returned to Bellefontaine." That was to be his last contact with formal education: war intervened.

The background of Julia Allison, with whom Owen Johnston Hopkins corresponded during the last years of the war, was quite different. She was the granddaughter of William Allison, a graduate of Dublin University, who was three generations removed from the Scotch Covenanters who fled to the north of Ireland in the seventeenth century to escape religious persecution. He emigrated to America in 1792, became a manufacturer of steel in Middletown, Pennsylvania, and was a major in the War of 1812. After the death of his first wife, William Allison married Juliana Brandon, daughter of Charles Brandon, a Revolutionary soldier from Middletown. To them was born, in December, 1820, Charles William Brandon Allison, Julia's father.

William Allison died in 1830, impoverished by the default of some young friends for whom he had given bond; and his widow with her ten-year-old son drove in a buggy across the Alleghenies to Wooster, Ohio, to live with her married sisters who had emigrated there.

By daytime work and nighttime study, young C. W. B. Allison was able to gain admittance to the bar in Columbus at the age of nineteen. Settling in Marysville, in Union County, he entered practice with the county prosecuting attorney (and his future brother-in-law), the "Honorable" Augustus Hall.

In the spring of 1844, Hall left for Iowa, taking with him his wife, Ellen Priscilla Lee, one of the three daughters of Dr. Elisha Guilford Lee. Allison then succeeded to the office of prosecuting attorney and entered practice with the locally famous Otway Curry. Later in the same year, he married Priscilla's sister, Susanna Sophronia Lee.

Susanna's father, Dr. Lee, the son of Moses Lee, who was of Massachusetts ancestry and a veteran of Valley Forge, had left Stephantown, New York, and journeyed westward over the Albany Trail, buying lands across the state and arriving in Ohio about 1812. For a time, it seems, he lived in Wooster. He married Elizabeth Israel, daughter of the Revolutionary soldier, Lieutenant Basil Israel, and Eleanor Mansell, who had come first to St. Clairsville, in Belmont County, in 1800, and later moved to Guernsey County.

Following his penchant for land speculation, Lee founded the little town of New Guilford, which once had five hundred inhabitants, then went on to Mt. Vernon, later to Piqua, and finally to Iowa, taking with him his wife and their one remaining unmarried daughter, Caroline.

In Iowa, Caroline Lee married a Virginian, William H. Seevers, who had emigrated to Oskaloosa. It was at his home that Julia Allison was visiting, in 1863, when Sergeant Hopkins addressed his first letter to her. The "Jennie" of whom he so often wrote was her cousin Virginia Ellen Seevers.

In 1848, Sophronia Lee Allison died in Marysville, Ohio. Left with the care of his two-year-old daughter Julia, Mr. Allison moved to Bellefontaine, where his mother joined him in order to make a home for them both. There he went into partnership with the Hon. Benjamin Stanton, a second cousin of Edwin Stanton, President Lincoln's secretary of war. Mr. Stanton had been a member of the lower house of the state legislature and a state senator (1841), and was prosecuting attorney for Logan County. In 1850, he was elected to Congress where he served four terms before he was chosen lieutenant governor of Ohio in 1862. Mr. Allison married his daughter, Mary Stanton, in 1851.

The law firm of Stanton and Allison had a very lucrative practice in the state, and Julia Allison grew up in luxury, somewhat spoiled by her doting grandmother and her stepmother. The Allison home was one of culture and religious observance. There were books and paintings (an oil by Huntington of "Mercy's Dream" from *The Pilgrim's Progress* presided over the living-room), music, social gatherings, and discussions of national affairs. The family was as active in the Presbyterian church as the Hopkins family was in the Methodist church. Daughter Julia was sent to the old Ohio Female College at College Hill, on the outskirts of Cincinnati, where she studied Latin, literature, piano, and the proper etiquette for young ladies. Life for her was sheltered, carefree, and urbane.

At the outbreak of the Civil War her father enlisted in the army and was commissioned Captain of Company E of the Eighty-sixth Regiment, Ohio Volunteer Infantry. Later, he was appointed Colonel of the Eighty-fifth. In 1862, he became the presiding officer of the rendezvous for drafted men at Camp Dennison, where he remained until that service was discontinued in January, 1863. Elected to the Ohio Legislature in 1864, he was made chairman of the Committee on Military Affairs and a member of the Judiciary Committee. Two years later he was elected to the Ohio Senate, and became its presiding officer. Having been a Whig before the formation of the Republican party, he became one of its most vigorous supporters. His death occurred in 1876, at Wheeling in the new state of West Virginia, where he and Stanton had set up their joint law practice after the close of the war.

These were the people who intimately or remotely helped to establish Julia Allison's pattern of living and to mold her character, who developed her ardent and deeply rooted moral nature and contributed to that keen sense of justice and the right that welded her to the cause of the Union and held her steadfast in loyalty to her country with a persistence and an intensity that the vicissitudes of life could not lessen.

Owen J. Hopkins kept two pocket diaries while serving with the Forty-second Regiment, Ohio Volunteer Infantry, during the Mississippi campaigns of the Army of the Tennessee, 1863 and 1864, under General Grant and General Sherman. The events chronicled in the diaries were put in the form of a continuous narrative toward the close of 1864, while the author was regimental quartermaster for the One Hundred Eighty-second Regiment, O.V.I., stationed at Nashville, Tennessee. In 1869, he wrote a fuller account of his war experiences, including his service with the Forty-second, O.V.I., commanded by Colonel Garfield, in the Cumberland Gap campaign of 1861 and 1862, and inserted in his notebook ink and pencil sketches based on his personal observation of places, people, and happenings. In the following pages references to these two manuscript narratives are indicated as follows: C(MS) refers to the 1864 version; D(MS), to the 1869 version.

Other sources have been utilized to supplement the diaries and narratives: letters addressed to Julia Allison between January, 1863, and July, 1865, some family correspondence and letters to old comrades, and letters and documents relative to certain aspects of Hopkins' service in the war.

Changes in the original texts have been held to a minimum, affecting only form and arrangement, and a few misspellings. It has not always seemed advisable to retain the underlining that Hopkins used so frequently in the diaries for purposes of emphasis. Hopkins was nothing if not forthright, and his underscoring left no doubt as to the intensity of his feelings.

I

THE CUMBERLAND CAMPAIGN [1]
1861–62

The writer of this history has had recourse to original diaries or memoranda of dates kept by himself during his term
of service in the army, and has endeavored to adhere strictly,
not only to dates, but to the truth, and nothing will be found
written in these pages but facts as they occurred and as witnessed by himself.

On the 25th of September, 1861, I entered the service of
the army as a private soldier in Captain A. Gardner's company, then in process of organizing at Camp in the new Fair
Ground at Bellefontaine, Ohio. A few days after found our
company of Volunteers assembled at the Depot, ready to
depart for Camp Chase, to be assigned to some Regiment.

Many friends, enthusiastic and otherwise, were there to
see us depart. Some were taking leave of fathers, sons, and
brothers, with prayers for our well-being and safe return. A
few hours later, we were being carried rapidly toward our
destination (Columbus), where we arrived late at night and
marched to Camp Chase, four miles west of Columbus, on
the National Pike road. Reaching the camp, we were assigned
quarters, and commenced upon the new duties which we were
to perform during the next three years.

The day following, being the 27th of September, the Company was examined and inspected by a mustering officer, and
all, with the exception of two men, were mustered into the

[1] In D(MS), the author writes: "Some parts [of this narrative] have been
copied from the works of others. They will be readily recognized in the details
of the Cumberland Gap campaign, the Siege of Vicksburg, and the Red River
Expedition, though interwoven with notes from my Diary." Pages 35–42 of this
chapter clearly show the influence of J. T. Headley's *The Great Rebellion*
(Hartford: American Publishing Co., 1866), II, 106–13, a copy of which had
been presented to Hopkins in 1866.

Military service of the United States. Recruits were added to our number from time to time until November, when Lieutenant Foskett with a number of men from Medina County joined us, thus filling up our Company, which was now assigned to duty in the Forty-second Regiment of Ohio Infantry Volunteers, and our Company letter changed from "F" to "K."

On the 25th of November, we were formally mustered into the Forty-second Regiment. Our Company organization was as follows: Capt. Andrew Gardner, Jr. (Bellefontaine), 1st. Lieutenant Thomas L. Hutchins (Bellefontaine), 2nd. Lieutenant P. H. Foskett (Medina), 1st. Sergeant Calvin C. Marquis (Bellefontaine), 2nd. Sergeant Robert W. Southard (East Liberty), 3rd. Sergeant George G. Douglass (Bellefontaine), 4th. Sergeant Wm. H. Leister (Bellefontaine), 5th. Sergeant Martin McAllister (Hinckley), 1st. Corporal Hiram W. Allmon (Bellefontaine), 2nd. Corporal Isaac Thompson, 3rd. Corporal Thos. Armstrong (Bellefontaine), 4th. Corporal Job S. Goff (Bellefontaine), 5th. Corporal Wm. C. Wilgus (Bellefontaine), 6th. Corporal Franklin S. Kaufman (Bellefontaine), 7th. Corporal Andrew J. Smith (Bellefontaine), and 8th. Corporal Orville N. MacClintock (Medina).

The Regiment remained in camp, receiving recruits almost daily, until the 14th of December 1861, when orders were read on dress parade that evening to be prepared to march for the front on the following morning, with three days' rations, our knapsacks neatly packed, and arms in good condition. This order was greeted with loud cheers, as we had grown heartily tired of camp duties and longed for active service in the field. Yet how little any of us realized the true sense of the term "active service"! How fraught with danger of sickness and death,[2] of hardships and deprivations! But when we marched out on that clear cold December morning to the step of martial music, every heart was buoyant and hopeful and fully resolved to battle manfully for the old Flag.

[2] The Forty-second numbered 990 men when it left Camp Chase; when it was mustered out in 1864, it had lost 19 officers and 345 enlisted men who had been killed or wounded.

Upon reaching Columbus, we found the streets lined with people assembled to witness our march through the city. Flags both great and small waved from window, terrace, and balcony, and the streets were boisterous with busy life. Long after, when marching through the desolate cities of the South, I remembered this scene in the capital of our old Buckeye State, and could not fail to note the contrast.

Marching to the Cincinnati & Columbus R.R. depot, the Regiment was formed in a hollow square and received from Governor Dennison a magnificent stand of colors, which the Governor said he hoped we would never trail in the dust,— or words to that effect. Our Colonel, James A. Garfield, in a short but appropriate speech, assured him that no enemy of our country should wrest that beautiful standard from us, but that it should be carried at the cost of our lives "through many a sanguine field to Victory." And many more such patriotic promises were made by the Colonel,—all of which we confidently hoped we would be able to do when, in the fullness of time, we had the opportunity.

Giving the Governor "three times three;" we embarked on the cars and were whirled on toward Cincinnati. At every station, the people were out with baskets of fruit and eatables of all kinds, and demonstrated their loyalty by showering upon Uncle Sam's soldiers every kindness in their power. One very pretty girl assured me that she would rather kiss a soldier than eat her dinner. I did not take the hint, but I took a cup of coffee from her hands instead.

Reaching Cincinnati, the Regiment left the cars and marched from the Little Miami R.R. Depot, through the city, to the foot of Vine Street, and embarked on board a river steamer which left the wharf on the morning of the 17th and steamed up the river, reaching Catlettsburg, Ky., on the 19th, where we found the Fourteenth Kentucky Infantry on the bank, awaiting our arrival. Their Regiment was dressed in *sky-blue* uniforms throughout, and made a fine appearance drawn up in line on shore, where they made the welkin ring with their cheers and shouts of welcome. Our work was now fairly begun. Our camp and garrison equipage, including tents, cooking utensils, mules, mule wagons, forage, and fodder, were transferred to the shore, and soon the white tents of the Regiment, pitched for the first time, were seen shining in the setting sun. Details were made to stand picket in Dixie for the first time, and we began to assume the airs of Veteran soldiers, if Veterans have airs peculiar to them.

The command, including the Forty-second Ohio and the Fourteenth Kentucky, took up the line of march toward Louisa, Kentucky, arriving at and occupying that place on the day following, going into camp the 21st.

The evening of our arrival, the boys were tired and footsore, as well as hungry. New recruits invariably eat their rations of hardtack and bacon before the allotted time expires for so doing, but gradually, as they become used to the diet, they learn to economize, and make their daily allowance hold out. The Regiment stacked arms in an open common west of the town, and scattered through the deserted village. Soon, the sounds of squalling hens and other noises denoted the reign of terror amongst the feathered tribe. I succeeded in unearthing two large cabbage heads and a wheel of corn pone, and my comrade had secured a brace of chickens, all of which we were preparing to make hash of, when the long roll beat and the Regiment flew to arms. Col. Garfield, commanding the brigade, formed the Forty-second into a hollow square, and we knew from the clouded face of our colonel that something had gone wrong. He sat on his horse, surrounded by the eager faces of a thousand men, and then, after a pause of several minutes, he spoke as follows:

"Men of the Forty-second, I thought when I left our old Buckeye State at the head of this fine-looking body of soldiers, that I was the proud commander of a Regiment of gentlemen, but your actions this evening, were I not better acquainted with each and all of you, would bitterly dispel that illusion. Soldiers, we came to Kentucky to help her sons free her sacred soil from the feet of the rebel horde now lying just behind that mountain range. Tonight, we go to dislodge them. Show these Kentuckians, who are your comrades under one flag, that you did not come to rob and to steal, but came to indicate the true character of the American soldier, and hereafter I shall believe that I command a regiment of soldiers, and not a regiment of thieves."

Many of us had, in our haste, carelessly slung our ill-gotten gains over our shoulders, and before the Colonel had half done speaking, every man had deposited his chicken, cabbage-head, ham, or sack of corn meal, on the ground.

In our simplicity, we then thought it wrong to confiscate rebel property, but as time moved on and our faces became bronzed, so also did our conscientious scruples, and we totally forgot the moral teachings of Colonel Garfield. And, also, like new soldiers, we were much given to cheering on the slightest pretext, and on this occasion the Colonel was rewarded with vociferous cheers.

Intelligence was received that the enemy, 5,000 strong under the command of Humphrey Marshall, had abandoned his position a few miles in our front, and moved on up the river, so we went into camp near the village.

(December 30th) Our Teams (*trains*) are reported to be within ten miles of our present position, and we are again on the march up the Big Sandy Valley. The appearance of our troops occasions a general stampede among Rebel sympathizers, but we are greeted by the Loyal citizens with open arms and smiling faces. A brush with the Rebels is expected hourly. The country is extremely mountainous, and mud deep.

January 1st, 1862, found us bivouacked on George's Creek, a few miles from the village of Paintsville. The halt was made to allow our trains to overtake the command. Our position here was very disagreeable, as we were without tents or any means of shelter; a few rails were all we had to keep us out of the mud.

On the evening of the 3rd. I was detailed for picket guard duty and stationed on the top of a high hill about two miles from the command. Here, in company with Dick Bailey of Company G of the Forty-second, we watched throughout the night in a heavy storm of sleet and snow. The dense pine forest was so thick that we could not see a distance of 50 yards down the side of the mountain, even when daylight came, and we saw the absurdity of watching such a position.

The snow was still falling and was now almost knee deep. We waited until noon, and no relief came; at once, we went to work to build a shelter. After shovelling away the snow with pieces of chestnut bark, we erected a rude hut of that material and the boughs of the cedar trees. Our scanty rations had been exhausted, having eaten the last hardtack for breakfast. My comrade suggested that we return to camp, but I reminded him of the danger incurred by sentinels leaving their posts, and we concluded to remain until relieved.

Night came, and no Sergeant of the Guard to relieve us. We watched through the night alternately, one sleeping in the hut as well as the cold would permit, while the other remained on duty. I was watching the last two hours before day. The storm had subsided, and the sun came up; but no relief guard. I thought I detected the sound of rumbling wagons moving over a distant mountain road, and rousing Dick, I informed him of my belief that our little army was on the move. Cold and stiff, we decided, "in council assembled," to *move* also from our position,—which we soon after did.

Starting down the side of the mountain, we found the route beset by some peril from loose boulders, which, upon being loosened from their position, would go bounding down the steep declivity, striking trees and scattering masses of snow from their boughs, then, with another bound, disappear entirely over a steep precipice. Occasionally, one of us would lose his footing and shoot down the steep as did the boulders, only saved from dashing his brains out by catching at the shrubbery.

On one of these races I shot over a projection of rock and landed some five or six feet below among a flock of sheep, making a scatterment in their ranks, which proved fortunate for us. They fled down the mountainside, following a path which the flock had formed by their frequent browsing expeditions, and we followed them to the base of the mountain and across a stream to a log cabin on the opposite side of the valley, occupied by an old man, his wife, and daughter. Here we rested for an hour, breakfasting on fried chicken, corn bread, and milk. Thanking the old people for their hospitality, and accepting the guidance of the little girl, we found the road by which the old gentleman said our troops had gone on, and pushed on rapidly after the Regiment.

The same evening, after a weary but rapid march, we overtook the brigade and reported our case to the Captain, who, in turn, reported to the Colonel, who, in turn, issued a special order reducing to the ranks the Sergeant of the guard who had neglected to relieve us. The picket guard that day had been formed into a *rear* guard, and our Captain supposed we were with them, until calling the roll just before our arrival.

(January 7, 1862.)[3] (Our Brigade occupied Paintsville and pitched tents on the outskirts of the almost deserted town. That night, a detail of 400 men was made from the Regiment, and crossing the Big Sandy on flat boats, pursued a trail across the mountains in hope of surprising a portion of the Rebel column resting at an entrenched position some thirteen miles east. The expedition was a severe one, owing to a heavy fall of snow and the desperate condition of the road. Wading streams of floating ice, climbing rocky steeps, and struggling through the half-frozen mud, made the march extremely tiresome, and many of the men fell exhausted and straggled back to camp, or were picked up by guerrillas.)

Near midnight, we stumbled upon some earthworks and rifle pits which had evidently been deserted by the enemy but a few hours and in great haste, judging from half-cooked pots of meat and many other signs betokening a hasty exit. Our advance guard once came near enough upon the Rebel rear to deliver a few shots, but the heels of the "Secesh" got the better of their courage, and the pursuit was abandoned. Now the hardest of our march began, as there was no longer any excitement to keep us up on our way back to camp; when the forces halted for a brief rest, many fell to sleep in fence corners, and were aroused with the greatest difficulty. Once or twice I was tempted to *give up,* but feared that I might fall to sleep on the cold ground and freeze to death.

Our officers, mounted on good horses, seemed to forget that they had a troop of tired and sleepy soldiers plodding on

[3] This and later sections have been set within parentheses since the author's intentions in lightly crossing them out in pencil in the manuscript are not clear. It has seemed best not to delete them.

behind them, and the march was conducted on the principle that men could endure as much as horses,—which proved to be the case! (Upon arriving at camp about nine o'clock the next morning, the horses seemed more exhausted than the men. Marching into the village, we found it occupied by the Fortieth Ohio Infantry, who had left Camp Chase about the time of our departure, and had come to join our brigade. As the Fortieth and the Forty-second were not on the best of terms at Camp Chase, their arrival was not greeted with any great display of enthusiasm on either hand. During this night march, I suffered more than at any other period of my service, having marched a distance of 26 miles during the night.)

The evening of the same day, 400 men from these regiments left camp in pursuit of the enemy, whose trail we had left the night previous, and coming upon his rear about daybreak, skirmishing began, the Rebels slowly falling back in the direction of Prestonburgh.

The balance of the command at Paintsville was now brought up by a forced march on the 9th., and overtaking the main Rebel force at Middle Creek on the 10th., the fight commenced. Humphrey Marshall had formed his line on the top of a crescent shaped range of high hills protected by a dense wood which covered the sides of the range; at the top, huge boulders formed an admirable protection for the Chivalry. At the base of the hill ran Middle Creek, now swollen by recent rains and breast deep, but through it, holding cartridge box and gun, dashed the Forty-second, and up the side of the mountain to our first battle.

Marshall had one small mountain howitzer, which throughout the fight sent its harmless, screeching shots high above our heads, doing more damage amongst the limbs of lofty trees than to any other living thing. The mountain side was almost perpendicular, and climbing this by the aid of branches of trees and under heavy fire from the well-protected rebels' entire line was extremely difficult, but the enthusiasm of the men was a motive power not easily baffled. Reaching a point near the summit, our line was formed, and a charge or two and heavy doses of minnie [4] balls soon dislodged the Rebs,

---

[4] The Minié ball or "minnie" was a conical rifle bullet, so named after its French inventor, Captain C. E. Minié.

who were now sent flying down the opposite side of the mountain, leaving their dead and wounded on the field.

They had no sooner abandoned the rocky summit than our discharges caused a great slaughter amongst them, and after the battle their dead and wounded were found in heaps. (A portion of the Fourteenth Kentucky took part in the engagement and fought with great gallantry, but after it was over, they disgraced the name of soldier by indiscriminate plundering of the dead and wounded, in some instances stripping boots and shoes from dying men and transferring them to their own feet. This heartlessness on the part of Southern soldiers in our army was remarkable throughout the War, probably owing to influences created by the Medusa head of their cherished institution: Slavery.)

The battle commenced at 3:00 P.M. and lasted until 5:00 P.M., when the enemy was driven from the field, and tired, completely saturated and cold, we occupied a higher spur of the rocky range until the next morning. We withdrew to Prestonburgh and bivouacked in that mud-cursed village to rest. Then we returned to Paintsville. The Fortieth Ohio was now assigned to our Brigade under command of Colonel Garfield, and we remained at this place, suffering from all the chronic diseases which beset new soldiers in an unhealthy climate, until the 22nd of February,[5] when the command embarked for Piketon, Ky., higher up the Big Sandy and thirty miles from Pound Gap, where Humphrey Marshall had taken refuge after his thrashing at Prestonburgh.

Arriving at this town, we found a dilapidated row of houses on the bank of the river, which here ran through a deep gorge formed by high precipitous hills on either side. Going into camp, we were joined by the Twenty-second Kentucky Volunteer Infantry and now numbered some 3,000 men, half of which force would have been sufficient to scare Humphrey Marshall out of his wits.

In March, a flood swept down from the mountains and deluged the town, making it necessary to pitch our tents higher up among the hills to prevent being washed away. I awoke one morning to find one side of my body immersed in the cold water, which was rising so rapidly that instant flight was nec-

[5] In C(MS), he gives the date as February 12.

essary. A half-hour afterwards, rail fences and drift-wood were carried by the flood over the spot where our tents had stood, washing away everything before it.

While at Piketon, we were engaged in several exciting chases after guerrillas, who understood the art of making themselves scarce, when necessary, to perfection.

(At Reveille one morning, volunteers were called for to take part in an expedition against a company of "Bush Whackers," reported to be lurking in the mountains some 35 miles up the river. The writer was accepted, with ten others of the Fortieth and Forty-second Regiments, and left camp with two days' rations and rifle and forty rounds of ammunition to the man. We were piloted over the hills by a specimen of the Southern "poor trash,"—a woman who rode without a saddle astride a very lean specimen of the genus horse, whose swaying bow legs betokened a slim allowance of oats, and bad usage.)

Our route was no route at all, but our course lay across the hills overgrown with cedar and laurel, wading streams back and forth in our devious windings, often accusing our guide of ignorance of the route, and threatening mutiny against her leadership, but finally, on the evening of the first day out, we came suddenly upon the corpse of a man suspended over a creek by the neck, who, our guide informed us, had been hung the night before by the guerrillas. The body was that of a man apparently forty years old, with an immense muscular frame, and the ground around the tree indicated that a severe struggle had taken place between the poor man and his executioners.

We cut the rope, took down the body, and carried it about a fourth of a mile up the valley to his house, which was a rude hut built of logs. On entering, we discovered on a cot in one corner an old man with a minnie ball in his side. The same party of guerrillas had shot him at the same time they had compelled his son to go with them, and whom they afterwards hung. The dead man's wife and four or five small children met us at the door, and their grief was intense. The old man was suffering intensely, but from him we learned all the particulars. His son had been accused of being a Union Man, and the guerrillas had tried to impress him into the Rebel service, but his steady refusal to fight against the old flag, his unswerving loyalty, had cost him his life. They took him by main force, but he probably resisted, and they hung him like a dog.

The old man's interference provoked the leader of the party, who, from his horse, shot him while standing in the door. That was the signal for the whole gang to fire a volley into the cabin. He pointed out the ball holes in the wall. It seemed a miracle that none of the children were hurt.[6]

We again took up the line of march up the valley, in close pursuit of the Rebels, and everywhere we found fresh traces of their depredations. Night found us bivouacked in a farm house, the occupants having fled from our approach. The "guilty fly when no man pursues," and we take it for granted that they are Rebels at heart. Chickens and poultry of all kinds fall a prey to our appetites, and we dine like Methodist preachers. After standing guard about two hours during the night, I retired to rest on a *straw* bed and slept soundly.

The next morning, after eating a hearty breakfast, we continued on the road by which the Guerrillas were said to have taken their leave, but this time they took some pains to deface any signs of their route, and we had some difficulty in following the trail. Wading several swollen streams repeatedly, we finally found it necessary to cross the Big Sandy, and were ferried across by a rather good-looking specimen of the Southern damsel. Her craft was only large enough to carry two of us at a trip, and it took some time to cross over. The fair but false one told us that she had seen nothing of an armed force in the neighborhood,—a statement that afterward proved to be even without a shadow of truth, as she herself had cooked breakfast for them only that morning, and they had crossed the river in this same boat.

After all were over, we took a mountain path and soon came upon the Johnnies. They had formed an ambush on the opposite side of a deep creek and among the rocks and trees on the side of the mountain.

The Major of the Fortieth Ohio Infantry called for Volun-

[6] This episode is described in full detail in F. H. Mason, *The Forty-second Ohio Infantry* (Cleveland: Cobb, Andrews & Co., 1876), pp. 80–81.

teers to wade the stream and commence the attack, where-upon we *all* volunteered, and plunging into the cold water with our rifles and cartridge boxes held over our heads, waded to the opposite shore and were soon hotly engaged with the bushwhackers. The Major, who had remained on the opposite shore with a reserve, was struck in the head with a rifle ball and mortally wounded.

The enemy soon fled, carrying several of their dead and wounded with them, but left one poor fellow, shot through the temple, on the ground; his body having rolled down a steep declivity, was partially hidden among the laurel bushes. We carried his body to the nearest farmhouse and left him in charge of the occupant.

Forming a litter of boards and poles, we started on the return with the wounded Major, and now commenced the most wearisome part of the trip. Relieving each other alternately at the stretcher, we were able to accomplish but a few miles before night, when we halted at a farm house with our burden. After eating a good supper, we rested until morning; then resuming the journey by a new route, found our task of carrying the wounded man becoming more and more arduous. He was unconscious most of the time, but groaned continually when we were in motion. The night found us several miles from camp yet, and we again bivouacked. On the following morning, our party divided, one continuing down the valley, the other going across the country by a nearer route to Piketon.

I was with the former, in charge of a non-commissioned officer. Soon after dividing, we conceived the idea of building a raft and floating down the river, but after spending a half-day in the construction of one, it proved too small for the purpose and had to be abandoned. Next, a leaky "dug-out" was chartered, but this was scuttled, after being condemned, and sent adrift.

Wading a stream shoulder deep, I lost my footing and was ducked head and ears, wetting my ammunition and gun, and almost losing the latter. The current was very strong and we had much difficulty in crossing. At length, tired and footsore, we reached camp, and most of us reported on the sick-list the next day. The other party, soon after, arrived with the wounded Major.

Some days after, another party made a raid on Pound Gap and destroyed the camp equipage and entrenchments of a small force of Rebels at that place, the enemy having retired precipitately toward Abingdon, Virginia.

On the 26th of March, 1862, our entire command, except a part of Wolford's Kentucky Cavalry, embarked on transports for Louisville. The Big Sandy was over its banks and we had many narrow escapes while descending the rapid and crooked stream. Frequently, the limbs of overhanging trees would rake the hurricane deck, carrying all before them. Negroes, old and young, came out upon the banks to greet us with joyful shouts, and occasionally white people would display their loyalty by waving flags and shouting for the Union.

Passing Catlettsburg and other towns on the Ohio, we reached Cincinnati. Stopping for supplies, we again steamed down the river, reaching Louisville on the first of April and going into camp near that city. After resting some two weeks here in a pleasant camp, drilling and holding dress parades in the presence of hundreds of visitors from the city, we again received orders to move. Taking the cars for Lexington, Ky., we arrived there April 14th. and again rested for further orders.

Then, joining General George W. Morgan's command, we marched southward through the garden spot of Kentucky, through Nicholasville to Camp Dick Robinson. Here, I was taken down sick with the *mumps,* and was left behind the command at the house of Mr. Robinson, an honest old farmer, who, with his kind wife and daughters, took every care of me that I could have expected of a mother.

The house was built of stone and surrounded by shade trees, while in the background there was a large orchard of peach and apple trees. A little negro girl was stationed in the hall outside the door of my sick room to go and come at my call, and the eldest of the daughters visited me frequently during the day. Seated by my bedside, she read me the news from different parts of the country where our boys in Blue were fighting for the old flag. I had half a notion to fall in love with her, as they do in ten-cent novels, but as I was but eighteen and devoted to "die for my country," I abandoned the idea. Still, I will remember her kindness forever. Her love for the old Union and all its defenders seemed a part of her existence; her unselfish desire to serve me in my sickness was like that of thousands of other noble-hearted women who administered so faithfully to our boys in the Hospitals throughout the War.

I had orders to remain at this place until I was entirely recovered, but my anxiety to rejoin the Regiment overcame my prudence, and in spite of their advice to the contrary, I shouldered my musket, bade them a hearty good-by, and trudged on alone, taking the road south by which the army had passed. I was still weak and scarcely fit to travel, but I made several miles that day and rested at a farmhouse by the roadside, where I was treated with the greatest kindness. The day following found me early on my way, much refreshed by my night's rest, and night found me some thirteen miles further on my journey. This night I passed in a haymow some distance from the road, and the next morning I traveled some distance before I could find breakfast. I found a Union man's log cabin finally, where I was fed and had my haversack replenished.

The country here began to assume a wilder aspect, and lost the old civilized appearance that had characterized the route this far. The substantial macadamized road abruptly terminated, and the winding excuse for a highway led off its miry course through dense forests, over steep hills, and down again into black, swampy, wooded valleys, crossing rapid streams, and losing one in its intricate windings. Were it not for some traces left by our troops, it would have been hard to follow.

At night, I overtook one of our trains on its way from Lexington to the front, on the top of a high hill. Several of the wagons were deeply embedded in the clayey soil, and the mule teams were unable to budge. The drivers, swearing by note, had no effect, nor had the lash which was "spared not." One wagon was overturned, and the load of hardtack in boxes scattered in every direction. I pushed on to the front of the train, which was some two miles long, and found the front wagons already preparing to camp for the night.

Joining the guard under a non-commissioned officer, I made up my mind to stay in company with them until we should reach the front and rejoin our regiments. They were a happy troop of young Kentuckians, and exercised their hospitality towards me as well as they knew how, and I shared their rations of bacon and hardtack with much satisfaction. After supper, we slept in the wagons, and a heavy rain during the night completely drenched my poor skin.

The train of wagons, numbering nearly one hundred, was in motion early, but the rain had reduced the roads to a quagmire, and progress was difficult. Many of us started out in advance to forage, but found poor picking in the trail of an army recently passed. One Kentuck stumbled upon a whiskey-still in full blast, and our canteens were filled immediately with the new fluid. I could only use it externally by bathing my joints in the sickening stuff, by means of which I kept off stiffness and soreness in marching. One dose taken internally acted like an emetic upon me, but it was panacea to the Kentuckians. They loved it even in its infancy, and swallowed "grown person's" doses of it.

We passed over the battleground of Wild Cat, where the Rebels received a sound thrashing. Many signs of the fighting were still plainly visible, and the dead were but partially buried. Here and there, a hand or foot protruded from the ground. A hard-hearted Kentuckian in our party grasped a skeleton hand thus protruding, and said: "Hello, old feller! Are you reachin' fer yer land warrant? I guess you've got all you'll ever git, so lay still and dry up." Many laughed at this as a good joke, but it struck harshly upon my nerves.

The trees were barked and riddled by minnie balls, and the branches torn and broken by cannon shot. Though, in reality, it was but a skirmish, compared with some of the battles fought later in the war, it was then considered a great fight, and its heroes honored in song and prose.

The day after passing Wild Cat, we reached the camp of our army at Morse's House, and I gladly joined the regiment, which occupied a pleasant position in one of the valleys skirted by the foothills of the Cumberland range. Here, we were assigned to the command of Colonel De Courcy, with the Fourteenth Kentucky and Sixteenth Ohio Regiments. Colonel De Courcy was an English officer who had procured a leave of absence from the British army, and coming to the United States, found his way to Wooster, in Ohio. Raising a volunteer regiment for the war—the Sixteenth—he was duly commissioned its colonel. A strict, rigid disciplinarian, he enjoyed more the confidence of his men than their love.[7]

His brigade numbered something near 2,500 men, able for duty, and was assigned to the most arduous duties of the campaign against Cumberland Gap by General Morgan. Always in the advance, removing blockades, cutting roads, and fighting their way, the "One-eyed Brigade," as we were called— De Courcy had but one eye—, enjoyed a reputation enviable in the extreme. Well-officered and splendidly equipped, we were a match for any corresponding number of Johnnies.

By climbing a high hill, we could get a distant view of Cumberland Gap. Procuring a one-day pass, I climbed the Young mountain and made a sketch of the Gap and surroundings as well as I could from this distance. My effort so pleased the Colonel that he granted us passes to go beyond the outposts some three or four miles, in company with two others, in order to get a nearer view of the Rebel works.

We set out early in the morning, avoiding the road, but traveling in its course, to prevent any disagreeable meeting with the Rebel scouts. After a wearisome climb to the peak of a high mountain, we had a splendid view of the Rebel works, and I made a draft of the same with the road leading to the Gap and the position of the enemy's pickets, a bird's-eye view of which we had from our position. Gazing long and earnestly at the formidable looking fortresses crowning the peaks on each side of the gap, we quietly and cautiously withdrew. Farther down the mountain, we caught sight of a company of Rebel Cavalry advancing up the road, and this

[7] "He had no personal attachments with any of his subordinates, and he set out to bring the volunteer soldiers of his regiment and brigade under the strict, precise, discipline of the British service."—*Ibid.*, p. 143.

sight greatly facilitated our retrograde movement. We got back to Camp in safety, and I delivered the draft to Col. Sheldon[8] of the Forty-second. I will not say that it was of any use in the campaign, but I do know that a project then in contemplation for an assault on the Gap was abandoned about that time, though the strength of the enemy's position might have been made known to Gen. Morgan through other sources.

It was now known that the enemy could not be dislodged by a direct attack, and Gen. Morgan resolved to try strategy. Breaking up camp, but leaving a small force to guard our line of communication and also to deceive the enemy as to the actual movement, we marched to the westward about forty miles, coming to the Cumberland Mountains again, at the foot of Roger's Gap. Here, repairing the road over the mountain which had been blockaded with fallen trees by the Rebels, with great difficulty our artillery was hauled up the steep ascent and down on the opposite side into Powell's Valley. So cautiously had we advanced this far that the enemy's pickets were completely surprised, and a number of them captured at the foot of the mountain.

A halt was now ordered to allow our trains and artillery to close up on the main column, and to afford a breathing spell to the men after the arduous march of the past twenty-four hours. Early the next morning, being the 14th of June, my birthday, volunteers were called for to participate in a scouting expedition, and I was among the number. Lieut. Clapp of Company A, Forty-second Regiment, was in command. We were in light marching order, some thirty in all, and proceeded rapidly in the direction of Cumberland Gap. Without any encounter with the enemy's cavalry, who were dodging in every road and lane, our party was finally placed in ambush, with a view to capturing a company of Rebel mounted men who were known to be approaching.

At some distance down the road we could hear their bugle calls and the clatter of their horses' feet. Every rifle was grasped in a firmer hold as the prospect of a pleasant little surprise to the Johnnies increased. Myself, and another pri-

[8] Lieutenant Colonel Lionel A. Sheldon.

vate soldier from Company A, were placed down the road some distance to signal our party when the entire Rebel force had passed a given point, and if there were still any heavier column approaching.

The Rebs drew nearer and nearer until we could almost distinguish the color of their eyes. I could have sent their leader to the "happy hunting ground" by a well-aimed rifle ball, but we were instructed not to fire. At this moment, a woman was seen to emerge from a house at the roadside and confer with the Rebels, whereupon their Bugler sounded the retreat,—and our expedition was a failure. She had, by some means or other, learned of our presence, and gave them a timely warning, very truly demonstrating that woman is at the bottom of all evil.

Returning to our main force, we found the regiment bivouacked in a cornfield at the foot of the mountain. At night, a heavy rain drenched us completely. The day following was devoted to straggling amongst the delightful scenery which here presented itself to the eye. High up the mountain a stream of water some two feet in diameter burst from the rocky soil, and taking its course toward the base, plunged over many miniature Niagaras and formed a stream transparent and clear, and further down was made to serve as the motive power for a sawmill, a gristmill, and a carding-mill. After passing over their wheels, it disappeared beneath the ground, and then again bubbled up from the ground near the base of the hills and continued on its course past our camps, supplying us with clear, cold, invigorating water.

From a high peak above our position a splendid view was obtained of the surrounding country. Powell's Valley lay like a mighty map to the eye. Far down the valley could be seen the smoke from the camp of a Confederate cavalry, and their vedettes, posted a mile nearer in the road, were plainly visible.

The following day, our Regiment undertook to capture a force of the enemy by a well-planned but badly executed ambush. The Rebel cavalry company had passed the ambush and their mounted infantry came next. Orders were quietly given along the line to prepare for a charge into the road as soon as the latter had passed. At this point, a cabbage-headed Dutchman in the regiment fired his rifle into the Johnnies,— and the game was up! We charged down from our cover into the field skirting the road as the Cavalrymen wheeled and precipitately retreated, firing their revolvers at us as they passed. The daredevil set made good their escape from our whizzing minnie-balls,—all but three, who were found further down the road, badly wounded.

Realizing that distance lends enchantment, the Rebels, from this time on, kept at a respectful distance from our column. Our Army now made a rapid march toward Cumberland Gap, De Courcy in the advance. Another day found us masters of the situation, holding the roads leading to Knoxville, the Rebel base of supplies. At night, we saw at a distance of ten miles the light of the setting sun reflected on the high peaks and forming battlements of this "Gibraltar of America." No flag waved from any of the forts. A few white tents still remained high up among the clouds, but the Rebel Stevenson had decamped. On the 18th of June, 1862, we marched and planted our flag on the highest point overlooking the defenses.

The Rebels had spiked some of their heaviest ordnance and tumbled them off the cliffs, but had left their earthworks intact. On the south side, their log huts still remained, having been left in some haste. They still contained many cooking utensils and other articles which proved of considerable use to us in our stay at the Gap. Many love letters from Rebel sweethearts were found in the cabins, and articles of interest lay scattered here and there.

Midway up the side of the mountain was the mouth of an extensive cavern. Fabulous tales of its vastness existed, and I resolved to explore its subterranean depths, so one day five or six others and myself, well equipped with torches, entered through a large doorway leading into a rocky chamber some forty feet high by thirty feet wide and sixty or seventy feet in length, from which a very slimy hole—a second "fat man's misery"—led into a long, dark, sloping corridor with overhanging stalactites. The least whisper caused an echo, and the effect of a pistol shot caused a thundering noise, deafening to hear.

From this room, we climbed up a difficult slippery ascent, and through another small orifice entered a vast hall larger than many theaters of the country. High overhead gleamed in the light of our torches what seemed to be myriads of diamonds and precious stones. Crossing this room on stepping stones over what appeared to be a bottomless lake, we came to a long hall with perpendicular walls on either hand, which appeared to be a mile or so in length. At the termination, water poured down from the roof in many small streams and disappeared under the stony floor. It was said that grander scenes than those already passed still lay beyond, but without a guide we hesitated to venture farther into the dark labyrinths, and we retraced our steps to the opening.

This description of the cave is a weak attempt; it would take a learned writer to give a satisfactory one. Old residents stated that the mountains all around the gap were hollow, and some had penetrated to a distance of five miles.

While in occupation of our Camp south of the Gap, we were joined by hundreds of East Tennesseeans, who were organized into regiments and mustered into the Army. They were nearly all accompanied by their wives and children. Awkward and uncouth in appearance, these men possessed great powers of endurance, but were hard to drill into precise and well-disciplined soldiers.

One day, standing on the parade ground, I heard one of their officers give the following commands: "From one string to two strings, git!" (Two ranks form Company; march!) and "Git into two strings and look smart like the Hioans!" (Ohioans). They would watch with the greatest wonderment our manoeuvering, and set us down as men from another sphere.

In July, our Brigade moved camp to the summit of the mountain east of the Gap. Our tents were pitched in a finely shaded position surrounded by plenty of beautiful mountain scenery, and with fresh spring water from the rocks to aid in demolishing Uncle Sam's hardtack and bacon. Frequent foraging expeditions were made into the country, but our field of operations became badly limited by the gradual closing in of Kirby Smith's army on the south. At times, our men would be gathering green corn from one side of a field while the Rebels were at the other side, and skirmishes occurred daily.

Picket duty was hazardous and beset by perils. While on this duty one night, I was stationed some fifty yards in advance of the main post, and a rifle ball was sent whizzing by my ears in uncomfortably close proximity by a concealed bushwhacker. Then, a dark form glided swiftly off in the gloom. The post was aroused by the shot and we kept diligent watch from then until morning.

Near the summit of the ridge over which the road crossed and a few feet from one of the bastioned forts, stood a large stone marking the intersection of the state lines of Kentucky, Tennessee, and Virginia. From this point, also, could be described the dim outlines of the Blue Ridge Mountains in Georgia and a great portion of East Tennessee spread out at our feet. No scenery, save that of the far-famed Yosemite Valley, equals this in sublimity and extent. It was worth weeks of arduous campaigning to see.

On August 6th, 1862, our Brigade was sent out under General De Courcy on an expedition of some peril toward the little town of Tazewell, East Tennessee. Ten miles out, we came upon the enemy strongly posted at a ferry over the Tennessee River. Because of a determined front presented to them, they abandoned their position and fell back towards Knoxville, our Brigade following close upon their rear guard and skirmishing with their cavalry. The enemy, at every crossing of a stream, posted dummy artillery to frighten us, but they soon found that we were not to be fed on chaff. Night found us in possession of Tazewell and the enemy occupying the hills a short distance beyond. Skirmishing continued throughout the night, and our main column rested on their arms until morning, when it was found the Rebels had fallen still further back in the hope of bringing us into battle with their main force, now marching to their aid from Clinch Mountain.

We cautiously followed, guarding every avenue by which a

flank movement could be made upon us. Our advance, now
held by the Forty-second O.V.I., with Companies B, G, and
K deployed as skirmishers, rested in a large orchard five miles
south of Tazewell. Here, the enemy contested our further advance. Lieut.-Col. Pardee of the Forty-second ordered the
writer and a private, Joseph Andrews, of the same company,
to crawl quietly to a high ridge covered with young shrubbery
and blackberry bushes, a quarter of a mile in advance of the
skirmish line, and to watch the Rebels' movements and com-
municate by certain signals the same to him.[9]

He cautioned us against making ourselves visible to the
enemy and to use every care against capture, but, if captured,
to remain stubbornly reticent with regard to the exact number of our force. We were not to fire unless absolutely necessary to preserve our lives.

The code of signals was unique in the extreme. If the enemy
were cavalry alone, we were to get down on our hands and
knees. If cavalry and infantry both, one was to stand while the
other remained on all fours. If advancing, we were to make
a feint of retiring to the rear. If stationary, a drop of the
cap so denoted.

On reaching the designated spot, we suddenly caught a
startling view of the whole Rebel army, cavalry and infantry.
The former were dismounted at a farmhouse by the roadside
nearly a mile away, their pickets stationed a good distance in
advance at a spring, from which we could see men filling their
canteens. At some distance to the right and in the rear of the
cavalry, was the infantry force of the Rebels; their arms
stacked at the edge of a wood glistened in the sun, and the
dirty gray uniforms flitting here and there were plainly dis-
tinguishable with the naked eye.

Keeping close under cover, we signalled all this to the rear,
where Colonel Pardee was now reading out our signals to
De Courcy, surrounded by other officers. The breaking of a
twig to be held up was the signal in case the enemy had artillery; this also was communicated, as we could discern several
pieces of brass ordnance planted near the farmhouse.

[9] See Mason, *op. cit.,* p. 115.

This piece of news was scarcely necessary, for we had no sooner imparted it than one of the guns was manned and trained in our direction. A curl of white smoke wreathed from its muzzle, and a shot came whizzing high over our heads, and striking the ground in our rear, burst and scattered dust and dirt in all directions. This was apparently fired to get the range, and seemed satisfactory, for it was not tried again while we were on the lookout. As near as we could make out, the enemy were about 5,000 strong, infantry and cavalry, with a battery of field pieces. Watching their movements for nearly two hours, we at last saw about 200 of the cavalry mount and ride towards us. Making the fact known by moving to the rear on all fours, we saw our men hastily form into order of battle. Lanphear's battery was placed into position, supported by the Sixteenth Ohio, while the Forty-second on the left guarded the road leading up the valley.

At this point, four or five men in Rebel gray glided out from a clump of bushes at a short distance directly in our front, and made a precipitate retreat towards their main column. They, too, had been trying to ascertain *our* exact position. Reaching the road which wound around the crescent shaped hill on which we stood guard, they were seen to confer with the cavalry, who now struck their rowels into their horses' sides, dashing towards us. We could hear the clatter of their horses' feet and the clank of their sabres closing around and to the rear of us, occupying the road between us and our command. This was endurable until another company was seen to let down the fence by the road and advance directly upon us. Capture seemed inevitable.

Our men were now engaged with the cavalry, and while they were occupying the Rebels' attention in front, we took the opportunity to make an effort to escape by crawling through the bushes back to the stone fence running along the base of the hill. Just as we reached it, the cavalry came dashing back, and we emptied our rifles at them. They returned the compliment from revolvers and carbines, but no one was hurt on either side. Fearing that possibly we might be a part of an ambushed party on that side of the road, they fled precipitately back towards their reserves, and we reached the command in safety.

Our line now advanced up the valley. Soon the Rebel army was in sight, marching in fine array towards us. A sharp fight commenced, and balls flew about our ears as thick as bees. Our field pieces made sad havoc among the gray coats, and that, with our well-aimed infantry fire, soon sent the Johnnies flying. De Courcy was ordered not to pursue the enemy beyond this point, and we held our ground until night, skirmishing occasionally with their cavalry during the afternoon. Our loss was slight; owing to the superior quality of our artillery, the enemy's loss was much heavier in killed and wounded.

Our Brigade now faced about and made a forced march back towards Cumberland Gap, where we arrived tired out and hungry. The Rebel army, now some 60,000 strong, were closing in upon us, and their advance was well on towards Tazewell. De Courcy's brigade was again called into line, and made another sally upon their advance guard and drove them from that town. The same night, we held their whole army in check for three hours by extending our line in single file and making a show of battle. The cheat was soon discovered, and the enemy came sweeping down upon us in overwhelming numbers. Like the meek little man, "we came away." Through a dark, rainy, night we were shelled and driven back into Cumberland Gap.

The next morning, looking from our camp down upon the valley, the sun shone on thousands of white tents which had sprung up like mushrooms in every direction in Powell's Valley, while upon the north side John Morgan's cavalry pickets could be seen upon the road leading to the Cumberland Ford. Interesting as this view was to the eye, to the *inner man* it was the opposite, and visions of captivity and a long tramp through the sunny South to Andersonville or Richmond stole upon the senses.

Our supply of provender was already meagre and now promised to be more so, which touched a tender spot in our composition. Foraging was still more restricted, and seldom if ever were our expeditions crowned with further success than the capture of a lean porker whose appearance conveyed the impression that he, too, was suffering from the effects of the siege.[10]

At length, the advance of Bragg into Kentucky left the enemy at liberty to push across the Cumberland Range by various routes and effectually cut off our little army from its base of supplies, thus leaving us alone to care for ourselves as best we might. Strong in position, we felt able to hold it against all odds, if we could be kept from starvation. Every avenue to the gap was besieged, and every foot of the advance of the enemy was contested. Foraging the country as far as safety would permit, though with poor success, General Morgan sent to Halleck and General Wright of Ohio for supplies, saying that if his communication could be kept open, he would hold the Gap against the whole Rebel army.

At different times, he sent out five expeditions under Col. De Courcy with the Sixteenth and Forty-second Ohio, and Fourteenth and Twenty-second Kentucky Regiments, in which he killed and captured 700 of the enemy, with a loss to our force of only forty men. For more than two months we waited, and saw the storm gathering thicker and thicker around us. But still strong in our faith in the perfect competency of our commander, we knew that all would be right.

As Buell fell back toward Nashville, the Rebel flood poured like a deluge into Kentucky. By the 21st of August, we found Kirby Smith with his Rebels guarding every road to the north, while Stevenson, like a fox, watched us from the south. Still our commander, as well as the men, kept cheerful. Not a despondent word escaped us. Our supplies grew shorter day by day, and even the horses and mules of the army were failing for want of forage. Morgan would not stir from his position, declaring that he would kill the horses and mules for food, did he see any movement set on foot to open his communications.

The country was alarmed for our safety. The very stubbornness with which we held the grim fortress, only insured our total destruction, if no relief should reach us. We were put on half-rations a good part of the time, without bread,

[10] Here begins the quotation, or adaptation, of Headley's account, interspersed with the personal experiences and feelings of the writer.

flour, or potatoes. The overwhelming enemy continued to draw closer and closer around us every day, narrowing our field for forage until, at length, starvation began to stare us in the face. The men looked lank and haggard from hunger and exposure, and were almost worn out by arduous duties in the chill mountain air at night, and as no man amongst the privates possessed a full suit of clothing, suffering from cold was added to that of hunger.

What was to be done? Answer, you who harped so incessantly on Morgan's "disgraceful abandonment" of Cumberland Gap! Or perhaps the Military Commission before whom General Morgan was tried for neglect of duty, could now answer?

We could hear of no movement for our relief, and we stayed, waiting for it, until every known avenue of escape was closed against us. The Rebel general telegraphed to Richmond that Morgan's army might be considered prisoners of war, for its fate was sealed.

True, one route was still open,—the wild, desolate region stretching for two hundred miles directly to the north.[11] But it was reported by the engineers as impossible for an army of ten thousand men, with artillery, to be supported there at all in the length of time it would take to traverse the country. Yet the Rebels seemed to think that a man who had dragged heavy siege guns up and over the cliffs of the Cumberland Mountains, might attempt to escape by this route; and so Humphrey Marshall of Prestonburg fame was sent to block it up, and early in September was making his difficult way through the sterile region to the northeast.

The only alternative now was immediate evacuation, or unconditional surrender. This being decided upon, Morgan chose the former, and determined to make a desperate effort to save his army and artillery,—all but the siege guns, which he resolved to destroy. It was a dreary prospect, at best. That frightful march of two hundred miles with ten thousand men before us, behind us, and on every side. But Morgan had

[11] According to Mason, *op. cit.,* p. 128, the region was "so barren and inhospitable that even the mountain corn-cracker and ginseng gatherer had abandoned it to desolation."

tried his officers and men, and knew they would do anything
short of a miracle, while he himself resolved to be annihilated
rather than surrender. Sending out officers to buy provisions
by way of Mount Sterling—who were purposely captured—
he completely deceived the enemy as to his intentions.

In the meantime, preparations were rapidly made to leave.
The mountain was mined so as to tumble the cliffs upon the
road in our rear; the heavy siege guns were destroyed, and
on the 16th, a large train started for Manchester, where the
brigade of Col. De Courcy was bivouacked, having left the
Gap on the 8th. and forced its way there, driving the Rebel
cavalry under the guerrilla Morgan before it. A mill there
was set in motion, grinding corn enough to supply the Brigade
with quarter-rations of corn bread. At night, we slept on our
arms, frequently repelling the charges of Morgan's Rebel
cavalry. Our Brigade was again moved on, opening up the
road for the remainder of our army, which was soon to leave
the Gap.

Throughout the night of the 16th., the work of the evacuation went on. At evening, the pickets were quietly withdrawn,
and Lieut.-Col. Gallup, with two hundred chosen men, was directed to hold the enemy in check, and if he attempted to follow, to give the alarm by blowing up the magazine. Before he
should finally leave the Gap, he was ordered to fire the military storehouse, Commissary's and Quartermaster's buildings
and tents, and then spring the mines that would unseat the
cliffs and hurl them into the road behind the retreating army.
Five picked men were stationed at each magazine, to which
the trains were already laid, and five more at a pit in which
were piled several thousand stand of arms, mostly loaded,
who at a given signal were to apply the torch and set the vol-
cano in motion.

Gallup, having stationed his pickets, went forward with a
flag of truce, and by adroit management effectually deceived
the enemy respecting Morgan's designs. When he knew, by
certain signs, that the army was well in motion, he took his
leave, saying he would call in the morning and get his answer
to the flag of truce. He then visited his pickets, telling them
to dispute every inch of the ground, and repaired to Baird's

Headquarters, where he found Morgan sitting on his horse, watching his retiring columns winding off into the darkness down the mountain road and away in the direction of Cumberland Ford.

It was now ten o'clock at night and the fate of the army was fast approaching. Turning to Gallup, Morgan said: "You have a highly important duty to perform. This ammunition and these arms and stores must not fall into the hands of the enemy. I hope you will not be captured. Farewell," he added, and bowing, rode off into the gloom. The night wore on, and Gallup, sending off his small force to a place of safety, detailed Markham, O'Brien, and Thad Reynolds (as he was called)—the boldest scout and spy in the army—to kindle the conflagration.

As the flames rolled heavenward, he gave the signal to fire the trains. To his astonishment, no answering explosion followed. Waiting a sufficient time, he put spurs to his horse and galloped to the spot. Not a soul was to be found; all had gone forward to the main column. Seizing some burning fagots, he fired the train with his own hands, and mounting hastily his horse, dashed down the Gap. He had hardly reached a safe distance when the first explosion followed, sending the huge rocks in every direction. The conflagration in the valley below was now in full headway and the scene, say eye-witnesses, was indescribably grand.

The savage precipices reddened like fire in the sudden illumination, and the whole midnight gorge shone brighter than at midday. One can imagine Gallup sitting on his horse, that glowed like a fiery steed in the intense glare of the flames, gazing with silent awe on the wild work his hands had wrought, every fissure and opening in the cliffs around him visible. The trees and rocks, at any time picturesque and interesting, now grand in their beauty. It must have been a scene more like enchantment than reality.

But suddenly the scene changed. The large magazine with its stores of fixed ammunition and powder exploded, shaking the mountains like a toy in the hands of a monster. The air was filled with dense smoke and huge masses of rock. Cartridge boxes, barrels of powder and other materials were blown to an incredible height, and went whirling through the air in wild confusion, falling in some instances, it is said, more than a mile from the exploding magazine. A moment after, the roof of a building 180 feet long, used as a store-house on the mountain, fell in and set fire to the shells stored there. Before the blazing embers that shot in a fiery shower heavenward had descended to the earth again, the explosion took place, sounding like a thousand cannon let off there at once in the trembling gorge.

Lighted on its way by such a sea of flame, and keeping step to such stern and awful music, did our gallant army move off into the night and turn its face towards the distant Ohio. But the terrific fusillade made by the discharging guns and burst-ing shells was kept up among the solitary crags until noon. The Rebel army beyond the ridge, in Powell's Valley, was filled with consternation as they gazed on the lurid sky and felt the earthquake shock, and knew not what the strange tu-mult meant. When at last they were informed by an inhabitant of the region that Morgan had evacuated the Gap, they dared not approach it until three o'clock the next day for fear of exploding shells and mines. When they did venture near, they gazed around in blank astonishment. Silence and desolation reigned throughout the gorge, while the rocks lay piled along it in a wild wreck, heaved there by the exploding mines.

The work was done thoroughly, but the mighty task before us was only just commenced. Two hundred miles of such a country as lay before them were never before marched over by 10,000 men, with artillery and no supplies, while a vast army was closing in upon them on every side. As if to cloud the beginning of our great endeavor with increasing gloom, towards morning of the 18th. a pelting rain set in, accom-panied with fierce gusts of wind that swept mournfully over the swiftly marching columns. Ten ladies (the wives and daughters of officers) were with the army to share its perils and its fortunes.

Marching by two parallel roads, the main army, by rapid marching, reached Flat Lick by daylight, 20 miles from the Gap which they had left the night before, and by evening were at Manchester. Here, they halted for a day to complete the organization of the force and gird their loins for the long and doubtful race yet before them. De Courcy's Brigade of well-disciplined troops were slowly driving the Rebel cavalry before them on the Proctor Road, and cutting out blockades and removing obstructions thrown down upon the route of our army by disloyal citizens and the enemy's scouts. Before Morgan was ready to start from Manchester, he heard the enemy's bugles sounding in his rear, while the scouts brought in the tidings that a brigade of cavalry under the notorious John Morgan was hovering around his line of march, between the main army and De Courcy's advance brigade. He learned, also, that Humphrey Marshall was moving to cut him off to the north. In fact, so precarious was the condition of our force that General Jones, afterwards taken prisoner by us, stated that had our retreat been delayed by a single day, the last avenue of escape would have been closed.

The storm was rapidly gathering on every side and nothing but swift marching could save us. A single inefficient or negligent officer, the capture of a picket guard, might work the ruin of the retreating army, but a truer set of subordinates and men never drew a sword or shouldered a musket. Generals Spears, Carter, and Baird, commanding brigades of Tennessee troops, and Colonel De Courcy, with the Sixteenth and Forty-second Ohio and Fourteenth Kentucky regiments, led their respective brigades with a skill that won the admiration of all.

It is impossible for me to give a detailed account of this extraordinary retreat. I lost the sole from my right boot a few days after leaving Manchester, and marching up and down the foothills of the Cumberland Mountains, over the rocky roads and thorny paths of the skirmish line, I suffered terribly,—but in this I was not alone. Hardly a man was fit to be seen for want of clothing.

Our route lay generally in the direction of Proctor, West Liberty, Grayson, and Greenupsburg, the army marching in lengthening line, winding over the stony, broken, sterile region like a huge serpent. The heavy rumbling of the trains and guns, the only music of the march. When we approached a crossroad, the army was concentrated to prevent flank attacks of the enemy's cavalry, and as soon as the danger was over, unwound again and pressed forward. Sometimes, water could be got only by pulling it up from crevices in the cliffs 80 or 100 feet deep; one day we marched 34 miles in order to reach water. So constantly and dreadfully did we suffer for want of it, that we began to talk of the distant Ohio as the end of all human desires. At another time, we were without water about fifty hours. Our tongues were parched with thirst, and when at length water was obtained in the horse tracks on a low, flat piece of ground, it was fought for by us like so many wolves. However, compared with the pangs of hunger which we almost constantly felt, our want of water was comparatively slight. Even the officers and women suffered from it. Occasionally, a field of standing corn was passed, which sufficed to keep us from starvation.

Our tin plates were converted into "graters," by means of which we reduced the hard corn to a coarse meal, and this, boiled to a "mush"; or else the corn was simply parched, serving as food in this way for the half-famished soldiers. A small slice of bread or a cracker—before either entirely disappeared —commanded fabulous prices; ten dollars offered, with more buyers than sellers. We frequently went 48 hours without a morsel of anything. Staring famine elicited no murmuring, no complaint.

The roads were blockaded with fallen trees and rocks which had to be removed, or a new road cut around them; and the crack of rifles from the thickets along our line of march and from barricades in front, and the report of forces gathering in advance, kept us always on the alert and hard at work, and constantly moving. The usual September storm, even a little delay, would probably have sealed the fate of the army. But the bright autumnal weather enabled us to march steadily, and thus keep the advantage we had gained at the start to the last. The Rebels Morgan and Marshall were both in our front, and an overwhelming force in our rear, but the latter could not overtake us, while we moved so rapidly that the former had no time to concentrate a sufficient force to arrest our progress. Many conflicts with small bodies of the enemy occurred, in which a few of our boys fell, and were hastily buried in the sterile fields past which we marched. Thus, day after day, for nearly a fortnight, this wonderful retreat was kept up until, at length, on the 3rd. of October, 1862, our Brigade in the advance, as we reached a lofty swell, caught a glimpse of the "Lordly Ohio," rolling its glittering flood through the distant landscape.

At the glad sight, a thrilling shout went up, and "The Ohio!", "The Ohio!", rose and fell in prolonged and jubilant acclamation for miles away along the weary column, recalling the day when the Roman army sent up in a wild shout: "The Rhine! The Rhine!", as they once more came in sight of their native stream, and joy and gladness filled every heart.[12]

Our loss from the time of leaving the Gap was eighty men. The women of Greenupsburg, where we struck the Ohio, were requested to stay indoors or leave the town until we had crossed the river, as our army was literally naked and unfit to be seen by the eyes of a respectable community. I had discarded one boot and had lost the greater portion of my pants from the knees down. A whole pair of boots or shoes was not to be found amongst the rank and file. Some marched in their drawers; others, without blouses; *all* looked like beggars. The town was ransacked by the voracious soldiers, but not enough was obtained to appease our hunger. On the contrary, it was only aggravated the more, and we now clamored to cross the river into Ohio, where *Rebellion was not and plenty reigned.*[13]

Our wishes were finally gratified. Messengers were sent on in advance to inform the inhabitants of our destitution. The citizens were aroused, and scouring the country in every direction, succeeded in accumulating at Wheelersburg, on the Ohio side of the river, a repast for the hungry men. Now, for the first time in months, we marched to the step of martial music through a loyal town with loyal inhabitants, in

[12] The author's adaptation of Headley's account ends here.

[13] "When the Forty-second left the Gap, it numbered seven hundred and fifty men, and while on the march there were issued to it two hundred and seventy-five pounds of flour, four hundred pounds of bacon, and two rations of fresh pork; the rest of the food consisted of corn, grated down on tin plates and cooked upon them. The distance marched was two hundred and fifty miles. . . ." —Whitelaw Reid, *Ohio in the War* (Columbus, Ohio: Electric Publishing Co., 1893), II, 268.

whose breasts loyal sympathies were beating and whose tears were shed for our suffering boys. Out beyond the village, upon the open common, a repast was spread for us, and never before was a repast so relished. We devoured roasted meats and pies, cakes, and every good thing that loyal and true hands had provided, like famished wolves. Men and women stood crying to see how near starving we had been. Every little article was asked for from us as relics, and even our tin plates which we had used for graters were begged of us for keepsakes. Such evident loyalty and love of the soldier by these dear people were highly appreciated by us, and we even parted with pieces of our garments to satisfy their requests. Anything we could do in return for their great kindness, was done willingly. A bevy of young ladies with baskets of pies and cookies and other delicacies besieged me for a tin spoon which I had carried from the Gap. I gave it to the prettiest one in the group; to another, I gave a piece of leather cut from my cartridge-box belt.

It was understood that our Brigade was to proceed to Camp Dennison for reorganization and to be reclothed, and the command marched to Sciotoville, remaining there in bivouac until the 9th., moving thence to Portland, Ohio, the order sending us to Camp Dennison having been countermanded. Here, the Forty-second was kept strictly within the limits of the camp until reclothed. Its depleted ranks were filled with raw recruits, and the Regiment was put through the drill for their benefit. Relatives of many in our ranks visited us there, bringing boxes of rich delicacies from our homes in the northern part of the state.

October 21st. found the entire force under Gen. Morgan en route for Gallipolis, Ohio. A march upon our green soil was a strange experience to us, and we felt more like soldiers upon leaving that place for Point Pleasant, Virginia, and thence up the Kanawha Valley to Charleston, encamping at that impoverished city on the 30th. The only Rebel force in this vicinity was a regiment or two of cavalry, who abandoned the country to our possession without a show of resistance, falling back through Gauley and into the mountains of this region. The Forty-second furnished the guard in the city, and

the writer was on the patrol force, whose duty it was to remain in the city and enforce good order in the streets. The
citizens were Rebels at heart, but said little on the War
topic. Our stay at Charleston was short, and pulling up stakes
on the 10th. of November, we marched back to Point Pleasant, embarking there for Memphis, Tennessee. We had
marched from Charleston, a distance of seventy miles, in
three days. When all were on board steamers, the fleet
steamed down the river, stopping a few hours at Cincinnati
before going on to Louisville.

On the 27th., the Command disembarked at Memphis,
after a pleasant trip down the Ohio and Mississippi Rivers.
Grant's victory at Fort Donaldson and the conquest of Island
No. Ten had driven the enemy out of this section of Tennessee, and we remained in quiet possession of the country. Our
Command, having been transferred to the Mississippi Department, made rapid preparation for the movement in process of organizing for the opening up of the River to New Orleans. The Fifteenth Corps from Holly Springs joined us.
Amongst the regiments belonging to the force was the Fifty-
seventh Ohio under Col. A. V. Rice, a brave and accomplished
officer with whom I was acquainted, as well as with many men
in his regiment.

II

THE VICKSBURG CAMPAIGN
1863

Private Hopkins was promoted to corporal on January 2,
1863. For an account of what happened to him between the
departure of the Forty-second, O.V.I., from Memphis, in De-
cember, 1862, to its arrival at Grand Gulf, Mississippi, in
April, 1863, we follow D(MS). His diary, A(MS), contin-
ues the narrative from April 29 until his return to Ohio on
special orders in August. Excerpts from C(MS), written in
1864, and a few letters complete the chronicle for the year.

On the 20th of December, 1862, our Regiment, with the
force under General Sherman, set sail from Memphis.

The army, consisting of about 15,000 men, with several
gunboats, arrived at the mouth of the Yazoo River, just above
Vicksburg, on Saturday morning, the 29th. A line of high
bluffs here fringe the eastern shores of the Yazoo and the
Mississippi. This bluff on the Yazoo is at a short distance
from the river, and the intervening space consists of a low
and marshy bottom often overflowed by the swelling of the
stream, and at all other times intersected by sluggish bayous.

The chain of bluffs frowned with batteries on summit and
sides, and with rifle pits near the base. The plan of attack
was for Gen. Sherman to assail these works in front, while
Gen. Grant, advancing by way of Jackson, was to charge them
in the rear. But by the inconceivable imbecility of a subordi-
nate at Holly Springs, a raiding party of Rebels had fallen
upon our magazines of supplies there and had destroyed
two millions' worth in a few hours. Grant was thus delayed.
On the very day of the disembarking of our forces, we pushed

across the marshy river bottom to near the edge of the bluffs, driving the enemy into their works.

The next morning, the engagement was opened with an impetuous fire of artillery, and then with an infantry charge upon the first line of rebel rifle pits. The enterprise was crowned with success, and as we swarmed into the captured works, the Rebels fled to their second line of defense. In the meantime, the enemy had concentrated a heavy force within their ramparts, while but one half of our army designed for the attack was in the field. Sunday and Monday were spent by both armies in preparation for the decisive conflict, while each endeavored to annoy the other by occasional artillery firing.

Having thrown several bridges across the bayous, Gen. Sherman ordered a general assault at two o'clock Monday afternoon. At the appointed hour, the storm burst in all its fury. The hill belched forth flame and smoke, with trembling of the earth under the cannons' roar, as though a hundred volcanoes were in violent eruption. We were compelled in the charge to wade the bayous and struggle through the swamps covered with fallen timbers and traversed by abatis.[1] General Blair's horse became hopelessly mired, and he slid from his back and led his brigade on foot.

De Courcy's brigade was next, but the boys pressed forward so vigorously in the daring onset that it was difficult to tell who was in the advance. Onward we swept through flame and smoke and blood, leaving the dead and dying behind us, climbing, crawling, fighting our way up the slope with the desperation of men resolved to conquer or die. Our thinned ranks, breathless, bleeding, reached the center of the enemy's works. Here, we were assailed by an awful fire from outnumbering foes nearly surrounding us. Bravely we had won our position, but it was found impossible to hold it. One third of our attacking party was placed *hors de combat*. We had taken both first and second lines of the rebel entrenchments, and yet we found but defeat in victory. Such a destructive storm of shot and shell was poured in upon us that we were compelled precipitately to retire. With saddened hearts, we yielded to the cruel necessity.

---

[1] These were defenses that were constructed of felled trees, the branches of which were pointed toward the invaders.

Such was the battle of Chickasaw Bluffs. It was a brave but desperate conflict.[2] We accomplished all that mortal valor could achieve. Those frowning heights could not be carried by charging them in face of all their batteries with but half the army commissioned for the enterprise.

We now withdrew to a point out of range of the Rebel field artillery, though their heavier guns shelled our position incessantly. At sunset, under a flag of truce, the two armies gathered their dead and wounded. This is the saddest duty devolving upon a soldier. The shrieks of the wounded, the groans of the dying, appeal to the sympathies of the most hardened nature, and our hearts grow heavy as we bury side by side our late comrades in arms. Glorious though the day may have been, this sad rite dispels every feeling of joy, when we remember how many mothers are made childless, how many children left without fathers, by the slaughter of the battlefield.

Our loss was 580 killed, 1400 wounded, and 550 missing.[3] The loss of the enemy could not be ascertained, though it could not have been as heavy as ours, as they fought under cover of their entrenchments.

A constant, though harmless, artillery duel was now commenced, and from breastworks along our front a perpetual fire from the infantry was kept up until the night of the 4th of January, when it was resolved to abandon the attempt of carrying this point, and to embark on board the transports, —which was successfully done, and our entire fleet sailed out of the Yazoo and into the Mississippi.[4]

The Thirteenth Corps, under General McClernand, after the failure at Chickasaw Bluffs, proceeded up the Mississippi as far as the little town of Napoleon, Arkansas. Turning into the Arkansas River, the transports laden with troops, under

[2] This was the first and worst defeat the Forty-second Regiment, O.V.I., ever suffered.

[3] "The Brigade, composed of the Sixteenth and Forty-second O.V.I. and Twenty-second Kentucky regiments, lost 1300 men."—C(MS).

[4] "The Rebels were heavily reinforced in the night by Breckinridge from Jackson, and their bands played martial airs on the fortifications by moonlight. Among the tunes played was 'Get Out of the Wilderness,' and we 'got,' for no sooner did the moon go down than we drew off our artillery, and the infantry followed, with the Forty-second as rear guard for our division."—C(MS).

convoy of several gunboats, threaded the dangerous channel of that turbid stream to a point several miles below Arkansas Post, a strongly fortified position in the hands of about 6000 of the enemy.

Here, we landed on the right bank of the river on the 10th of January, and bivouacked for the night. The gunboats sailed forth up the stream and anchored in sight of the fort. The morning following, one division of our corps crossed the river with two batteries of artillery, and forming a line diagonal with the river, advanced in conjunction with the division on the right bank upon the Rebel works.

The battle was opened by our gunboats, moving in line with the land forces. Soon the Rebel guns responded to their fire, and afterwards the Water batteries were loosing shells into *our* advancing columns. Colonel Lindsay, commanding the brigade, adjacent to the river and the right bank, pushed forward his troops so vehemently that they were the first to open fire on the enemy.

Morgan's division of the Thirteenth Corps was the next in the fight, and soon the whole line was engaged. An assault was repulsed the second time, but we were resolved to make up for our defeat at Chickasaw Bayou, and every man fought with a courage and perseverance seldom equalled. At the second onset, a few entered the Rebel redoubts, and the white flag was hoisted. The firing ceased along the lines, and with cheers we dashed across the open space in front to enter the works, but no sooner had we advanced within fifty yards of their rifle muzzles than the white flag was lowered, and we were greeted with a treacherous and deadly fire of infantry and a raking discharge of grape and canister.

At this unparalleled treachery, our boys dashed into the ditches, and climbing on each other's shoulders in lieu of scaling ladders, with deafening cheers and cries of victory, entered the rebel works, driving the traitors before them at the bayonet point. This breach was effected by Morgan's division, and the whole line of Rebels gave way. The white token of surrender was again run up in place of the Rebel flag, and the Victory was ours. Four thousand, eight hundred prisoners fell into our hands, and two batteries of artillery, besides sev-

eral valuable pieces of heavy ordnance. Our loss was comparatively slight.

Our success was followed soon after by the reduction of
Forts St. Charles, Duval's Bluff, and Des Arc, on the White
River, and thus were the two rivers—the Arkansas and the
White—again returned to free navigation as far as Little
Rock, Ark. Guerrilla bands still infested the banks on either
side, but our transports, generally moving under convoy of a
gunboat, were seldom molested, as the bushwhackers entertained a wholesome dread of these savage looking engines of
war.

The Rebel force captured at Arkansas Post was composed
chiefly of Texans, and appeared to be the off-scouring of crea-
tion. None of them could explain or even conjecture any of the
issues involved in the war, and like thousands of others in
the Southern Army, they knew not what they were really fighting for. Their convictions, however, were that we were wag-
ing a war of extermination, and they expressed their determination of resisting to the bitter end.

Our fleet now sailed back into the Mississippi, and on the
29th of January landed at Young's Point,[5] opposite and above
Vicksburg, which is situated upon the east bank of the river,
on a high bluff near the point of one of the most majestic
bends of the stream. On the opposite, or west, shore of the
peninsula formed by the bend, the land is low and protected
by a dyke. Our first attempt now was to open the old Williams
Canal[6] across the peninsula of Young's Point. Day and night,
the troops were kept busily at work upon this ditch, until the
work was nearly two-thirds done, when an unfortunate break
in the dam flooded the immense *cut* with water, effectually putting a stop to all further work.[7] Before this injury could be
repaired, the period of high water had passed away, and the
enterprise was abandoned.

Soon after, the Thirteenth Army Corps was ordered to
Milliken's Bend, several miles above Young's Point, and go-

---

[5] At this juncture, General Grant took command of the siege operations in
person.

[6] In 1862, General Thomas Williams had come up from New Orleans and
cut a ditch ten or twelve feet wide and as deep across the peninsula.

[7] The work ceased March 8, 1863.

ing into camp there, awaited further orders. The country around was low and marshy and often flooded for leagues in the swellings of the stream, expanding often into an almost illimitable ocean, spreading through somber forests and over gloomy morasses through a region of hundreds of square miles, where Nature, by the slow deposit of ages, is preparing soil for future tillers, [but] now presents bogs and lakes and sluggish bayous, the congenial home of alligators and all unclean reptiles. Mosquitoes, the vilest of earth's tormentors, darken the air. Majestic trees, draped in funeral moss, overhang these gloomy waters, while the rankest undergrowth of every creeping, climbing, intertwining shrub renders the boundless thicket almost impregnable. Where the land is sufficiently raised above the water to be cultivated, it is protected from the spring and autumnal freshets by dykes, or levees— artificial mounds of earth about ten feet high and fifteen wide, constructed at immense expense along the river banks.

As soon as the spring floods had sufficiently fallen to render it possible,[8] we were ordered to advance by land, through the forests and threading the edge of the morass on the western shore of the river, entirely concealed from observation, and to march from Milliken's Landing, above the Rebel ramparts, to New Carthage, below. In this movement, Gen. McClernand with the Thirteenth Corps led the advance. It had been necessary to delay the enterprise until the waters in the river and the bayous should recede; still, the road was all but impassable. It lay through a vast bog, intersected by numerous bayous half flooded with water.

The heavy artillery wheels cut through the slime and the mud, making the path a perfect mortar bed through which we waded knee deep, and where the hubs of the wheels often disappeared out of sight. The advance of the army was found to be utterly impracticable, except by the building of corduroy roads, cutting outlets for the egress of the water, and bridging the bayous. The army had to build for itself, under the most difficult circumstances, a military road as it advanced. Twenty

[8] From December, 1862, to April, 1863, the river was higher than its natural banks, and there were heavy rains along its lower course.

miles of levee had to be most carefully guarded, lest it should be cut by the enemy and the whole country flooded.

The vigilant foe got some intimation of the movement, notwithstanding it had been very carefully concealed. As we approached New Carthage, we found that the levee had been cut by the Rebels, and the surrounding country was so flooded that New Carthage was converted into an island. After ineffectual attempts to bridge the rushing waters or to cross them in boats, it was found necessary to march in search of some point farther down the river. Inspirited rather than discouraged by such obstacles, we pressed on, and after having constructed seventy miles of road and about 2000 feet of bridging, we reached our final destination.

A considerable part of the army was now south of Vicksburg, but on the wrong side of the river, which here rushed along, a wide, deep, turbid torrent. We had no means of crossing, and as the Rebels had a strong array of batteries at Port Hudson, no transport could be sent up the river to our aid. But, without transports, the river could not be crossed. General Grant was prepared for the emergency. We had resolved to undertake the apparently desperate enterprise of running the terrific batteries with the steamboats then at the landing of Young's Point and Milliken's Bend.

Three transports and eight gunboats, in a bend of the river where they were secluded from all observation, were secretly prepared for the trying ordeal. The transports were plain wooden boats; speed was essential to their safety. The boilers were carefully protected by bales of cotton and hay on the sides exposed to the batteries. Volunteers were called for to engage in the desperate enterprise, and more came forward than could be accepted. One single regiment furnished 132 such volunteers. The contest was so great that a boy who was accepted was offered $100 for his chance. He rejected the offer, held his post, and passed the batteries in safety. Such was the spirit which animated the American soldier in this war against rebellion.

A little before midnight, when most of the lights had disappeared from Vicksburg, and silence reigned over both camps, the gunboats were to pass down in single file, and when opposite the batteries were to open on them a terrific fire. Under cover of this fire and protected by the gunboats, the transports were to endeavor to run by unseen. The gunboats—huge masses of blackness—emerged from their concealment and moved silently down the stream. Breathlessly, the army at Young's Point watched the movements of these clouds of darkness from which War's most awful thunders were soon to burst.

Three-quarters of an hour of silence elapsed, when two flashes from one of the Vicksburg batteries, followed by a roar that shook the hills, announced the opening of the grand drama. In an instant, the whole line of bluffs was ablaze with fire. The three transports—the *Forest Queen, Henry Clay,* and *Silver Wave*—were now on the most impetuous rush down the stream. The ironclads lay squarely before the city, from twenty-five guns pouring their storm of shell and shrapnel directly into the streets. Suddenly a gleam of light appeared, and an immense bonfire blazed from one of the hills of Vicksburg, converting night into day. The beacon flames lit up the hills so brilliantly that every boat was exposed to the careful aim of the batteries.

The *Forest Queen* was disabled and was taken in tow by a gunboat and carried without further injury down the stream. The cotton on the *Henry Clay* ignited from a bursting shell, and that steamer burned to the water's edge. The crew in both escaped to the western shore. The *Silver Wave* was not touched, and reached our lines below in safety. The eight gunboats reached their destination without injury. On Porter's flagship, the *Benton,* one man was killed and two wounded. No one on the transports was injured. The batteries extended for eight miles along the river, from the upper end of the city to the fortifications at Warrenton. One and a half hours were spent in passing them.

The injuries which the boats received in running the batteries were speedily repaired by volunteer mechanics, who came forth from the ranks, ready to perform any work in wood or iron, and who were skillful artisans in all the most difficult branches of mechanics. The success of this experi-

ment was so gratifying that on the 22nd. of April six more
transports were sent down the stream, towing twelve barges
loaded with forage. One of these transports, the *Tigress,*
received a shot below the water line and sank on the Louisiana
shore. The rest, with one half the barges, got through with
but trifling damage. On the 29th, the fleet and army, now
rendezvoused at Perkins' Plantation, were ready for action. A little below Vicksburg and on the same side of the
river, is the town of Grand Gulf. The Rebels, anticipating
the danger of Grant's seizing upon this and using it as a base
of operations against Vicksburg, had planted heavy batteries
there and had dug rifle pits. It was not supposed that their
works were very formidable, but that under the protection
of the gunboats a sufficient force could be landed to carry
them by storm.

The army embarked on transports and barges, and moved
down toward the batteries on the 29th of April, while Ad-
miral Porter's gunboats opened a heavy fire upon the rebel
works, continuing the bombardment for four or five hours. On
the steamboats, hardly out of range of the enemy's shots, we
watched the grand sight, which but few witness in a lifetime.
The ironclads often moved up to within pistol shot of the
batteries, and poured their deadly hail right into the enemy's
embrasures. The attempt, however, proved a failure. The
gunboats, having exhausted all their energies of valor and
skill, a little after noon were compelled to withdraw, leaving
the principal batteries apparently uninjured.

During the bombardment, the army impatiently awaited
upon the transports the moment when our advance should
be ordered. The withdrawal of the fleet caused general disappointment, for it seemed the whole expedition had been a failure. Our commander, however, was prepared for this emergency as he had been for all others. The troops disembarked
and continued on the march down the western bank of the
river three or four miles, to Bruinsburg. Our movements were
buried in the forest so that the foe could not perceive them.
The same night, the fleet steamed by the Grand Gulf batteries, and the next morning gladdened the vision of the army
by moving near our bivouac. A hasty breakfast, and the

troops were ferried across the river. This movement in landing our Corps of the army (the Thirteenth Corps) on the
eastern bank of the river was bold even to audacity.

The enemy, in superior force, was strongly entrenched just
above, commanding the river. Our line of communication was
long and liable to attack. The troops felt the extreme danger
of the enterprise, but were resolved to do their duty, and having strong faith in the sagacity of their leader, had no fears for
the result. Sherman's army was on the Yazoo, ready to strike
simultaneously with Grant. All the provisions of the army had
to be conveyed down the western bank of the river over the
military road we had constructed. The country through which
we had to advance, was wild and entirely unknown, very
sparsely inhabited, full of hills and gloomy ravines most admirably adapted to defensive warfare. Everything depended upon
celerity of movement and almost reckless bravery . . . .

*During the bombardment of Grand Gulf, on April 29,
1863, Corporal Hopkins made the first entry in his diary. In
following it day by day through the Vicksburg campaign,
one should recall that the writer was an eighteen-year-old
village boy, limited in formal education, untraveled until his
enlistment, whose deep convictions of right and wrong had
led him to volunteer his services in the Union cause, but who
because of his experiences in the war had already matured beyond his physical age. The boy and the man appear con-
jointly in these pages.*

April 29th. Witnessed the Bombardment of Grand Gulf
by U.S. Gun boats *Louisville, Cincinnati, Tuscumbia, Franklin, Benton, Carondelet,* and ———. Bombardment lasted
six hours when the Iron clads withdrew after silencing all
the enemies Guns but two. 5 P.M.—McClernand's Corps disembarked and march below the Rebel Batteries and Bivouac
for the Night while our Transports run the Guantlet of the
still uninjured guns of Grand Gulf. At Mid-Night we are
awakened by the tremendous thunder of artillery as our transports attempt to run the Blockade. We listen with awful
suspense until the shrill whistle of half a dozen Transports

tell us that all is well, and in a moment after Comd. Porter's Fleet lands in silence near our camp.

April 30th. This morning we cross[9] the Father of Waters and draw five days rations Preparatory to a long march Who knows where. 3 P.M.—Take up our line of march toward the interior of the State of Mississippi on the road leading to Port Gibson. Continue on the march until the Morning of the 1st of May, when we halt and prepare a cup of the Indispensible, everlasting, and never-ending Coffee. Add to this the Unconquerable hardtack and slice of "sowbelly," our breakfast is finished, and amid the noise of rattling wheels, the Clarion notes of the Bugle, and Neighing of War horses, we move onward. A mile beyond, the enemies[10] guns from Thompson's Hill (*or Plantation*) open upon us, for Osterhaus[11] has the advance. The usual amount of skirmishing goes on while our Columns deploy into line of battle and by 10 A.M. the Battle rages with all its fury.[12] The enemy resists stubbornly to the last, but before nightfall his Columns slowly give way and the Victory, though dearly bought, is *ours*. A sullen silence prevails for a moment, when a shout of Victory went up from thousands of Yankee throats, and the Noise is louder than the roar of Battle which preceeded it. We do not persue the flying and disordered Traitors but Bivouac on or near the Battle Field. The roll is called and the Forty-second is minus 100 of its best men. A low murmur of revenge sounds through our ranks and we retire to our "downy" (?) beds of ease,—the ground for our Mattress, our Knapsacks for Pillows. We gaze at the Stars and moon until sleep takes us into Forgetfullness on the Night of that First Day of May, 1863.

May 2nd. The Bugles sound the Reveille at early dawn and we prepare our scanty breakfast of crackers and coffee, and at an early hour we are on the track of Bowens' Rebel army.

[9] The crossing was made five miles above Bruinsburg, Mississippi.

[10] A portion of Pemberton's army commanded by General Bowen.

[11] General Osterhaus was in command of one of McClernand's four divisions.

[12] Corporal Hopkins had his cartridge box shot from his side by a shell fragment at the battle of Port Gibson.

Arms and legs of dead Rebels, Broken wagons and Artillery, dead horses, dead mules, and dead Rebels show the extent of the Victory and the enemies loss. Continue the Persuit to Port Gibson where the Rebels cross Bayou Perre [Pierre], a tributary of the Big Black River, and destroy the Bridge. We halt [13] until Pontoons are thrown across. At 5 A.M. we cross on the following morn; Bivouac near the town of Port Gibson.

May 3rd. This morning at daylight we move forward. Everywhere we find evidences of the Panic of the Rebels. Skirmishing with the Rebel Rear Guard commenced very early. The weather very warm. We halt on the Banks of Big Sand Creek at 4 P.M.[14] Our cavalry constantly bringing in prisoners.

May 4th. Still in our stopping place of Last night. Expect a train of supplies soon. Our rations few and far between.[15] Corn bread our only supply and that without salt. Our five days rations gone the way of all rations and "who Knoweth what the Morrow may bring forth?"

May 5th. Moved across Big Sand Creek and Bivouacked one mile beyond. The looked-for train not yet arrived. Faith and hope now mixed with a greater portion of Economy is our only living. But few complain, knowing that it is all for "The Union."

May 6th. Had Battallion drill and Review this afternoon by Generals McClernand and Grant.

May 7th. Lay in Camp until Noon when orders came to march. Move 8 miles and Bivouac for the night. Confiscated

[13] "Last night, the two armies bivouacked close together, and Federal and Rebel soldiers stole chickens and hogs off the same plantation. Rebel deserters are coming in constantly. . . ."—C(MS).

[14] ". . . reaching it just in time to save the bridge from burning, it having been fired by enemy."—C(MS).

[15] ". . . Many of the men having lost their haversacks on the march and in our battles, the rest have to *share* with deficient, and the consequence is that hardtack is at a premium and corn-bread and coffee compose the *bill of fare.*"—C(MS).

contraband articles, *viz*. One old Rooster aged 8 years 3 months and one day; One hen with a large family of Chickens; one Yearling Pig weighing 75 pounds; and a shoulder of mutton. (Bully for us!)

May 8th. March again in the afternoon and Halt at the Junction of the Rodney and Raymond Roads. Sherman's corps will be there tomorrow.

May 9th. Our Company sent out on a foraging Expedition, alias Stealing tour. I filled my Haversack full of the dainties of the country. We succeeded in Finding a wagon-load of molasses and Bacon which we shipped immediately for the especial Benefit of the Forty-second Regiment Ohio Infantry Volunteers, U.S.A. Returned to Camp tired But *not* hungry. Sherman's corps passed in the evening; it is believed we will move on Jackson.

In C(MS), Hopkins describes the expedition in greater detail:

Captain Hutchins' company (which is *us*) was detailed on a foraging expedition, much to the delight of every man in it. Striking off across the country in the direction of Vicksburg, we came to a plantation where no Yankees had ever trod, and after putting to flight a pack of blood hounds and frightening half out of their wits a motly group of alternately black and white darkies, I discovered the *garden,* now full of early vegetables, while Jim W—— [Whitsell] had the honor of discovering a well-filled *smoke-house,* and Don Van D—— [Van Deuren] accidentally fell over a barrel of dried peaches, Jake C—— [Caskey] in the meantime capturing three or four fat hens, while Adam D—— [Dellman] encountered a porker with such violence that Porker was killed and his hams amputated with great skill. Massa and the white folks having fled the premises, our search extended to the mansion and bureau drawers, where I succeeded in finding a dozen pairs of cotton socks, a welcome discovery as my only pair needed the tender care of a mother who could darn. I'll be darned if they didn't! Having secured all the provender on the premises, we "hired" a "colored individual" to hitch up the *ox and mule* teams, and hauled our prisoners and Wedgetables to camp, arriving tired but *not hungry* about dusk, receiving as a reward from our ravenous comrades a round of hearty cheers, and before morning chickens, turkeys, calves, pigs, and everything had become food for soldiers.

May 10th. Still no movement of our Division. Forage comes in slowly.

May 11th. March at 10 A.M.; Twenty-second Kentucky in the advance, we are on the Raymond Road. Halt!—Stack arms!—Unsling Knapsacks!—Make your fires for the night!

May 12th. Move but a short distance today owing to the Number of troops on this road.

May 13th. Our Columns are in motion early, and the sun pours its vengeance on the heads of Grant's noble Army of the Mississippi. In the afternoon, the Programme of the weather is changed and we struggle Forward through mud and rain until night. Halt 5 miles from Raymond.

That night, Corporal Hopkins and his buddy, Jim Whitsell, set out on an unauthorized foraging expedition of their own that is related in C (MS).

After a hard day's march of fifteen miles, the bugles sound the "halt," and commands are given to unsling knapsacks and rest for the night. Feeling sort of emptyish, says I to Jim, says I: "Jim, let's go for some provender." And says he, "Agreed!"—and we started, I taking a revolver and Jim, a knife. Dodging the camp guard, we soon found ourselves in a large timbered tract, and after a search of an hour succeeded in starting a spring calf. I fired with the revolver hastily, while Jim flourished his knife, the ball striking the calf's nose, causing it to bawl most melancholy, and we at once started through the brushwood in persuit. Making a flank movement, I got another shot, and with more success this time, for the veal fell, and in the next instant Jim's knife was in his throat.

We amputated a hind quarter, and by this time other actors appeared upon the stage, namely, three or four of Company D boys, who soon finished the amputating process, and the calf was soon on the way to the bivouac of the "invaders," —as we were styled by the natives. A slice of veal steak was our countersign and pass through the line of guards, and soon our meat was in the pot. It was cooking under difficulties, however, as a severe storm of rain extinguished our fire and lasted until twelve o'clock at night. By the time it was cleverly boiling again, an orderly galloped to the Colonel's quarters, and soon the bugles sounded "Fall in!" . . . We moved off at a dog's trot toward Raymond, leaving our *veal* simmering on the fire, not having even snoozed.

May 14th. Last night's rest was not very comfortable. It rained until Midnight, when we were ordered to roll up our Blankets for marching Immediately. Of course this was no welcome order, But we might as well be marching as Sleeping in the rain (for we had seen no tents since leaving Carthage). Mud and water, broken bridges and deep ditches, were all the go; no moon, no stars, but utter darkness prevailed, and at daylight we entered the town of Raymond. Not with Floating banners or swelling strains of music. Not with Bright Bayonets gleaming in the sun. Not as a victorious army generally enters a city of the enemy. But tired and dejected, hungry and almost disheartened, our boots full of water, our clothes wet and covered with mud, we entered, and No wonder Raymond Citizens looked at us with fear and trembling!

C(MS) gives the following description of the entry into Raymond:

On and on we tramped . . . till daybreak when we entered the town of Raymond on the double quick amid the barking of dogs, cheering of men, and skedaddling of retreating Rebels, males and females, cows, horses, hogs, and sheep. Our line was formed around the east side of town, the position of the Forty-second being in the Court Yard, and our company resting on the Court-house steps, where many of us,

tired, in fact almost exhausted, soon fell asleep. By broad daylight, however, the Brigade was astir, and a regular pillaging
of the town commenced; the rain poured in torrents, and the
streets were a quagmire, rendered so by the tramping of men
and mules . . . .

May 15th. The rain still pours in torrents, and Raymond
streets are tramped into a quagmire. A general Plundering
prevails. Stores and ware-rooms, Kitchen and dining-room,
Parlor and Pantry, undergo alike the ordeal of being Searched
by the prying "Lincolnites." Furniture and Crockery, Glass-
ware and tinware are scattered and Broken promiscuously,
and the Forty-second Boys are wreaking their vengeance on
the China ware in a Whole Sale establishment just across
the Street. The Eighth Missouri Boys are taking the lead, followed closely by the gaunt sons of Indiana, while the Buckeye
Boys do not quite bring up the rear. Go ahead, boys! It all
belongs to Rebels; go in on your "mus" [muscle]! March
again at 3 P.M. toward Vicksburg; rout the enemies Pickets and Lay in Line of Battle. Enemy expected to attack.

May 16th. Champion Hill. Early this morning we were on
the move and everything betokens an early collision with the
enemy. About 10 A.M. Skirmishing commenced, and ere
noon the two opposing armies are engaged in all the Fury of
Battle. The Rebels charge on us, and we charge on the Rebels.
But no ground is gained until a late hour in the day, when
General Blair moves on the left Flank of the Rebels. They
slowly and sullenly give way at First, But pressed as they
are by Osterhaus, who now has the advance, their retreat
soon became a rout, and the Victory Belongs to Us.[16] They
were whipped more completely than at Thompson's Hill, and
their loss heavier. Guns, caissons, ammunition, small arms,
and dead and wounded, are abandoned in their retreat. We
follow until night puts a stop to pursuit, and we halt at Edward's Depot.

[16] "All along the route are evidences of the complete demoralization of the
Rebel forces: dead horses, disabled guns and carriages, dead men, wounded
ones crying for water, headless bodies, legs and arms with no visible owners
—these are the scenes connected with Victory!"—C(MS).

May 17th. Big Black. Sees us in motion early. By this time, the swift-flying Rebels have reached their dens at Big Black, and we will soon be stirring them with a hot stick. Stragglers from their scattered ranks are constantly being taken. Near noon, we are greeted with a volley from the Rebel 20-pounders at Big Black, it being a signal to prepare for warm work again. Our Column was soon deployed into line of battle, and the thrilling command of "Forward!" was given, and again the Rebel Batteries open with all their fury upon the ranks of our advancing line. The Fight soon became general and lasted with great Fury for six hours, when a charge was ordered, and Yelling like Demons, we went for the Rebel Breastworks, and were greeted with one withering Storm of Grape and Canister, and the Rebels fled, leaving their Artillery Unspiked and loaded to the Muzzles with Grape-shot which we turned against them and paid them off in their own coin. The Forty-second captured the Twenty-sixth Tennessee Rebel Regiment with its colors and Officers.[17] The Victory again is a complete one. The Rebs Fled across the Big Black, Destroying the Bridge and Firing the Railroad Bridge and Trusslework across the River. We have a Pontoon Bridge to build before we can follow.

That same May evening, back in Corporal Hopkins' home town, Bellefontaine, Ohio, one William Kernan was writing a letter to a former schoolmate, Julia Allison, daughter of Colonel Charles W. B. Allison, lately of the Eighty-fifth Regiment, O.V.I., and at present chairman of the Committee on Military Affairs in the state legislature. Miss Allison was not yet seventeen, and William was conceivably no older.

FRIEND JULIA,
Having a little leisure this evening, I have concluded to pass the time by writing to you a few lines which may not be devoid of interest.

Somebody told me that last evening, as I was walking up Columbus Street with a couple of boys, you asked why I went with those boys. It reminded me of a question I had in-

[17] ". . . who, after being formed in line, gave three cheers for the Stars and Stripes, declaring that *under that flag they had plenty.*"—C(MS).

tended asking you. It is this: why do you go with Fannie Riddle? Ever since she disgraced herself by engaging in that
"Butternut mob" [18] at the school-house, I have had no respect
for her whatever. Any one that would take a part in such
proceedings is devoid of all self-respect and should be shunned
by every one.

But we will let that pass, and I will tell you something about
Frank Marsh. One evening—it was when you were in New
Jersey [19]—I asked Frank to take a walk up past your house
with me. "No," said he, "I don't want to see the casket when
the jewel is gone." Ever since then we have called your house
"The Casket."

Why don't you come to school? We have some "gay and
festive" discussions up there about every day. I am the only
one in the room who will stand up for Vallandigham [20] and
his principles, and it is for this reason chiefly that I am called
"Secesh."

I often ask them questions which they cannot answer, and
they call me "Rebel Sympathizer" for daring to ask such
questions.

Here are a few of the questions still unanswered. If you will
answer them for me, I will be much obliged, and I will, in my
turn, answer any question which you ask me about Democratic loyalty:

1st.—Why was Gen. Banks given a command after he had
said, as late as 1860, that he was willing under certain con-
tingencies to let the Union slide?

2nd.—Why were the leaders of the Dayton mob [21] arrested,

[18] Northern partisans of the Southern states were derisively called "butter-
nuts" because of the brown homespun clothing worn by the Confederate militia.
[19] She had been visiting the Roeblings, cousins of the Allisons.
[20] In May, 1863, General Burnside caused the arrest of an Ohio Democrat,
Clement L. Vallandigham, on a charge of openly sympathizing with the South
and uttering opinions prejudicial to the cause of the federal government. He
was tried by a military commission, convicted, and imprisoned in Boston. President Lincoln commuted his sentence but banished him from Union territory.
General Bragg sent him to Richmond, and from there he went to Canada,
where he remained until the close of the war.
[21] On the night of March 5, 1863, two hundred men—most of them soldiers
from Camp Chase—gathered in front of the office of the Columbus *Crisis,* an
anti-administration and Peace Party organ, edited by Samuel Medary, broke
in the door, demolished furniture and equipment, and threw the files into the
street. The police did not interfere. There was a later attempt to burn the
building, but it did not succeed. The affair in connection with the Republican

and the leaders of the mob against the "Columbus Crisis" let go scot free?

3rd.—Why wasn't Greeley arrested for calling the star-spangled banner a "flaunting lie"?

4th.—Why isn't Abe Lincoln impeached for breaking the Constitution?

But I haven't time to write any more this evening. Answer soon, and oblige

Your Friend,
W. KERNAN.

Monday, May 18th. This morning at 9 A.M. the Bridge was completed, and we crossed the Big Black, the Forty-second in the advance. General Lee has command of the Ninth Division, Osterhaus being wounded in yesterday's Battle. Sherman had crossed farther up the river, and the movement on Vicksburg—the boasted stronghold of the Rebels—commenced. The sun was extremely hot and water scarce, But highly elated at our repeated Victories we marched on in good Spirits, resolved to Follow where Ulyssus S. Grant, Unconditional Surrender or United States Grant, led. The movement of so many Troops on this one road, of course, was very slow, and we halted for the night with six miles of road between us and Vicksburg. Strange were our Feelings as we made our beds on the ground that night. Well we knew that a collision would soon take place, for Pemberton's Army was cornered with no place to escape, and the Morrow would tell the tale whether he surrendered without a struggle, or [would] Prolong the contest and increase the loss of so much life. An early Reveille in the Morning was the order for the Night, and the Union Camp relapsed into Silence, except for the "Measured tread of watchful Sentinels pacing the Lonely Beat."

Dayton Daily Journal was more serious: On May 3, following General Burnside's arrest of Vallandigham, a mob of several hundred men, some of them armed, surrounded the newspaper office at nightfall, shot out the windows, set fire to the building, and wrecked the fire engines, causing a widespread conflagration that destroyed several stores, a stable, and a market before it was brought under control. An appeal by city officials to General Burnside brought troops and martial law. So many arrests were made that the jails overflowed. See R. S. Harper, "The Ohio Press in the Civil War," *Civil War History,* III (September, 1957), 3.

Tuesday, May 19th. The Thirteenth Corps was early on its way this morning toward the Heroic Little City. The March was uninterrupted until 2 P.M., when we came in sight of the enemies old Fortifications around the City, and even a portion of the city itself was visible over the hills; as we neared the Hostile Batteries, a curl of Blue smoke was seen to ascend from a Fort directly in our Front, and soon after a shell came flying over our heads, and passing rapidly to the rear, exploded over some wagons loaded with Ammunition. This was Pemberton's Compliments to Grant, and though sent in rather a rough way, was politely answered a short time after by three of our 34-pounders. Some time was occupied in Deploying into line, But by 3 o'clock we were ready for action, and again "Forward!" was the cry.

The Enemy reserved their fire untill we were within close range, when they opened with shot and shell, grape and canister. Men fell like chaff before the wind, But we moved steadily on to within rifle shot, when we halted in a deep Gorge and Partially sheltered from the enemies fire. "Sharp Shooters" were thrown out, and soon the Rebel Artillery fire was almost Silenced. We crept up so close to their batteries that we could fire into the muzzles of their guns, and very seldom did a traitor show his head above the Breastworks. This kind of fighting lasted untill dark, when we retired to the Gorge to rest, supperless and tired, our faces black with Powder, and no water to Wash. Our supplies non-present, and many of our comrades non-respondant.

> 'Tis the lot of a soldier.
> Soldiers we are and none complain,
> Though all feel dejected.

Corporal Hopkins was one of the "sharp shooters":

Sergeant McAllister from Company K called the following names, which were eagerly responded to (with lots of volunteer offers from others), namely, Corporal Hopkins, Privates Allmon, Baldwin, and Van Deuren. We climbed along the summit of a hill in front of the main line of battle, which had now ceased firing, and retired to a ravine out of reach of the Rebel fire, until within close musket fire of the Rebel batteries; here, hiding in gullies washed by the rain, we opened upon the Secesh gunners with such true aim that they were forced to abandon their artillery, while ours came into position and ready to throw "pots and kettles" into their works. A half-dozen men crawled to us with a fresh supply of cartridges, and we continued the fire, cutting down the Rebel flag on Fort Hill and keeping it down, with all heads that tried to look over their breastworks . . . ."—C(MS).

Wednesday, May 20th. Today the Programme of the Battle has been the same as yesterday. No advantage gained over the Enemy.

Thursday, May 21st. Firing still continues along the lines. Our batteries are being placed closer to those of the Rebels. Our Regiment has been engaged all day. I fired 95 rounds at the Chivalry of the South, But with what effect am unable to state.

Friday, May 22nd. (Bad luck to ———!) Will ever be remembered by the Soldiers of Grant's Army as one of the Bloodiest of the campaign. In ordering the Charge on the entrenched Position of the Enemy, May 22nd., General Grant Sealed the fate of Hundreds of his best Soldiers. It was not a charge; it was not a Battle, nor an assault; But a Slaughter of Human Beings in cold Blood. We done our best; we struggled manfully; we fought desperately; all would not do, we were repulsed and with fearful loss.

The charge was made on the Rebel center in columns by Battalion, the Forty-second leading the advance of the Brigade, with the Sixteenth Ohio and Twenty-second Kentucky in the rear. Grape and canister, buckshot and ball, fell in showers, thinning our ranks at every step. We gained a position so close to the enemy that we could aim at the buttons on the Johnnies' coats, holding our ground under heavy fire till dark, when the main force moved back to our old line, while the stretcher bearers carried off the wounded and details buried the dead. Our loss is fearful. Let history tell . . . . —C(MS).

Saturday, May 23rd. Found us again at our Posts in an advanced position which is gaining. We were compelled to run a gauntlet of Rebel Musketry. Kept a continual Fire on Chivalry all day, our batteries crawling *slowly up.*

This morning, our regiments moved out to the *extreme front*, and continued the firing on the enemy's line, while our batteries advance slowly to better positions,—deep gullies washed by the rain, with stumps and trees for protection. We make the dirt fly around their ears, and have cut down one regimental flag four times, when a bold Secesh secured it to an iron rod, and it floated in shreds tonight over more than one dead Rebel killed "beneath its folds."

Under cover of darkness, we crawl back to the ravine to clean our rifles and eat our hardtack, having been relieved by a detachment from the main line, which rests in a ravine a half-mile back from the front. Here, we roast our fresh beef over fires half-smothered, and after cleaning our arms lie down for the night, while the ceaseless clatter of small arms, mingled with an occasional shriek of a shell over our heads, render the situation "sublime."—C(MS).

Sunday, May 24th. Our Camp—as it is called—is three-quarters of a mile from the rebel work, and every night we are relieved by fresh troops and retire to camp to sleep a portion of the night away, and have time to make our Corn mush and roast a piece of Fresh beef, as this is all we can get.

Monday, May 25th. The Forty-second remained quiet in Camp all day, or at least untill dark, when we were ordered out on Picket duty with one day's rations. About 12 M. today Great Excitement prevailed, the occasion of which was a flag of truce Sent from the Rebel lines to ask Permission to Bury the dead, though at the time its object was not known to the soldiery, and all Believed it to be a surrender of the city. Hosts of Rebels Flocked upon their Breastworks, and the Yankee Skirmishers advanced to converse with them. Hostilities ceased for four hours, and on due notice being given at the close of the armistice, Yankee and Rebel went to work, and the rattling of Musketry and the Cannons' roar were louder than ever.

Tuesday, May 26th. This morning the same old Tune commenced from Rodman, Parrot, Howitzer, and Enfield Rifle.[22] We have our entrenchments within a few yards of those of the enemy, and death is dealt out to the Rebel who is Brave enough to show his head above the parapets of the enemies Breastworks. Deserters from Pemberton's army state that their Supplies are going down rapidly, and their only hope is for Joe Johnston to concentrate a force sufficient to raise the siege within thirty days. Every night we are ordered to sleep with our clothes and accoutrements on and be ready for action at a moment's notice. The Rebels are daily expected to Break our lines and escape by the Jackson and Vicksburg Road.

Wednesday, May 27th. The Usual slow firing of musketry and artillery progresses. But the General feature of the Siege is unchanged. The Capitulation and Surrender of Vicksburg, the "Heroic little City," the "Confederate Sentinel of the Mississippi," is only a matter of time, and Grant's soldiers are as confident of success as though the white flag already waved from the tallest spire. We are Bivouacked on a hill side, and of course the opposite one from the enemy, but not altogether sheltered from interruption by his Shells, as they often drop in our resting place, But seldom ever disturb our composure and the general cheerfulness of the camp.

Thursday, May 28th. Nothing has transpired today to interrupt the Prosperous condition of the siege. The usual amount of Powder and Balls have been thrown at the "Brave Defenders" who seem determined to hold out untill the last Dog is Dead. We Yankees admire their grit and Perseverance,

[22] Both Rodman and Parrott were cast-iron, muzzle-loading, large calibre cannon, the former having a smooth bore and a hollow water-cooled core, and the latter a rifled bore. The Enfield used by the Union troops was a muzzle-loading, rifled musket of .577 bore of British make.

But would sooner they possessed less of such mettle, as they cause us a great deal of daily inconvenience by such Stubborn Conduct.

Friday, May 29th. Last night, Companies K and B of the Forty-second were sent out on Picket, But was fortunately held as Reserve and had an opportunity of sleeping a few hours. The Twenty-second Kentucky had marching orders, and left in the night for Big Black. At Present, the Sixteenth and Forty-second Ohio are all that is left of De Courcy's old "One-eyed Brigade," and we cannot muster 500 men. Were relieved at 8 A.M., and returned to Camp.

Saturday, May 30th. Sleep is so precious that we take the most of it in the daytime, as our ardent duties call us out every night, Consequently I have been improving the day as above.

Sunday, May 31st. Last night, K and B Companies were again sent out on Picket in the Rifle Pits, But were relieved at 10 o'clock by order to report at Head Quarters. Were sent from there to build a Fort of Cotton Bales in front of Smith's Division. We worked hard all night within Speaking distance of the Rebels, But as they were at the same business, both parties kept quiet until morning. The noise of the Rebels rolling Cotton bales could be heard plainly, But the darkness prevented any conflict between us, and the two separate works were finished in silence, to gaze in astonishment upon one another when day dawned. We returned to Camp this morning as one hundred guns opened their thunder on the doomed heads of the traitors.[23]

Monday, June 1st. One year ago today, we were among the mountains of Eastern Kentucky, preparing for our suc-

[23] That night, according to his declaration for invalid pension, filed in 1889, Corporal Hopkins "was ruptured in the right groin while aiding to move one of the 20-pounder Parrott guns of Foster's Wisconsin battery, his company being them engaged in building an advanced earthwork and moving the artillery thereto on the left of the Jackson turnpike and railroad. He was never treated in hospitals and continued to perform his duty without medical treatment for this injury up to date of muster-out."—Department of Soldiers' Claims, Columbus, Ohio. File SC-590876.

cessful Expedition against Cumberland Gap. Today, we are closely Besieging a stronghold of the enemy, the fall of which will be as a thrill of Joy throughout the Loyal portion of the United States, and a nerving to greater deeds for the Army of the Mississippi. *Babylon shall fall,* for great is the sin thereof.

Tuesday, June 2nd. Last night, we were called out in line of Battle at 11 o'clock, and stacked arms, remained closely on the watch for several hours, and were then ordered back to our "downy" beds with accoutrements and clothes on our arms close by, and to be ready for a muss on short notice. The alarm was occasioned by Picket firing. One o'clock at night, our Batteries Simultaneously opened upon the enemy. The roar and reverberation was tremendous. Our Mortars also played upon the city. It is truly a grand sight to see these messengers of death ascend to the skies, and forming a graceful curve, descend with a roar like thunder, to explode and scatter its missiles of destruction over the shrinking Rebels, or Strike the ground with a jar that shakes the earth like an earthquake.

Wednesday, June 3rd. Out on Picket in the Rifle Pits all last night and all day today, But relieved tonight by the Sixteenth Ohio. Returned to Camp, eat Supper, and turned in.

Thursday, June 4th. Crawled out a little late this morning and drank a cup of Coffee, eating a solid foot of hard tack and a Slice of Pork (not ham), and felt as well as I would, had I eaten Breakfast. In the Afternoon, we moved our Camp to a position farther to the Right. Here, we had to make new Nests of Brush and leaves; digging a level place in the side of the hill, we place four Forks in the ground, and on these we place poles, and cover the whole with leaves, bark, and brush. These are our tents, and when it rains we lay Still untill the rain is over; just like they do in Spain, we let it rain!

Friday, June 5th. All quiet in Camp, but Skirmishing on the outposts. The Siege progresses favorably.

Saturday, June 6th. This forenoon, had Inspection of Arms and a short drill. Vicksburg still holds out.

Sunday, June 7th. Guns of heavy caliber are daily arriving and being placed in position. This morning, two eleven-inch guns arrived from off the Gun Boats, and by night will peal their notes of thunder with their peculiar neighbors.

Monday, June 8th. No Surrender yet.

Tuesday, June 9th. We have our daily drills down here in this gorge while shells and minnie balls are whistling over our heads. All are apparently as happy and contented as though we were walking the streets of Old Bellefontaine.

Wednesday, June 10th. The Rain Poured down in torrents all day, and like the beasts of the field we "Poor Soldiers" have to grin and bear it. Very disagreable, But it's all *"for the Union."*

Thursday, June 11th. Brings nothing new except a clearing up of the wet weather.

Friday, June 12th. This morning at 4 o'clock, the Enemy opened on our batteries quite briskly. The shells fell pretty fast in this ravine, but I believe no one is hurt in the Forty-second. Had Inspection of Arms and general appearance of the men, and the day closed without further incident.

Saturday, June 13th. Today, I procured a horse and rode along the lines as far as Steele's Division, which rests on the Yazoo. I had a fine view of the Mississippi River and the low shores of Louisiana on its western banks. The sight was truly sublime after such a rigorous campaign as we have had among the hills of Mississippi.

Sunday, June 14th.[24] All day, over a hundred guns have played unceasingly upon the doomed city. The object is to kill

[24] This was Corporal Hopkins' nineteenth birthday. Perhaps the sight-seeing jaunt on horseback, the visit to the berry patch, and, later, the letter to his mother served to properly mark the occasion and replace the usual celebration.

as many as possible, making the less number of prisoners to keep when the Brave Pemberton Surrenders his noble little band of Patriots to "Unconditional Surrender Grant."

Monday, June 15th. Went out after blackberries this forenoon, But as the Enemies shells fell so fast in the patch, concluded that blackberries were not good for a soldier, and we returned to Camp.

Tuesday, June 16th. Wrote a letter home today under a tree while Minnie balls were clipping off its Branches. They were all too high, however, and I finished my letter in peace.

Wednesday, June 17th. Last night, the Rebels opened a brisk artillery fire on our Batteries, but were soon silenced by a few well-directed shots from our 11-inch guns.

Thursday, June 18th. The Usual slow Bombardment from Land and water is kept up on the City; the Rebels must suffer terribly. Today I was delighted by receiving two of Harper's Illustrated Papers from Toledo.

Friday, June 19th. No change in affairs.

Saturday, June 20th. Remained under arms all day, while our Batteries, numbering 150 Guns, shell the City. An assault was looked for, But was not ordered, and all is quiet again at Vicksburg.

On this day, Corporal Hopkins found time to write a letter to Julia Allison. It was Sergeant Hiram Allmon who prompted him to do it: Hopkins had thought of her for a long time, but had lacked the courage to begin the correspondence.

BIVOUAC IN REAR VICKSBURG, MISS.
June 20, 1863.
Enclosed is a rough Sketch of Black river Bridge, a scene after the late battle in that place. If curiosity prompts you to make any inquiry as to who the "artist" is, address Second

Corporal, Company K, 42nd. Reg., O.V.I., 9th. Division, 13th. Army Corps, Vicksburg, Mississippi.

"PATRIOTIC."

Sunday, June 21st. In the evening was detailed on duty. Took a squad of men and marched out on the Vicksburg and Jackson Rail Road 3 miles to guard a train of cars loaded with Quartermaster's Stores.

Monday, June 22nd. Was relieved of duty this morning, and returned to Camp, where we had the best dinner I have helped to dispatch since the beginning of the Siege. At 5 P.M. the Forty-second started on the march toward Big Black to join the Division we belong to. We kept the Rail Road all the way, and arrived at Big Black 2 o'clock at night.

Tuesday, June 23rd. Our Camp is a beautiful one Situated in a grove of trees. We have been busy making shelters, not from the rain, but from the scorching rays of Old Saul. Hi Allmon, Jim Whitsel, E. J. Allmon, and Myself are in pardnership and have erected what can be justly styled a Palace of Willow Branches. Yankee skill is rapidly developing itself. Axes, picks, hatchets, and spades are Busy at work making shelters for tents we haven't seen since the 28th. of April last.

Wednesday, June 24th. After cleaning up the Camp of rubbish and loose leaves, we were marched to the Colonel's quarters and Received $26 of the legal tender from Uncle Sam's Paymaster.

Thursday, June 25th. Sent $35 home by Express. Our Captain has gone to Haines' Bluff to express our money via Memphis.

Friday, June 26th. This has been a very warm and sultry day, the murcury at 110 in the shade. The Soldiers lay around in Camp panting like dogs.

Saturday, June 27th. Vicksburg still holds out with a determination worthy of a better cause, but old General Starvation will surrender to U.S. Forces before long.

Sunday, June 28th. Very little firing has been heard in the direction of the City today. Joe Johnston has not made his appearance yet, and we almost fear he will *not.* Should he come, however, we will teach him a lesson.

Monday, June 29th. Today, was detailed for Picket duty. Was stationed with a squad of men at Gen. Lindsay's Head-quarters.

Tuesday, June 30th. Was relieved this morning by a detail from the Sixteenth Ohio; returned to Camp Alice.

Wednesday, July 1st. Our tents arrived yesterday, and to-day our Camp presents a more military appearance.

Thursday, July 2nd. Mail arrived for the Forty-second, gladdening many a soldier's heart with a letter from home. I have one from Toledo.

Friday, July 3rd. Today the two opposing armies ceased hostilities at the sending out of a flag of Truce by Pemberton to propose terms of Surrender.

Saturday, July 4th. Today will ever be remembered by the soldier that fought at Vicksburg, for on this day the Block-ade has been removed from the Mississippi, and the only bar-rier to its Navigation now in the hands of the Union army. We are all rejoiced at the happy result of our Campaign, and ready to give all honor and praise to our noble leader Ulysus S. Grant.[25]

Sunday, July 5th. Our Division[26] received orders to be ready to march at a moment's notice with nothing but Gun and Cartridge box and Blanket, but did not start today.

[25] "The Union Army marched into Vicksburg this morning and took posses-sion, while the Rebel Citizens and Soldiers came out of their *caves* like Elijah of old."—C(MS). In his *Personal Memoirs* (New York: Charles L. Webster & Co., 1885), I, 572, General Grant states that "31,000 prisoners were surrendered, together with 172 cannon, about 60,000 muskets, and a large amount of ammuni-tion."

[26] Under the command of General Osterhaus.

Monday, July 6th. Took up our line of march toward Jackson about 8 A.M. Continue on the move untill within two miles of Edward's Depot, a distance of 16 miles from Vicksburg. Here, we halted for the night after a tiresome day's journey. Many of our Number were Sun-struck, and a great many who were entirely exhausted were sent back to Camp at Big Black.

Tuesday, July 7th. Resumed our march very early this morning, and pass our old Battle Ground at Champion Hill. The Rebels at Bolton Station made a bold stand until we deployed into line of battle, and then they vanished. There, we stopped for the night, and after roasting a few ears of green corn to eat with our coffee and crackers, we made our beds for the night. Myself and Jim Whitsel made a bed of green fodder on a pile of rails to keep us out of the mud, as the appearance of the weather had suddenly changed. The glaring streaks of lightning played around the Bayonets of our Stacks of Arms, and the thunder sounded not unlike the siege of Vicksburg, only this was heaven's artillery and was more sublime and calculated to inspire the soldier with awe, while gazing with admiration at the Grand scene.

The rain came at last. It was none of your northern Summer Showers, But a regular Mississippi Pour-down. We had no alternative but to lay and take it. Thank fortune I kept one side dry—the side next to the rails—but this was accomplished by laying still all night. The Storm lasted untill daylight, and few have dry rags to boast of. This is not playing soldier, but acting it out to the letter.

Wednesday, July 8th. Were early on our way this morning, skirmishing with the enemy as we advanced. No general engagement took place, though hourly expected. Halt and rest for the night at Clinton, Miss.

Thursday, July 9th. Our column again in motion, closely crowding three Regiments of Rebel Infantry and 1,500 Cavalry. They slowly fall back as we advance, and if pressed too closely, they show fight. At night, we halt five miles from the

Rebel Capitol, and tomorrow a fight will probably occur with Johnston's Rebel Force.[27]

Friday, July 10th. We advanced cautiously again at dawn and about noon reached Jackson. Attacked the enemy in his entrenchments. Osterhaus' Division in the centre advanced under a heavy artillery fire, and gained a position in the woods in front of a heavy battery of the enemy and within rifle shot of his works, and opened a brisk fire of musketry which soon silenced his largest guns. This continued untill night without any favorable result, and we slept that night in a ravine partially under cover from the Rebel shells, our Cartridge boxes on and our trusty rifles in our hands.

Saturday, July 11th. The fight commenced again at daylight and lasted all day, but nothing except a Better position for our Skirmishers was gained. Our rations are played out, and the prospect looks dark for more.

Sunday, July 12th. Company K deployed as Skirmishers, and engaged the enemies Sharpshooters for six hours. I fired nearly a hundred rounds at the traitors. "Damage to the enemy not Known." Corporal D. P. Wallis was wounded, and his leg will have to be amputated.

Monday, July 13th. Lieut. A. L. Bowman of K Company was wounded today while we were engaging the Rebel Skirmishers. Was under fire six hours, and returned to our resting place of last night.[28]

Tuesday, July 14th. An assault on the Rebel Intrenchments is expected to be made by our entire force, but has not been ordered yet. There is very little artillery firing today on either side.

[27] "Our march has been a very severe one owing to scarcity of supplies and the extreme heat of the weather. Hundreds have been sunstruck and sent back to Vicksburg, and others, seized with fever, have been transported to the rear, yet we hope to be able in our weakness to cope successfully with the Johnnies." —C(MS).

[28] "I was stunned by a bursting shell. The *front* today was a *hot* place, and many good men were killed. The enemy hold out admirably, but a movement of our cavalry in their rear will force them to evacuate, if not surrender."— C(MS).

Wednesday, July 15th. Last night our company was out on picket within seventy-five yards of the Rebels' entrenchments. Myself, Jim Whitsel, and Bob Smith were thrown out several yards in advance of our lines to watch the movements of the enemy, should he attempt to advance on us. We were ordered to lay flat on the ground in the bushes and keep perfect silence. I placed my Rifle on a bush so as to swing it in any direction like a *pivot gun,* and remained thus all night. Towards midnight, I could hear the Rebel relief come to relieve their Pickets, and was surprised to hear how close I was to the enemy. I could plainly hear all *that was said.* Their officer cautioned them frequently to keep silent, as *the Yankees would crawl up on them and pour in a volley on them, if they didn't stop their d——d noise.*

The Rebels were very busy all night working on their breastworks, and I could hear them beating the earth with their spades, as the gravel was thrown out to strengthen their works. Morning dawned at last on a few tired and sleepy soldiers, But before the daylight had advanced, we were called back to a safer distance, and opened fire on the Chivalry until relieved long enough to get breakfast.

Thursday, July 16th. Today, Osterhaus' tired and exhausted Division was relieved by Gen. Carr, and retired to the rear to rest. The men were getting sick very fast from exposure.[29] My health is excellent, though I am tired and sleepy. The Rebels evacuated in the night.

Friday, July 17th. We are enjoying the few leisure hours allowed us for rest and are thankful that matters are no worse. I was in Jackson a while this afternoon. It is on fire, and will be destroyed before night. Citizens are leaving in *herds.*

Saturday, July 18th. This morning our Regiment marched eight miles on the Mobile and Ohio R.R. to destroy the track. The heat was almost unbearable and many fell exhausted

---

[29] "Our Company, which started from camp with 41 men, is reduced to 15 or 20 by casualties and sickness, the sick being taken back to Vicksburg in ambulances."—C(MS).

"by the wayside." We arrived at the commencing place and the Rail Road ties flew like feathers. We finished our job and encamped for the night, had a hearty supper of Roasting ears, and stretched out about 5 feet 11 inches of Hopkins and snoozed.

Sunday, July 19th. Returned to Camp tired and hungry and in no very good order, but all are in except those who are still straggling behind.

Monday, July 20th. This morning, Ord's Corps took up its line of march toward Vicksburg on the Road leading via Raymond. Night finds us fourteen miles from Jackson, encamped at Mississippi Springs for the night. The march has been very tiresome, and hundreds have given out and were obliged to be conveyed in wagons. I stand it admirably except for sore feet.

Tuesday, July 21st. Marching ever since daylight. This morning, our Company reduced to ten men able to march. Men drop dead in the ranks from sunstroke; the heat is intolerable, and dust suffocating. We halt for the night in an open field, and the gathering clouds threaten a storm. No army ever underwent the hardships that this one has.

Wednesday, July 22nd. Continue the march this morning, and men are beginning to feel in better spirits as we approach Vicksburg, where we expect to rest for a while. It rained all night, and our clothes are drenched, but will dry when the sun shines. Encamp at night beyond Edward's Depot, the scene of former trials.

Thursday, July 23rd. Our army of veterans and tired soldiers arrived in Camp this afternoon. Glad to get back to Camp Alice, and to sleep in tents once more; I never was so tired before. Our Company numbered eight men in ranks when we arrived.

Friday, July 24th. Our marching was not over, as we expected when we returned to Big Black, For this morning we upset our Beautifull Camp and marched to Vicksburg. Those who were too much exhausted, were taken on the cars. This is a finishing touch to our hardships. Human nature fails often with our stoutest men and they sink exhausted by the road side. At dark, we reach the scene of the late siege, and encamp temporarily untill the officers decide upon a regular Camp Ground.

Saturday, July 25th. Today, we marched through the City of Vicksburg and encamped on the Bank of the river, Below town. I don't like the situation, But I am not the Judge. We are all too near worn out to pitch our tents, But they must go up, and the war must be carried on. Richmond must be taken, the Rebs must knock under.[30]

Sunday, July 26th. Had a hard Storm of wind and rain today, and several dead trees blew down in our camp. One fell across three tents, but as all its occupants were out taking the rain, no one was hurt. Furloughs are being granted to three men from each Company.

Monday, July 27th. Today, we have been busy in clearing the underbrush around our camp, But it will take a great deal of work to make it a comfortable Camp.

Tuesday, July 28th. Had Company drill for the sake of exercise, as we have had none of that in the last few months.

Wednesday, July 29th. Was on duty today. Had a very pleasant time, as all my men were prompt in appearing at the right time for Guard.

Thursday, July 30th. Nothing to write,—and I write nothing.

[30] "Having rested very quietly last night, we felt *bully* today, and marched into the City with colors flying and band playing 'The Girl I Left Behind Me.' After marching and counter-marching and establishing lines and breaking into columns a few hundred times, we halt on the river bank and stack arms, after which the grub situation is considered, and we lie down on our blankets to rest for the night."—C(MS).

Friday, July 31st. Hurrah for the Union and Johnny Brough![31]

Saturday, August 1st. The Expenditionary Army, composed of Sherman's, Ord's, McPherson's, and the Ninth Army Corps, is resting quietly from all its labors after taking Jackson, and our enjoyment is complete. Our Regiment was Paid off to-day, and Uncle Sam's Greenbacks are rapidly going into Circulation via Sutlers, Hucksters, and News-boys.

Sunday, August 2nd. Inspection of Arms.

Monday, August 3rd. Moved our Camp closer to the City. The situation is a beautiful one with "Nice drill ground attached."

Tuesday, August 4th. Was improved by cleaning Camp, etc. etc.

Wednesday, August 5th. Passes off quietly with no interest.

Thursday, August 6th. Dieu et mon droit!

Friday, August 7th. Death to Copperheads in the North!

Saturday, August 8th. Down with the traitor Vallandigham, and up with Johnny Brough!

Sunday, August 9th. Where is the Chaplain? Echo answers: Dead drunk!

Monday, August 10th. Tom Armstrong told me something today that, should it be true, I shall be a happy soldier.

Tuesday, August 11th. Corporal Owen J. Hopkins was detailed from the Forty-second Regiment, Ohio Infantry Volunteers, to report to Camp Chase without delay, for the pur-

[31] John Brough was the Republican candidate for governor of Ohio. He opposed Clement Vallandigham of the Peace Party.

pose of taking charge of the drafted men from Ohio, and to escort them to the Regiment. Tom Armstrong told the truth!

Wednesday, August 12th. Today was spent in getting my papers signed and ready to start in the morning. The detail from this Regiment for the same purpose is as follows: Co. A, Capt. I. S. Ross; Co. K, Lieut. A. L. Bowman; Co. E, Lieut. John Flynn; Co. I, Sergt. Leedom; Co. B, Sergt. Hecouphs [Hicocks]; Co. C, Sergt. Groescoup; Co. K, Corp. O. J. Hopkins; Co. C, Corp. Dick Bailey; Co. A, Corp. O. C. Hill. The commissioned officers are at home on leave of absence.

Thursday, August 13th. Have been waiting at the landing all day for a boat to leave for the North, but none have started yet.

Friday, August 14th. Last night, our Regiment left for New Orleans [32] on the Marine boat *D. J. Adams,* and this afternnon, at 3 o'clock, we started up the river on the steamer *Albert Pierce.* The Twenty-third Connecticut 9-months men are aboard, but they are not soldiers,—only imitation of soldiers! Bully for the Pilgrims! Hurrah for the heroes of Plymouth Rock!

August 24th. [33] After many delays and much Vexation of Spirit, we find ourselves at last in America and among White People who [look] like the Inhabitants of another clime. [34]

August 25th. At Home. [35] *Hurrah for Brough!*

The following is the last entry he made in the diary of 1863:

[32] The Thirteenth Corps had been transferred to the Army of the Gulf, under the command of General Banks, for the campaign in western Louisiana, which was to culminate in the invasion of Texas.

[33] There are no entries between the fourteenth and the twenty-fourth, when he was en route.

[34] ". . . where they live in houses and eat off of dishes and tables with knives and forks. Something new all the time, and we soldiers gaze on things around like young Horace Greely on the Youth from the rural districts."—C(MS).

[35] In Toledo, where his mother had gone to live with her eldest son Almon.

Sunday, October 8th. This afternoon, received orders to return to my Regiment. Will start day after tomorrow, Tuesday the 10th., the day set for starting from Elyria, Ohio.

Hopkins' leave expired on October 10, and he left with his squad of new recruits to rejoin the Forty-second Regiment, then in New Orleans. He was now Sergeant Hopkins, having been promoted to that rank on August 31. Between October 8 and January 1, 1864, his adventures are known only from four letters addressed to Miss Allison and a few pages in C(MS).

His acquaintance with Miss Allison had made but little progress since that late September day in 1861 when she and a bevy of other girls presented bouquets to the new recruits as they marched down the street to the Bellefontaine station. She had sworn to give her flowers to the handsomest soldier there. It chanced to be Owen J. Hopkins. Three years later, at a gathering of friends in her home, at the time when he was preparing to leave for the front, they promised to correspond. He lost no time.

HEAD QUARTERS, LOGAN HOUSE, BELLEFONTAINE
October 9, 1863
MY FRIEND JULIA,[36]
    There is always an object in view with everyone when beginning a new correspondence, and of course the case must be the same with us, though not always comprehended by both parties at once. The only one in view, however, in the present instance, is mere Friendship on the part of the writer, who is ever and always willing to forward and promote the interests of a Friend, whether in need or otherwise.
    I have convincing proof that I can count you as an addition to my list of Friends and "Fellow Sympathizers" in the good cause of the Union, and as none but such are entitled to the confidence of a Soldier, I think we can carry on our acquaintance thus hastily formed, though miles of Rail Road intervene.

[36] This letter is addressed to her in Oskaloosa, Iowa, in care of Judge Seevers, the husband of her aunt Caroline Lee, whom she was then visiting. Virginia ("Jennie") Seevers was a favorite cousin.

I was prevented from saying a "Last Farewell" to you last Thursday by receiving orders to report to Headquarters. I have just returned to Bellefontaine, where I shall remain until next Thursday, when I shall start home to Toledo to stay until I receive orders to go to my Regiment. I am afraid we will have to stay home all winter. If that is the case, I want you to come back to Ohio, as it is very lonesome here since you left for the "Far West."

I saw Mary Knapp [37] last evening and enquired if you left any parting words of advice for me. She said your advice was for me to never desert the army, and to stand by the Stars and Stripes forever. This I thought was very good, But hope you could not Believe me so base as to desert the cause I am sworn to sustain. As to Standing By the old Flag, I promise to do so until death, under penalty of Forfeiting your Friendship and esteem, as well as that of the whole world. My lot is cast with the Glorious old Army of the Union so long as it Battles for Freedom and the Right, and the only compensation I ask is a grateful country Blessed with Freedom and Individual Liberty.

How it cheers a soldier's heart to know that there is some one still left at home, who will sympathize with him and his cause, and how goading to know that we have such bitter enemies in our rear while we are vanquishing the Traitors in Front, namely, the Copperheads [38] of Ohio. But my space is limited and I must close. My Regards to your Fair little relative, [39] and my best wishes for Your happiness.

Yours truly,
O. J. HOPKINS

TOLEDO, OHIO
November 9, 1863

DEAR JULIA,

Your very kind letter was received Saturday, but please pardon the delay in answering. I have orders to be ready to start to my Regiment on the 12th from Cleveland. [40] Will leave in

---

[37] A close friend of Julia Allison's, who lived in Bellefontaine.

[38] An epithet that was applied to Northerners who were sympathetic to the South; the reference is to the copperhead snake.

[39] Her cousin, Virginia Seevers.

[40] A month has passed without further orders. Miss Allison is still in Oskaloosa.

the morning (tomorrow) at 5 A.M. Am very busy preparing for a "long march."

Julia, I flatter myself that when I return to the old Forty-second, I will number you among the list of interesting correspondents to keep me posted in the affairs of civil life while I am defending the flag of the Union,—unless that Cavalry Soldier who gave you "hard tack" should claim too great a share of your leisure moments. Your good judgement, however, will here manifest itself by preferring the Infantry service to that of Cavalry, since the former has been so much more beneficial to the Government.

I hardly know what explanation to give in regard to the emigrating scheme mentioned in your letter. Suppose it must be some of Mary's own arrangements, as I am perfectly ignorant of such plan in existence.

The name of my new acquaintance was Anna Lawton: are you acquainted with her? I presume not very intimitely.

Do you intend to keep that great secret from me untill you see me again? I think it very cruel to keep me in suspense so long. Why not tell it now? What is going to happen when the War is over? Don't think paper is scarce; have plenty.

Should like very much to see the cousin who complimented my personal appearance so highly. As a reward for his good judgement and refined taste, please give him my best wishes for Rapid promotion and great distinction in the service, and tell him I never fail to extend the *Right Hand of Fellowship* to all the *Sons of Abraham.*

Don't forget to send me the full length *counterfeit.* I had concluded something had happened, or you would have sent it before. Hardly know where to have you direct it, But think it would be safe to direct to Forty-second Ohio Volunteers, Thirteenth Army Corps, via New Orleans. I will write again soon. Love to Julia.

Sincerely your best Friend,
OWEN J. HOPKINS
Sergeant K Company, 42nd. O.V.I.

P.S.—Jennie, I will send you a Photograph before long; have not fit to send now.

P.P.S.—Beware that dangerous Copperhead. Let me hear from Julia often,—SERGEANT. (I fights mit Banks.)

COLUMBUS, OHIO
November 14, 1863.

FRIEND JULIA,

I am on my way to the South; am in splendid, *splendid* Spirit. Will be Glad to get back to the old Forty-second. All of the Detachment is here, and we will start from Here early Monday morning (16th).

Had pretty hard time getting away from the Toledo Girls. Shed many briny tears, etc., etc.

Can you write once a week? If so, I will promise to write as often. Probably can interest you more since I am going to act soldier, instead of playing it. We are bound for the Gulf. My love to all. "Julia, fare ye well."

In haste, but truly Yours,
—JOHNS.

N. B.—Dick Bailey (one of my comrades who is a very handsome Young Soldier) says *give her my never dieing love.* I will be "shure" to do it, won't I?—J. H.

CAMP AT PLAQUEMINE, LA.[41]
(120 miles above New Orleans)
December 3, 1863

FRIEND JULIA,

I received yours, dated at Delaware, Ohio, this morning, and haste to answer.

In company with the detachment of Forty-second Boys, I embarked at Cairo, Ill. on board steamer *Sultana.* The trip down was a pleasant one, though it is generally understood that traveling on the Mississippi steamers is not the most pleasant thing on earth. Had quite an enthusiastic lot of Passengers, and they displayed in many instances a love of the novelties attendant on a Mississippi voyage. Nothing happened to relieve the monotony of the trip until some distance below the mouth of Red River, where a few *ungentlemanly*

[41] Postmarked New Orleans, December 12, and addressed to Delaware, Ohio, where Miss Allison was visiting a cousin, Annie Lee Humphrey.

Guerrillas secreted behind the Levee on the right bank of the river had the audacity to fire into our boat.

The scene which followed this unlooked for calamity beggars description. A portion of the passengers were just sitting down to dinner, when the Leaden messengers of the *Gorrillas* entered the cabin very unceremoniously, singing the tune so familiar to old Soldiers, whizzing uncomfortably close to the ears of the Dandy in Broadcloth, the Quiet gentleman, and the man of Business. A general rush for the *larboard* side, a twinkling of negro waiters' heels as those "gemmun" took refuge under the table and behind cotton bales, shrieks and screams from the female portion of the passengers, many of whom fainted and fell into the arms of any who chanced to be near. The "brass coats and blue buttons," grasping sword and musket, hurried to the Hurricane deck, where we delivered a few volleys at the Chivalry before the boat had passed out of danger.

Then, we returned to the Cabin—after reporting to the bar, but be it understood I never drink—to discuss the subject of Guerrilla warfare and laugh at the woe-begone countenances of Mr. Broadcloth and the other non-combatants, as they crawled from their numerous hiding-places.

We had a dance the night before in the same cabin where just now had been such confusion. How different the scene!

Had several theatrical Performers on board. These were the first to drop on their knees and plead for that worthless object: Life. (I have since learned that their prayers did not ascend higher than the Hurricane deck of the Steamer *Sultana*.)

Had but a short time to look around in New Orleans, but what I saw of the Crescent City satisfied me that it is the most prosperous and beautiful place in the South. The scene on the Bay was one of interest: merchant vessels and men-of-war from almost all nations. Resting at anchor in the middle of the river was the trim English war vessel with the Cross of St. George floating from the mast head, the neatly rigged Frenchman with tricolors of France in the breeze, and the sullen old Yankee Ironclad watching them all, as it were, with mistrust,—The old Banner of Stars waving gracefully at

Stem and Stern, Uncle Sam's Gunboat Boys lounging on deck, or playing "seven-up for the Beer." 'Twas a scene for an artist's pencil, But not very easily sketched by new beginners, and so I didn't undertake it.

My Regiment had no fighting while I was at home. Glad to hear it; I can say I have been in every battle in which the Forty-second has been engaged. The Boys are all going into the service for three years longer when our time is up, which will not be long. I am going into the Regular service, if nothing happens.

What a sad thing! The very thought of me being killed! Would I be the first soldier killed in this war?

I own that was very ungentlemanly conduct on the part of that Sergeant Sunday afternoon. Had I been a witness of his impious conduct, would have punished the Fellow severely.

Mary must be mistaken, as I never ask permission to write to anyone,—always write without permission. I belong to the Independant Rangers; Go it on my own hook; Never ask favors. Perhaps Jons is handsome enough: am not personally acquainted with him. Am intimately acquainted with Alice Jones, But Mary Walker? *Vraiment, je ne la connais pas!*[42]

You seem to have a high opinion of that Johns: he is a Soldier, of course, or you would not speak of him in such high terms. *Je comprends que la belle aime le militaire. L'on ne peut pas blâmer ce noble essor.*

Ours is the Third Brigade, First Division, Thirteenth Corps. All but this Brigade have gone to Texas, and not to Mobile, as was expected. We are fortifying our position more to keep the men at work than of any fears of the enemy. Old Billy Rumor reports a large body of Rebel cavalry a short distance from here. How soon they will attack, am not able to say. Think we can hold our own against any force the Rebels may have in Louisiana.

My fighting weight is 173 pounds: let them come!

Here, we gather the oranges from the trees ourselves.

[42] Hopkins' occasional use of French is limited to the time of his stay in Plaquemine. He may have become acquainted with the language through Lisette Hirsch, whose name and the date appear on the flyleaf of a presentation copy of V. Value's *New Method French Grammar.*

Have all we can eat; would like to send you some, But am afraid they would sour before they reach you.

I don't think of anything more, so excuse short letters, and write often to your Friend,

J. H.

P.S.—Direct to J. H., K Company, 42nd. O.V.I., 13th Corps, "Plaqueville," Iberville Parish, La. Love to all,— SERG'T.

[Marginal notes] Oranges are plenty. We gather them from the trees. I send an orange leaf from the garden of a fine old Rebel, whose daughter[43] and myself are on the best of terms. A sprig of Palmetto and a specimen of Louisiana moss, which grows on all kinds of trees. We soldiers use it to make beds of.

Dieu, dans sa bonté sainte, protège ton bonheur! Do you ever read your letters after writing them?

A summarizing statement of what happened between November 18, 1863, and January 1, 1864, is given in C (MS):

Left Cairo, Illinois, October 18th,[44] on steamer *Sultana,* for New Orleans in company with the "detachment" and a number of recruits, arriving at New Orleans on the 28th, and learned that our regiment had marched for the Teche country, and we started to join them. Arriving at the command, we were warmly welcomed by the boys of the Forty-second. The Teche country, in which the Corps was now operating, is a fertile region, plentifully watered, with here a belt of woods and there a stretch of prairie, whose principal bayou—the

---

[43] She may have been the lovely Annie Robinson, whose photograph he kept in his album and whose tender farewell message is written on the last page of his French grammar. If so, his poetic effusions (including his quotation of the poem "Oui" in the entry of January 8), his reference to "the eyelash of a pretty girl" on January 18, and his frequent visits in the city during the winter months, have special significance.

As F. H. Mason points out in *The Forty-second Ohio Infantry* (Cleveland: Cobb, Andrews & Co., 1876), pages 244–47, the regiment had never before garrisoned a permanent post, so it made the most of the social welcome accorded it by the citizens of Plaquemine. The men were dined and entertained, and while the "maidens and the soldiers wooed and sighed," the prosperity of the town rose to hitherto unknown heights.

[44] An error: It was November 18, as his letters above indicate.

Teche—was valuable to the Army as a highway for transportation of its supplies. The forces of the enemy, commanded by Gen. Dick Taylor, were said to be numerous and well-armed. They had gunboats on the Teche; the most formidable of these, however, the *Cotton*— so named after a citizen, not the staple—had been destroyed by an expedition under Gen. Godfrey Weitzal, who had penetrated as far as Pattersonville, and this officer is now with the Army to point out the road and lead the way.

They had also entrenched works at Camp Bisland. These, Gen. Banks attacked, with Gen. Emory's division and the brigade of Gen. Weitzal, while Gen. Grover with his division was sent on transports through Grand Lake to a point eleven miles to the enemy's rear, in the hope that he would be able to secure his capture, but his superior knowledge of the country enabled him to make good his retreat. The two Corps, the Thirteenth and Nineteenth, proceeded as far as Opelousas, the enemy making but little resistance, and after lying there a while, returned as far as Franklin, the principal town on the Teche. There, the Ninth Corps went into winter quarters, while the division of the Thirteenth Corps were scattered at various points in Louisiana and on the coast of Texas. The Forty-second Ohio, with the Twenty-second Kentucky and the Sixteenth Ohio, were stationed at Plaquemine, on the River, remaining here at work on the fortifications until March 26, 1864.

Years later, in his history of the regiment,[45] *F. H. Mason of Company A wrote of the stay at this winter base:*

For more than two years the Forty-second had been in the field, without a week of what was known in the army as "soft" duty. Not a man in the Regiment had seen the inside of a barrack, or—with exception of the few weeks of hard work —had it at any time formed part of the garrison of a permanent post. Always in the field, often without tents, the men had learned to take life as it came and ask no questions.

[45] Mason, *op. cit.*

Plaquemine was a clean, healthy, beautiful town; the people were intelligent and cordial, and the Regiment settled down to its winter in the South with bright anticipations.

By January 1, states Mason,[46] the troops had completed a bastioned earthwork, two acres in area, with a magazine, a drawbridge, a neatly turfed slope and glacis, and fourteen guns. Old buildings in Plaquemine had been torn down, and the lumber was used to erect comfortable barracks. A provost guard was organized, and rigid garrison discipline was maintained. Relations between the Yankee troops and the Southern citizenry soon became "intimate and cordial."

One of the residents, a French soldier of fortune, musician, and fencing master, took charge of a class in fencing organized by members of the Forty-second, and introduced his new friends to families to which he had a ready entree. The soldiers were "dined and entertained," and the young ladies acknowledged that "these Ohio soldiers are not Yankees, but Western people like ourselves."

Packets plied up and down the river, carrying passengers, cargo, and letters and newspapers from the North and South. The camp—dubbed "Spiegelville" after Colonel Spiegel, commander of the 120th Ohio—even published a weekly, single-sheet newspaper entitled "Picket Post," [47] which was a most informative and entertaining dispensary of gossip, rumor, quips, anecdotes, and news, with occasional articles and verse. Local merchants and army sutlers proclaimed their wares in it. Costing only five cents, it made a major contribution to the life in the barracks. The issue of December 24, for example, ran the first installment of a "History of the 22nd Kentucky from Its Organization up to the Present Time"; an anecdote about Zollicoffer's troops in their advance on Wild Cat, Kentucky; General Bragg's farewell address to the Army of Tennessee, which he delivered at Dalton on December 2; [48] an obituary notice on the death of Captain Evan D.

---

[46] Entries in Sergeant Hopkins' diary for 1864 indicate that the work on the fortifications was not completed until March 15, 1864.

[47] Captain Jack Hughes, publisher. Vol. I, No. 3 (December 24, 1863).

[48] General Orders No. 214, copied from the New Orleans *Picayune*.

Thomas of Company G of the Twenty-second Kentucky Regiment; a column of late news items concerning happenings in the Confederacy; and, in a lighter vein, paragraphs like the following:

ONE CENT REWARD,—Strayed or stolen, one bottle of the pure yellow of the egg from the Head-Quarters of the 42nd Ohio Vol. Inft., on or about the 11th of December, 1863. Said bottle contained about one quart of the delictious [sic] fluid. Any person finding the same and delivering it to me will not only be entitled to the above reward, but, in addition, will receive one snort and many thanks.

—Gumbo

(Special for the *Picket Post*)
THE CAPTURE OF VICKSBURG

Adown the stream the gunboats run
To pass the batteries one by one,
Death flashing forth from every gun,
    Pemberton, my Pemberton.

At Thompson's Hill Mc Clernand's Corps,
Drove back the enemy o'er and o'er,
The rebs that ne'er were whipped before,
    Pemberton, my Pemberton.

[And ten stanzas more.]

NOTICE,—Theodore Manvielle will open an Academy in Plaquemine, on Monday the 4th day of January next. Mr. Manvielle will be assisted by competent teachers. The English, French, and Latin Languages will be taught. Especial care will be taken to establish industrious methodical habits, and to qualify young gentlemen for active business positions . . . .[49]

SPIEGELVILLE,—This cleanly village is one of the rising provincial towns in this parish [Iberville]. It is situated east of Plaquemine and is noted for its comfortable and elegant appearance. It is settled almost exclusively by Ohioans. Col. Spiegel is the chief magistrate.

[49] A copy of Value's edition of Ollendorff's *New Method French Grammar,* inscribed: "Lisette Hirsch, presented to Sgt. O. J. Hopkins, Co. K, 42nd Ohio" indicates that he may have taken French lessons at the Academy while he was at Plaquemine.

TO VISITORS,—Our paper is delayed this week and justice compels us to state that it is owing entirely to the influx of inquisitive and curious visitors in our office. No one can be more hospitable or social than ourselves, but it is at another time and in another place. So look at the notice on the door, and if you have no business to do, do it outside of the office.

NEWS FROM MOBILE,—A Mobile dispatch of a late date informs us that Plaquemine was attacked by General Green, of the Rebel army, capturing the town, killing, wounding, and capturing 2,000 Federals. It stated also that the navigation of the river is suspended. It said nothing about the 15 gunboats blown up, the two million of the Corps d'Afrique's returned to bondage, the 5,000 400-pounder Parrotts captured and spiked, the capture of 16 Major Generals and Pay Masters with all of Chase's Treasury in their hands; the utter rout of Bank's army, or last, but not least, the suppression of the *Picket Post*. Come, Mr. Editor, don't be modest, put it all in.

If one may judge by the advertisements, Christmas, 1863, would not be like the previous Holiday season: in 1862, the Union troops had lain under a heavy cannonade in front of Chickasaw Bluffs all through Christmas week. If the sutlers had their way, this season would be different.

S. Herold, sutler of the Forty-second Ohio, advertised in bold type: "Fruits (of all kinds), Oysters, Lobsters, Clams, Sardines, Cigars, Tobacco" as well as "Condensed Milk, tinware, cutlery, clothing, and all the various articles needed in camp life."

J. Spiegel, sutler of the 120th O.V.I., announced as "Latest Arrivals: 20 kegs of fresh Ohio Butter, sweet and nice; 10 kegs new Ohio Apple butter; 20 barrels green Apples; 10 barrels Oranges; and many other eatables of the choicest kinds."

Not to be outdone, Keller and Hollander, sutlers for the Seventh Kentucky, had in readiness for the festivities "Canned Fruit, Fresh Oysters, Cigars, Tobacco, Boots, Shoes, Hats, Shoulder Straps, Military Uniforms, and LAGER BEER, available at a stand opposite the Q.M. Depot in Monroeville." And in New Orleans, at Cassidy's Saloon on Gravier Street, could be had "Little Neck Clams, Capons, Fresh Oysters,

Eels, Lobsters, Fresh Salmon, Fresh Halibut, Turkey, Venison, etc. Constantly receiving from New York."

Twice a week the packets *"Jennie Rogers," "Meteor,"* and *"New Orleans"* offered passenger service to New Orleans and Baton Rouge for those who had passports and permits from the proper authorities.

Understandable, therefore, was the editorial advice of Lieutenant Shanks in the *"Picket Post,"* the day before Christmas: *"Let the soldier rejoice tomorrow, not get beastly drunk and make himself a nuisance, but enjoy Christmas rationally, take his egg-nogg with his friend, his glass of beer where it is for sale, his stroll through the street, and if an elegant man and the ladies are willing, he can pay a visit to his lady friends. We doubt the less of his fighting qualities, if he enjoys himself when he can, for who should do so, rationally, more than the soldier."*

Christmas passed. On January 27, the Kentucky regiments were transferred to Baton Rouge, leaving the post to the care of the Ohio troops and the artillery. Two months later, orders came for their removal also. On the same day, the first outfit of dress coats that they had received since enlistment were issued to the members of the Forty-second.

On March 26, the Ohio regiment, resplendent in their new uniforms, marched through Plaquemine to take the steamer for Baton Rouge. *"The citizens of all colors, ages, and both sexes,"* says Mason, *"crowded along the line of march to wish the departing braves God-speed. The young ladies were unconsolable and wept and waved their handkerchiefs as their cavaliers marched away."*

Miss Annie Robinson—may she not have been one of them?

III

KEEPING WATCH ON THE MISSISSIPPI
1864

The diary of 1864 is a small, cloth-covered, pocket-size book with a back flap that can be brought forward and tucked into a slit in the front cover. Besides the daily entries, it contains copies of several army orders affecting the writer, a few pen-and-ink drawings and decorations, two or three bits of verse, some accounts of loans made or received, a table of the distances from New Orleans of various points on the Mississippi, a key to river-boat signals, the names of the states and the battles in which the Forty-second had maneuvred, and so on. The end papers are covered with drawings of spread eagles, banners with inscriptions, and a Union soldier in a sergeant's uniform.

Throughout his diary, when mentioning the receipt or sending of letters, Hopkins conceals the identity of the correspondent from prying eyes by using a symbol in place of his or her name: a heart, a spear point, a pocketknife, an envelope, a book, a shield, the flag of the United States, a flag with a crescent, a key, and so on. A key to most of these symbols, giving the initials and residence of the person for whom the symbol stands, has been found on a separate sheet, which is much worn, patched, and stained. In transcribing the diary, I have replaced the symbol with the initials given in the key, or, when identification was possible, with the full name.

The following entries were made at Camp No. 1, Plaquemine, Louisiana.

Friday, January 1st. This morning was relieved of Picket. Was on reserve; the night was the coldest one I have felt since entering this state. Was up all night. Feel the effects today.

Had one corporal and eighteen men "under my command." This is my first time on duty as Sergeant.

Saturday, January 2nd. The *Jennie Robinson* arrived from New Orleans, bringing the mails for this place and Baton-Rouge. I received a letter from [lozenge], dated Elyria, Ohio, Dec. 6, 1863. One also from [pocket-knife],[1] dated Dec. 3, 1863. Spent the larger share of the day reading *The Scout, or Sharpshooters of the Revolution.*[2] Good night.

Sunday, January 3rd. Improved the day in writing letters. This forenoon, I answered Miss ———'s letter; Have not answered ———'s yet. Had bread and coffee, fried beef and pork for dinner, after which Dick Bailey and myself took a stroll up town. Saw two pretty dark-eyed Southern Creoles who looked at us as though they liked the looks of us pretty well. Long live Abraham Lincoln, President of the United States of America!

Monday, January 4th.

> "Be thou like yon mountain oak
> A sturdy man, in purpose strong,
> And prove thyself to be unchanged
> In every sense from right to wrong.
> Let not success unbalance mind;
> In adverse times be honest; then
> Support the truth, and thou shalt march,
> A monarch, in the van of men."

Tuesday, January 5th. The day has been wet and cheerless. I passed the time in "visiting" down in the city. Started to write a letter to [candlestick],[3] But failed in the attempt, as the weather was too cold on the fingers. Am expecting a letter from [heart],[4] a resident of Bellefontaine.

[1] Neither correspondent is identifiable.
[2] By William Gilmore Simms; published in 1841.
[3] "An old friend and teacher, in Kalida, O." Hopkins had lived there several years in early childhood, following his mother's marriage to Judge McClish.
[4] Julia Allison.

Wednesday, January 6th. The undersigned is on camp guard duty, the guard consisting of three corporals and eighteen men. The weather is cold and disagreeable, with snow on the ground and more falling. The citizens of Plaquemine are going around humped up like winter calves. "But let the cold winds blow as they will; I'll be gay and happy still."

Thursday, January 7th. The weather moderating. Ten thousand of the Potomac Army re-enlisted. Our Champion prize fighter whipped in England.[5] Also reported that two Regiments are ordered from here to Lake Ponchartrain, La. Hope it is not the Forty-second Ohio! (The misterious signals and tokens in this book can be solved by referring to "Memorandum of Letters.")[6]

Friday, January 8th.

Oui (or "Yes")[7]

"O miracle étonnant par ce mot enfanté!
L'humble esclave, soudain, a relevé la tête.
Le monde entier, pour elle, a pris un air de fête.
    Je viens aussi, de mon côté,
De terminer une excellente affaire . . .
    J'en suis enchanté!
Je sens pourtant qu'elle m'est chère."

Voilà tout!

Saturday, January 9th. Commenced to build a new fireplace this afternoon. Worked untill dark, think we have shoved an ox into the pit to be lifted out on the Sabbath, as the old Quaker said. Have had no news from home since the 10th November, 1863. Have concluded to stop writing untill I hear from them.

Sunday, January 10th. Today finished our fireplace. It draws finely. The weather threatening rain. "Spades is trump"; "I'm

---

[5] One of the last of the prize fights with bare fists.
[6] The key mentioned above.
[7] The author of this poem is unknown. The last four lines, however, are most certainly the invention of Hopkins, who applies the thought of the first three lines to his own case.

High, Low, Jack, and the Game"; "Puts me five to your
Make-some,"—this is all you hear from morning till night,
on your left and right! "Never trump your pardner's ace."

Monday, January 11th. Was on duty as guard for forage
train. Went 4 miles below Bayou Gouley, making a distance
of 19 miles. Returned to Camp about 8 P.M. with 8 wagons
loaded with corn. Had one corporal and 20 men for the guard.
Reported G. M. Wallis to Major Williams for the crime of
fighting and conduct prejudicial to good order and military
discipline.

Tuesday, January 12th. Private G. M. Wallis sentenced to
ten days imprisonment in the jail and fed on bread and water.
The way of the transgressor is hard, and George will find
there is truth in the saying. Mud! Mud! Mud!

> Oh, tell me, ye winds that round my pathway roar,
> Do ye not know some quiet spot where "Mud" is trump
>   no more?
> The cold winds whistling round my face
> In sorrow answer: "Narry place!"

Wednesday, January 13th.

> "The night grows wondrous dark; deep swelling gusts
> And sultry stillness take the rule by turn,
> While o'er our heads the black and heavy clouds
> Roll slowly on. This surely bodes a storm."

(And at dark it came: and such a storm!)

> "They did not know how hate can burn
> In hearts once changed from soft to stern,
> Nor all the false and fatal zeal
> The convert of revenge can feel." [8]

Thursday, January 14th. Last night, received a letter from
[pen],[9] and answered it today. Also sent a letter to ———

[8] Hopkins indicated the personal significance of these lines by drawing a
hand with one finger pointing to them in the margin.
[9] His younger brother, Livingston Yourtee Hopkins, who later became the
famous cartoonist "Hop" of the Sydney, Australia, *Bulletin.* At this time,
Yourtee—or "Yourt"—was seventeen.

at Kalida, Ohio, an old friend and school teacher of mine.
Weather fine and drying. My two letters, I fear, will not leave
until Monday next, as I learn the mail does not go until then.

Friday, January 15th.

> From my youth upward,
> "My spirit walked not with the souls of men,
> Nor looked upon the earth with human eyes;
> The thirst of their ambition was not mine.
> The aim of their existence was not mine.
> My joys, my griefs, my passions, and my powers
>   Made me a stranger." [10]

So says the subscriber O. J. Hopkins, Co. K, Ohio Inf't Vols.,
13th A.C.

Saturday, January 16th.

> "Sadly sighs the north wind,
> And multitudes of dense white fleecy clouds
> Are wandering in thick flocks along the sky,
> Shepherded by the slow unwilling blast."

The Regiment was out on General inspection this morning in
its clean and orderly appearance. Arms and accoutrements in
good order.

Sunday, January 17th. Company had Photos taken, while
standing *en masse,* by Professors Hall and Judkins. The
weather not very favorable, it being too windy. Mail arrived
without a letter for the Author. Too bad! too bad! Should
have had three or four! Three cheers for the Red, white and
blue!

Monday, January 18th. Laughter, sleep, and hope are the
three bounties with which kind Mother Nature compensates
us for the troubles of a life which few, perhaps, would accept,
if they were asked beforehand. The lash that a "soger" does

[10] These lines are also accompanied by a hand with a pointing finger.

not object to having laid on his shoulder: the eyelash of a pretty Girl.

Tuesday, January 19th. Was destined for Picket this A.M. Am stationed at 2nd Post with a guard of four men. Citizens, from the humble slave to the proud aristocratic master, are passing hourly; our duty is to see that their passes are correct and that no goods are taken through the lines. Gentlemen and ladies must undergo our search.

Wednesday, January 20th. Having been relieved of Picket, I returned to Camp, where I found lumber and implements for the enlarging and improving of our "quarters." Have been busy all day, and tonight I write in a new room added to our former dwelling. The hour for tattoo is not far distant. Then, O Morpheus! wrap me closely in your embrace, for my eyes are heavy, and I fain would sleep.

Thursday, January 21st. The Steamer *Meteor* arrived from New Orleans with mail and late papers. No letters were handed to the Subscriber. The day has been one of unusual calmness. No excitement to relieve the monotony of Camp life, and all is dull as a hoe. Work is still progressing on the Fort. Heavy details are at work daily, and "Fort Plaquemine" will soon be finished.

Friday, January 22nd. Was calm and beautiful as a summer day in our old Northern home. One year from today, if nothing happens, I intend to be a partaker of the hospitalities of that home. Hoping that period will see the end of this disastrous war, with the old flag floating in peace over all the states of our Union, I will retire to my couch for a soldier's dreams and a soldier's repose.

Saturday, January 23rd. For Picket tomorrow, says Orderly Sergeant O. J. Hopkins, and the following Privates: Caskey, Delman, Fawcett, and Fenton. Hope it won't rain and drown us out, like it generally does. All quiet on the Mississippi. Banks' army in winter quarters. No news from the front or rear.

Sunday, January 24th. Weather so warm we are compelled to "draw our blouses,"—and this in January! Stationed on 2nd Post, South Picket Line. Not troubled much with travelling humanity or Rebels in arms, though at times a few Rebellious looking ladies pass in Carriages, armed with "darts of fire" from bright eyes. Not dangerous, though.

Monday, January 25th. Relieved of Picket this A.M. Returned to Camp, found the Boys cleaning quarters and renovating generally. By order of Maj. Wm. H. Williams, Com⁴, Reg. Cotton in immense quantities is coming in daily. No news from the North, and none from N.O.

Tuesday, January 26th. Several steamers arrived today, But without late dates.[11] All continued northward, laden with Cotton and other merchandise. The fort will soon be completed, and will mount four heavy guns, beside pieces of lighter calibre. Fresh fish for dinner.

Wednesday, January 27th. The steamer *New Orleans* arrived today with mail. I rec'd three letters: one from [Julia Allison], one from [Mary Knapp], another from [spear].[12] Company K had Photo retaken *en masse,* as the former one, taken the 17th., was not a good one. This time, I think we have a perfect one. I will send mine home. Weather continues warm. It is hard to find *items* fit for insertion in this quiet folder, and I fear, if we stay here long, my Diary will play out.

Thursday, January 28th. On Picket at 2nd. Post. A large house to stay in, and everything is lovely, and the goose hangs high. The weather threatening rain. Don't think it will, as the wind's from Nor-West. In the P.M., the clouds scattered, and "Old Saul's" rays are doing their best to dry up the duck-ponds.

Friday, January 29th. Relieved, and returned to Camp, but found nothing of interest going on. Everything dull. Rained

---

[11] The term "late dates" refers to newspapers of recent issue.
[12] The letter was from "M—— J——," in Bellefontaine, whose identity is not known.

very hard last night, though I did not get wet, as we had a very good shelter in a cotton shed. The guard consisted of 17 men, one corporal, and Myself.

Saturday, January 30th. Spent the day in writing. Answered the letter of my "very dear friend" [i.e. Julia Allison], sealed and mailed it, and sent it double quick to destination. Rebels have stopped the cotton business in this quarter for the present by confiscating all they find coming in. Yankees have also closed the lines for a time.

Sunday, January 31st. Had Regimental inspection at one o'clock and Dress parade at five. Regiment looked respectable, as usual. Arms and accoutrements in the most perfect order, as is generally the case with the old Forty-second. The *Mittie Stephens* took on a cargo of cotton for N.O.

Monday, February 1st. The Steamer *New Orleans* was arrested today for smuggling liquors to the enemy between here and Baton Rouge; was sent under escort to Cairo, where she will be confiscated and sold for the benefit of the Federal Government, as a warning to all smugglers. Permits and Passes for goods have to be signed by Provost-Marshal Capt. M. L. Benham, of the Forty-second Ohio.

Tuesday, February 2nd. Wrote a long letter to M—— J—— today. Also finished one for [Mary Knapp] in the evening. Had Battallion Drill and dress parade at half-past five this afternoon, with a number of spectators. Looking for the Paymaster daily, but has not made his appearance yet. Some of the boys are strapped. Figuratively speaking, I have to reach down pretty deep to find a greenback in my pocket.

Wednesday, February 3rd. The Steamer *Meteor* arrived from N.O. with mail. I rec'd two letters: one from [book],[13] and the other from [crown].[14] Also a Bellefontaine *Republi-*

[13] His niece, Sarah Eliza ("Lide") Wilcox, daughter of John and Jemima Wilcox of Eddyville, Iowa. She was a devoted correspondent.
[14] His sister Hester Jane, wife of John Knox, of Eddyville, Iowa.

cain sent by [Julia Allison]. Answered [crown] today. Had no Battallion drill in consequence of the Major's absence. Long life to the citizens of Plaquemine!

Thursday, February 4th. Today, I answered ["Lide's"] letter, but did not mail it. Dress parade at half-past five. Detailed for Picket tomorrow. Bully for Picket! Unless it should happen to rain; then it wouldn't be so bully. Duty is pretty heavy here. "Do they miss me at home; do they miss me?"

Sergeant Hopkins dated his letter to his niece ahead to Sunday, February 7. She was the same age as he, and teased him by calling him "Uncle." The letter was written on a double sheet of foolscap and was decorated with a drawing of the American flag, bearing the legend "Mort au traître" and flying from a masthead tipped by an army saber. The Sergeant was in a jovial mood.

CAMP OF 42ND OHIO INFANTRY, U.S.
VOLUNTEER ARMY, PLAQUEMINE, LOUISIANA.
Sunday eve, Feb. 7th 1864.

DEAR LIDE,

My Patience and long forbearance has at last been rewarded by receiving your letter this morning, dated 17th Jan.

I am surprised to see how you improve in writing—surely you can't be so dumb as you pretend.

When I opened your letter, one of my comrades happened to glance at the writing. He said, "She writes a very pretty hand, Sergeant." Then he wanted to know the name. I told him it was from a "fellow I was acquainted with out in Iowa." Couldn't make him believe it was a *fellow's* handwriting.

Your letter came with one from Jane [Knox], and also a *Bellefontaine Republican* sent by my best Friend in B——. I wish you could see this friend of mine; am shure you would love her, if but for my sake. She was on a visit to Oskaloosa last fall; was there five weeks. Has been going to school in Delaware [Ohio] this winter, but is at home in B—— now. Her Grandfather is Lieut.-Governor of Ohio.[15] I have eight

---

[15] Julia Allison's stepmother was Mary Stanton, whose father, Benjamin Stanton, was elected lieutenant-governor of Ohio in 1862.

other correspondents who write regularly, and this is my chief
employment to pass away the long winter hours . . . .

When you join Church I want you to be a Methodist, or I
shall call you a secessionist from the old principles of the
Family. However, we will not quarrel about that, as I am not
either one.

I must tell you how I was fooled out on Picket the other
night:

It was about 12 o'clock at night as I was going the Rounds
to see that all were diligently on the watch. I found everything satisfactory and was returning to the Reserve Post
through a dark woods. When reaching the trunk of a large
cypress tree, I halted, and as the night was unusually calm,
though dark, I seated myself for rumination, such as only soldiers are acquainted with. I was taking a *general review* of
my past life—all its incidents and connections, and was just
gaining the victory at Champion Hill when I was startled
from my deep reverie by the breaking of a weed at no great
distance. I was upon my feet in an instant, and peering through
the darkness in the direction of the noise, I could discover the
outlines of some dark object crawling on all fours across the
line.

Now be it understood my nerves are never shaken by Rebel,
Devil, or any of his imps. But *This* was taking my Garrison
of courage by surprise, and I was about to challenge the in-
truder when a second thought struck me. I concluded a plan
to take the enemy by a regular *coup de main,* and all the prisoners I took would give me something to talk about for days
when I returned to camp. I also dropped on all threes, with
my trusty Enfield in my fourth, and advanced towards the enemy's position, but without skirmishers deployed on either
flank or in front, determined to risk a battle with his main
body. I had posted my cap and blanket at the tree for reserve to fall back upon in case of a repulse or total defeat,
and was now advancing gallantly to the conflict with (out)
colors flying gaily in the night breeze. I soon drove in the hostile Pickets (or would have, but it seems he had neglected this
precaution), and when within a very few yards of his intrenchments in the tall grass and weeds, I gradually but noise-

lessly regained my slantendicular and now stood up and
stretched toward the skies about six feet of Yankee Sergeant.
Then, drawing a long breath for the onset, with one single
leap I placed my enemy *hors du combat,* and in another instant he was rolling on the grass with the sharp point of a
Yankee bayonet against his ribs, to which was attached a very
bright Enfield rifle in the strong grip of a very determined
looking young fellow, demanding the while an unconditional
surrender in the name of the United States, and in the name
also of snakes, and alligators, Niggers and secessionists.

The enemy responded thus: "Foh de Lor's sake, massa,
don't shoot, don't shoot! De good Lor bress me, I'se a gone
nigga shuah! Oh! mussy! mussy!"

He begged so piteously that I could not help but laugh so
loudly that a sentinel came running immediately, expecting to
find a maniac roaming in the forest all alone at that late
hour. But discovering the ridiculous cause of the mirth, he
joined in the laughter, and together we tormented the big Nigger, threatening him with the Provost Marshall (all Nigs have
a special dread of that dignitary), and told him he would be
hung early in the morning for a spy.

After the descendant of Ham recovered enough to speak,
he told us that he had presented his passport to the guard
about dark, but it being after six o'clock, he was not allowed
to pass the lines, and he had concluded to go to his home outside the lines in the manner just described, but had failed in
this attempt also. Says he: "Its no use tryin' to pass you-alls
nohow! De Yankees hab got eyes gis like a possum; see gis
as well afer dark as de broad daylight. I passed de cornfed-
eracy's pickets more'n onct gis dat-a-way."

Such adventures are very common here; it is very seldom
anything more serious happens, as there is no enemy within
fifteen miles, save an occasional Bushwhacker.

Tell Addie if she don't answer my letter, I will be tempted
to commit suicide. If some other soldier occupies all her leisure moments, just let me know. Should he be a non-combatant, or a stay-at-home Ranger, tell her to inform him I am
learning the sword exercise.

You say she is smart, pretty, and only seventeen—just as

though these three virtues were all that is necessary to insure a Soldier's Friendship, or secure his Admiration! What kind of an Idea have you of my disposition? Can't you see I am inclined to be *sentimental,* if I knew how? Much soldiering hath made me what I am, and should the critical eye of a schoolgirl detect in my "short" letter a single mistake, or an omission of proper grammar, orthography, syntax, or prosody, please attribute it to the extreme ignorance of your

Affectionate Uncle,
O. J. H.

P.S.—Write as soon as you get this; tell me "tales out of school," and write long letters. Remember, it is a long distance from here to Eddyville. Perhaps 1600 miles. I am waiting with the greatest of Patience for that facsimile. Say to Miss Addie: "Sans toi, ma vie est un désert. Enfin, tu n'en peux plus douter!" *Voilà tout.*

Friday, February 5th. On First Post, South Line of Pickets, on the Donaldsonville road. Business lively. Girls plenty. Cotton. Citizens and Negroes passing continually. Having a very pleasant time. Plenty of company. Contraband articles and produce of every kind coming in.

Saturday, February 6th. Was relieved promptly this morning, and returned to camp after reporting Private Peter Carlen of Co. G, 42nd., to Head Quarters for the crime of disobedience of orders. The said Peter Carlen having positively refused to go on guard last night at the hour of eleven.

Sunday, February 7th. Regiment had Company and Regimental Inspection and Dress parade in its usual fine appearance and soldierly cleanliness. Finished the book entitled *Ella Adams, or the Demon of Fire,*[16] a tale of the present Rebellion. Green Back library not worth a ———!

Monday, February 8th. Today, had negative taken for Photo; will get them in a few days. Had a very pleasant Bat-

[16] By Ned Buntline (New York: F. A. Brady, 1863).

tallion drill this P.M. at one o'clock. My comrade, Jim Whitsel, is on Picket; I will have to sleep alone this cold night.
Sickness is increasing in the Regiment, and more strict Sanitary rules are being daily enforced. Soldiering in Plaquemine
is a nice thing, and just suits the dispositions of some men,
but, for one, *I* can't see the nicity of it, tho we have all the
luxuries a soldier could wish or expect in the army.

Tuesday, February 9th. Am out on Picket duty towards
Bayou Gouley.[17] Business lively. Citizens, Ladies, Soldiers,
and Negroes passing constantly, keeping me busy examining
Passports. The weather threatening rain; hope it won't,
though, until I get back to Camp,—don't like rain at all!

Wednesday, February 10th. Today rec'd a letter from
[Yourtee], and one from ["Lide" Wilcox]. Answered the latter this evening. Also rec'd a *Toledo Blade* sent by "Bro." at
Toledo. All quiet on the Coast. "Au revoir." Family were all
well at home, according to Yourtee's last letter.

Thursday, February 11th. An ineffectual effort was made
by Col. Sheldon today to get the Forty-second to reenlist as
Veteran Cavalry. Not much inclination manifested by the boys
to reenlist. About a dozen of us signified our willingness to
Volunteer by stepping to the front. Think it will be a success
finally.

Friday, February 12th.

> "Calm is the firmament
> Over the clouds,
> Clear shine the stars through
> The rifts of the shroud.
> There our repose shall be,
> Thither we tend,
> Spite of our waverings
> Approved at the end."

This poetry, of course, is not original, or at least not of my
composition. Active service in some other Department is

---

[17] Bayou Goula.

preferable to this killing inactivity. Oh, for the glorious old days of Vicksburg and Chickasaw Heights!

Saturday, February 13th. The Boys are rapidly reenlisting as Veteran Cavalry. Our Company has already turned out fifteen men. Other Companies are excelling ours in the work. Sent a Photo to [envelope];[18] one also to [Mary Knapp], and one to [Yourtee]. The mail leaves on Monday for the North and America.

Sunday, February 14th. Mailed one letter to [Mary Knapp], and one to [Yourtee, M—— J——, Jane Knox, and "Lide" Wilcox], all containing my Photo, except ["Lide" Wilcox].

> "My peaceful home has no charms for me,
> The battle field no pain.
> The lady I loved will soon be a bride,
> With a diadem on her brow;
> Oh, why did she flatter my boyish pride?
> She's going to leave me now."

Bully for Cox![19]

Monday, February 15th. Companies I, K, G, and B were out on a foraging expedition today. Crossed Bayou Groestat at Indian Village and routed the enemies Pickets, and loaded five barges with lumber to finish our Fort. Started back for Plaquemine 5 P.M. and arrived about eight at night.

Tuesday, February 16th. Today we cleaned up our arms and accoutrements, they having been rusted and soiled considerably by the heavy rain that fell while we were out at Indian Village. Company F, formerly consolidated with our Company, has been removed, and Capt. Willard now commands it.

---

18 His sister Hester Jane, wife of John Knox.

19 In December, 1862, Representative Samuel Sullivan Cox of Ohio had introduced a resolution in Congress, initiating the movement that resulted in the general suspension of habeas corpus for the duration of the war in September, 1863. The Vallandigham trial was a case in point.

Wednesday, February 17th. Today, the Forty-second had Battallion drill and dress parade. The Mail arrived from N.O., but I did not get a scratch of the pen. This P.M., wrote a letter to [lady's hat],[20] Huntsville, Ohio. My Health excellent, my Spirits excellent; Fighting weight, 175 lbs.

Thursday, February 18th. Brings quite a sudden change in the weather. This P.M. it commenced to snow quite briskly, putting a dreary mantle upon the beautiful green grass, and killing the Peach blossoms that the last four weeks of fine weather brought forth. Everything of the vegetable nature was prospering finely.

Friday, February 19th. Preparations are being made to send men north to receive the conscripts destined to fill up this Regiment. Sergeant McAlister is selected from Co. K to go. Will probably leave on the first steamer. Weather moderately cool.

Saturday, February 20th. This blot was caused by the carelessness of the owner of the book in dipping his pen into the Ink bottle too deep and bringing up, instead of an *Idea,* a pen full of writing fluid, and letting it drop on the page, as you observe. He tried to lick it off, but the effort proved a failure. Bad luck to the old tipsy ink bottle that upset and made this ugly blot on my book, and badder luck to my own carelessness!

Sunday, February 21st. Am on Picket today on First Post, and having a busy time examining Passports, searching for contraband goods, etc., etc. Orders are very strict with regard to Goods and provisions passing the lines. All undergo a rigorous search. Weather *warm.*

Monday, February 22nd. Am quite sleepy today, having slept but two hours during the last night. Regiment was drilled by Maj. Williams today in Firing. The place selected for the drill was on the river bank, and our balls reached the

[20] Probably his sister Sarah Eliza ("Lyde"), wife of Dr. Thomas Thompson, who was serving with the 182nd Ohio as a hospital assistant.

opposite shore, a distance of 500 yards,—pretty long distance for a musket ball.

Tuesday, February 23rd. Today, was detailed to take charge of the working party on the fort in place of Sergeant McAlister, who has gone home for drafted men; find it a pleasant duty. Had fresh beef for dinner today: the first we have had since coming to the place. Mac took our Photos home. The ocean breeze from off the Gulf makes this country inhabitable; otherwise, no white man could thrive in it.

Wednesday, February 24th. Kept the men at work today on the North-west Bastion of the works. The work progresses finely. The mail arrived today. Rec'd one letter; from Mother. The weather continues fine. A rumor of small pox in camp is going the rounds.

Thursday, February 25th. Chief Engineer J. T. Baker, Capt. U.S.A., made an inspection of our Fort today, and planned a few alterations in the construction of the parapet and slope of *banquette;* also intends to form a *glacis* over the *counterscarp,* to range with the top of the parapet. Had 25 men at work.

Friday, February 26th. The Guns for the fort arrived today on board the Steamer *Col. Colburn.* Will be mounted as soon as possible. My working party today consisted of 56 men and a sergeant. The work progresses rapidly. The armament will consist of 14 heavy guns *en barbette,* with small ones in embrasures. I see no need of fortifying this miserable little place, as the Rebels would never get rich, or subsist a corporal's Guard in it.

Saturday, February 27th. Ends our labors for this week. The Steamer *Constitution* passed en route for the North, also several other boats. The *General Banks* brought a load of ordnance stores for this Fort. One 30-pounder was moved into the Fort this P.M., but not mounted. The others will be moved in and mounted soon.

Sunday, February 28th. This morning, answered a letter to Ma, and one to [cross].[21] Commenced the book entitled *Three Times Dead, or Secret of the Heath.*[22] Have just seven months to serve yet to finish three years. It is not expected that the Forty-second will take the field soon. The Second Ohio Brigade left today for Algiers.[23]

Monday, February 29th. Regiment was mustered for pay at 2 P.M. The paymaster is expected soon. The wind shifted from the south, and tonight a brisk Nor-wester is blowing, changing the atmosphere to a cold, chilly dampness. Was engaged but two hours on the fort today, when I relieved my men for Inspection and general muster.

Tuesday, March 1st. March comes in like a lion, and according to the old Quaker sign, it will go out like a Lamb. The day is cold and stormy. All outdoors duty is suspended, except that of the guards. A big fire is necessary for comfort, and my Great Coat is my best friend.

Wednesday, March 2nd. The Steamer *Black Hawk* brought the mail, and I have a letter from ——— [Julia Allison]. Commenced the answer tonight, but did not finish it; have been busy on duty at the fort today. I received the *Christian Advocate,* but know not to whom I am indebted for the favor. Ike Davis.

Thursday, March 3rd. The Ocean Steamship arrived from N.O. at 3 P.M. with freight for this Post. Still filling in the Bastions of the Fort, and will soon be ready for the floors and Guns. Today, had two Sergeants and one Corporal and 89 men at work on the Fort under my direction. Have not answered my letter yet. Weather pleasant in the extreme.

Friday, March 4th. Mechanics of every description are at work on the Fort. Another detail will be sent tomorrow to

---

[21] His sister Elizabeth, wife of Theodore Swiggart of Attica, Indiana.

[22] By Miss M. E. Braddon (New York: Dick & Fitzgerald, 1864).

[23] A small town located on the west bank of the Mississippi, opposite New Orleans.

cut sod for the revetment of the interior slope. Advices from New Orleans state that General Sherman and Staff arrived in that city on Wednesday ahead of his expeditionary army, now on its return from the interior.

Saturday, March 5th. Reports are current this P.M. that McClernand is fitting out an expedition for some point in Texas, and it is thought that our Regiment will be ordered back to our old place in the Thirteenth Army Corps. I received orders this evening to relieve all men in fatigue belonging to the Illinois battery. I suppose they are going to leave.

Sunday, March 6th. This P.M., answered [Julia Allison's] letter and mailed it, but the mail leaves not until the morrow. The letter was a long one,—pretty saucy in its nature, but nevertheless containing some very plain unavoidable truths. Over a month will have to elapse before I will get an answer.

The following is the letter to Julia Allison.[24]

CAMP OF 42ND. GEORGIA VOLS., C.S.A.
PLAQUEMINE, March 6, 1864.

DEAR FRIEND,

Your letter, in company with four others, was handed to me a few days since, and strange to tell, I didn't swear once while reading yours, though, like the *Indian's Hawk,*[25] I *thought* pretty loud.

I have been on daily duty at the fort; have charge of about 80 men engaged in finishing the interior works and mounting heavy Siege Guns, consequently have very little time to write a very long letter, so have selected this small sheet[26] to "express myself" on this Sabbath morning. Captain J. T. Baker of the Regular Army is in charge. The work will soon be completed, and will be one of the strongest Forts on the river. Citizens passing cast mournful looks up at the *grim dogs of*

[24] The bravado and persiflage in these early letters to Julia Allison were doubtless matched by her teasing quips and innuendos; each displayed a sort of protective camouflage and feinting.

[25] No source for this reference could be found.

[26] The "small sheet" was eleven and one-half inches long and eight inches wide.

war bristling over the parapet, and with doleful shake of the head they wisely come to the conclusion that their Confederacy is played out in Louisiana.

An effort was made by Col. Sheldon to get the Forty-second into the Veteran service as Cavalry, but Gen. Banks refused to accept us as such. To obtain the consent of the Regiment to be mustered as Veteran Infantry for another three years was out of the question. Eight of us from our company reenlisted, as did about the same number from every company in the regiment, But were not accepted unless the Regiment would go *en masse*. We just told General Banks he might go to . . . Mobile!

I intend *now* to serve my term in the Forty-second, at the expiration of which I expect to join my Brother-in-law, Major of the Seventh Iowa Cavalry, now in active service in Nebraska.[27] Am bound to wear Soger Clothes and live in a tent as long as I am able to carry a musket, or there are no snakes in my boots. I truly admire that youthful gent of the legal profession, if for nothing else but his meek resignation to the will of his *aged parents*. His obedience is a virtue certainly not to be overlooked in making up the character of a *nice young man*. Oh! cruel even the thought, to tear him away from his home, his *aged parents!* To leave them so helpless on the cold charity of the world! And he, so young, so handsome, so accomplished and promising, to drill by the side of a rough soldier! Oh! I see it now: he fears to enter the ranks! A happy thought strikes me: tell him that there's a vacancy in our Company for an eighth Corporal, and fine prospects for promotion to the *rear rank*.

I think I know this gentleman's name. In fact, am certain of it, and hold myself responsible accordingly. I entered the ranks of the Army with no thought of position or promotion, with no other ambition than to perform every duty assigned to me as a soldier and a defender of the *Good Cause*, leaving a widowed mother whose love for her Son was as great

[27] Jemima's husband, John Wilcox, had raised a company of one hundred men who were mustered in at Davenport, Iowa, as Company B of the Seventh Iowa Volunteer Cavalry. He was commissioned its captain and was sent into the plains of Nebraska "to quell an uprising of the Indians." When he returned, he had been promoted to major and was in command of the regiment.

as that of any mother, Yet she has been no less proud of her Boy, I hope, for his past career, or for standing up for his Country's flag when all was dark with *blackest treason.* Over two years of active service has not lessened my love for home and its associations; still, I could not linger in idleness around that Home, while Traitors were threatening its very threshold.—"Shakespeare."

Love of Country is rather poorly developed in a man who, under no consideration but high salary and shoulder-straps, could be tempted to enter the service of Uncle Sam. Very slight indeed must be his patriotism.

What is your opinion?

Who was the fellow who said that my Company must have been in the rear? Does he wear citizen's clothes? If so, all right!

No one knows anything about your *condecension,* nor shall they through my agency. But why do you ask? This Chick always burns his letters as soon as they are read, though for once I have departed from usual habit in the case of your last letter, as I have not read all of it yet. Am perusing at my leisure; got to where you ask for my counterfeit. I have three left out of a dozen, but can't send mine, or Dick's [28] either, until you send or destroy those old ones. If you assure me of this next time, you may look for both mine and Dick's, taken not in the stylish, unbecoming rig of Photo N.2, but in such as Abe's Boys wear down in Louisiana. Am almost certain you will fall in love with Dick. You can't help but like the *cut of his jib,* but remember, he isn't as fast a sailer as I am, being iron clad fore and aft, and nothing but a Second Corporal, at that. Some soldiers it don't take long to demoralize. *I* am reforming gradually, but surely. Don't put on half so much style as I used to. Can't afford it . . . don't smoke but three cigars per day . . . hardly ever take my bitters as I used to—take them sweetened now! . . . don't swear, except when very angry . . . abandoned blacked boots and paper collars entirely . . . Seldom ever think of home, and *never* dream the soldier's dream (of Home). That's played out! And seldom ever heard to sing, but sometimes

[28] Dick Bailey, of Company G.

whistle to myself the good old tune, "Southern Rights," or *The Bonnie Blue Flag.* Don't play *Several-up;* only at times for who shall go to the river after water, when it is raining.

Falsehood, Gambling, Drinking, Swearing, and the "Union forever" were erased from my calendar long ago. As to the two you named for my selection, I beg time for consideration. Certainly the virtues you enumerated, namely, the *natural* beauty you say they possess, are matters of no small importance, since *false teeth, false hair, false shoulders, unnatural bright eyes,* and *false hips* have become the order of the day. By the way, do you think the roads will be in condition for an overland journey to the West by the last of next August?

Al Bowman is from Medina, Ohio; Lieut. Hubble [Hubbell], from Newburg; Dick Bailey is from East Cleveland. Lieut. Hubble of Company A is the most handsome officer in the Regiment, a perfect soldier in his bearing, and a true Gentleman. Al Bowman is handsome, too, but very *wild.* Dick beats them all in each of these characteristics.

Sergeant Sid [Sidney] Alden, Sim [Simon] Oatman, and others are very anxious that I should send their compliments, but none of them know who to. When one soldier writes a letter, everyone that happens in, says: "Give her my love," when perhaps the letter is to some aged relative or father. I have had three letters from my little bright-eyed Sis in Illinois; the second one contained a Photo. I tell you, she is beautiful; *natural,* too, I *think,* though of course am no judge.

Our nigger says supper is ready. Can you write a sentimental letter? Hurrah for Vallandigham! Long live Jeff! Death to Abolition nigger-lovers! Down with the Invaders! Up with the Stars and Bars!

Your Bitter Enemy,
"FIVE MONTHS" [29]

[Marginal notes] I've found several white spots on this letter, and am resolved to cover them with black ink. We have a very nice little P.O. in Plaquemine where we mail our letters, but when the mail arrives, it is separated and sent to each company commander, when it is distributed to the com-

---

[29] Those who had volunteered for three years of service held those who had been recruited for five months in contempt.

panies, as directed. Does anyone know you write to me? Hope not. Was Mary disappointed in her expectations the day you wrote? Did she get the letter? Hardly think I shall send a sketch to a young lady I am not acquainted with. I received a very long "political" letter from an *old friend* in Bellefontaine the day yours came. He must pardon me if I do not exactly coincide with his views of the present situation of affairs.

Monday, March 7th. Revetment of interior slope progresses finely. Also the filling in of the bastions. The detail for my "relief" today was 2 sergeants and 65 men. The duties for the day have been unusually active and promise to increase tomorrow.

Tuesday, March 8th. The Mail left today for N.O., from where it will be started north, bearing my letter to [Julia Allison]. This evening, staked off the ground in rear of the Sally Porte. Will commence in the morning to build it with earth from the ditches, unless it rains tonight.

Wednesday, March 9th. Am the recipient of several papers sent by some unknown friend, but no letters by this mail. Has been raining every few moments in small showers since daybreak; the ground is covered by ugly muddy water, and labor is postponed on the Fort.

Thursday, March 10th. The weather is making a desperate effort to clear off, but showers of rain will force themselves on, in spite of the efforts of "Old Saul" to pierce the thickness of the flying clouds, which look dark and lowering yet. Time hangs dull over the hearts of soldiers who have six more months to serve.

Friday, March 11th. Private Jack Wilson returned to the company; has been absent from the Regiment since August last, on furlough. Received a paper containing General Garfield's speech in Congress.[30] Tried operations on the Fort, but

[30] James A. Garfield took his seat in Congress in December, 1863, as a Representative of the district of the Western Reserve.

the earth was rather damp and adhered to the tools too much to work.

Saturday, March 12th. Am reading the book entitled *Minnie Grey, or Who is the Heir?* [31] The weather moderately fine, with a fresh Gale blowing from the south-west. Farmers (or planters, rather) are making preparations for tilling the soil. Many have already begun to plant. No paymaster yet: the man above all to elicit a Soger's hearty welcome.

Sunday, March 13th. Today, perhaps, our friends at home are reaping the benefits of the seventh day. For us, its blessings do not come. The Catholic Church is the only one open today, but to me their mode of worship is like the performance of the Theater more than the worship of Christian people.

Monday, March 14th. The river is raising rapidly, and I think, in the course of a week, it will be bank full. This P.M., the sodding party commenced the revetment of interior slope of bastion. Think by Saturday will get "Old Abe" mounted.

Tuesday, March 15th. Finished one platform in the northwest bastion, and mounted one 30-pounder. Work is progressing rapidly. A rumor is again prevalent that Col. Sheldon is expecting marching orders; for what point, is undecided. The river still continues to rise. But very little cotton is coming into our lines. Weather warm and pleasant.

Wednesday, March 16th. Steamer *Black Hawk* brought the mail. I received one paper from some unknown friend, also a letter from [Mary Knapp], dated March 1st. A very interesting letter, confirming me in the belief that [Mary] is my 2nd best correspondant. Can't tell when I will get time to answer it, as I am on duty constantly.

Thursday, March 17th. The Paymaster has arrived at last, and has paid off the 120th Ohio. Our Regiment will be

[31] Published by Garrett & Co., 1852. Author not known.

paid off tomorrow. My account against Uncle Sam calls for four months' pay, but this time will only get half of it ($34). Weather cool, but *windy;* just cool enough for comfort, and that's all.

Friday, March 18th. Regiment was paid off for two months. I received $61. Several of the boys didn't get a cent, for the reason that they had lost their descriptive lists, or were not here at the time of muster, and will have to borrow enough to last until next time.

Saturday, March 19th. Nothing has yet occurred to confirm yesterday's report of our leaving, and many do not credit the rumor. For my part, I believe that we haven't got long to tarry, but will leave for some other Port soon, if not sooner.

Sunday, March 20th. Bought a Photo Album and filled it in less than *no time.* Hardly know whether to send home any money this time or not; the chances of its ever reaching destination is doubtful. But guess I will risk it by Express.

Monday, March 21st. I mailed a letter to [Mary Knapp], Bellefontaine, O; also the *Gazette* and *Sentinel*[32] to the same. Rained hard all last night and today; the country is navigable for ducks. River still on the rise. Colored troops are being sent up Red River; three transports loaded with troops of A.C. passed since morning.

Tuesday, March 22nd. All quiet on the Mississippi. River rising. Steamers are being chartered by the Government to transport supplies to our forces on Red River. Also to ship troops to Alexandria. Received no late papers today from either south or north.

Wednesday, March 23rd. The 120th Ohio left for Baton-Rouge on the Steamer *Empire.* We are expecting to go as soon as other troops come to relieve us. The *Empire* brought

[32] These may have been the Logan County *Gazette* and the Cincinnati *Sentinel.*

a portion of our mail, and I received a letter from my Brother [Almon] at Toledo.

Thursday, March 24th. 6:30 o'clock. Have packed up everything ready to move at a moment's notice. Will leave perhaps tonight on the first boat. The Fourteenth Rhode Island Regt. "Corps de Afrique" [colored troops] disembarked this morning, and will garrison the place until further orders. Rains by fits and spells, making ponds and little rills, etc., etc.

Friday, March 25th. The day closes and finds us still in our old camp at Plaquemine. No boats have come up since last night capable of transporting troops, but it is thought the close of another day will find us at Baton-Rouge, the Capitol of Louisiana.

The following entries were made in Baton Rouge, Louisiana:

Saturday, March 26th. The Regiment embarked on board the U.S. Gunboat #27 at half-past two P.M. at Plaquemine upper landing, and arrived at Baton Rouge at quarter-past 5 o'clock. Marched to camp in south-east suburbs of the City and near the statehouse. Weather very fine, and our trip was a pleasant one.

Sunday, March 27th. The 156th New York Volunteers was formerly encamped on the same ground we now occupy, and we have been busy all day cleaning up and renovating quarters. Capt. Willard has command of the Regiment in the absence of Major Williams, whose severe illness detains him at Plaquemine. Lieut. A. L. Bowman still has command of the Company, but Capt. Hutchins is expected back soon.

Monday, March 28th. Was distinguished from all other days by the very heavy rain that fell in the forenoon. The Steamer *J. H. Russell* was burned last night at Plaquemine landing by the accidental catching of the turpentine and cotton from the fire of a torch, while preparing to land.

8 UNDER THE FLAG OF THE NATION
Tuesday, March 29th. A steady nor'wester has blown ever since morning, and our tent was capsized in a squall and torn from stem to stern; don't know where we will sleep tonight. Morning, on camp duty today; have three corporals and six men. The gale has somewhat abated, 6 P.M.

Wednesday, March 30th. We have been looking for mail today, but as yet we are disappointed. Rumor says that the Steamer *N. P. Banks* is aground below here with mail on board, but I hardly credit the tale, since the present high stage of the river would hardly admit of such an incident.

Thursday, March 31st. Regiment was paraded for inspection at one o'clock, and looked in good trim. Also, dress parade at half past five o'clock. The picket detail is not so heavy as common: generally a non-commissioned officer and four or five men. The close of the month dry.

Friday, April 1st. The mail arrived per Steamer *Bella Donna.* I received a letter from ["Lide" Wilcox] and [Jane Knox], dated respectfully March 13th and 4th; also a letter from M—— J——, dated March 9th; also one from Mother at Toledo, dated 15th of March. Good news all round. I will expect several letters next mail.

Saturday, April 2nd. Answered and mailed letters to the following: [Jane Knox, "Lide" Wilcox, M—— J——, and Sarah E. Thompson]. Bought a new cap today of the latest style. The weather is quite pleasant. April came in *like a lamb.* Business is growing lively here. Brig. Gen. Patrick St. George Cook, of the regular army, is in command of the Post.

Sunday, April 3rd. Maj. Wm. H. Williams has again taken command of the Regiment. We are all glad to see him back. The Major is the favorite officer of the 42nd. Had dress parade at 5 P.M., and at night, with a squad of 10 men, I attended Methodist Church.

Monday, April 4th. My pard has gone on picket, and I am left alone in my mess to spend the day as best I can. Have

almost finished the book entitled *Under the Spell*.[33] Pie ped-
lars and hucksters of both sexes and all kinds, without number, invade the camp.

Tuesday, April 5th. On Picket at Post No. 4—high land
round south of the City. An expedition composed of the 22nd
Kentucky Vols., a section of a battery, and several companies
of Wisconsin Corps made a successful reconnaissance on the
Wilmington Road. After a slight skirmish with the enemy,
they returned with several prisoners.

Wednesday, April 6th. After being relieved, and delivering
instructions to the new Guard, we mounted a planter's wagon
and returned to town; thence to camp, where I expected to
get some mail, but the Steamer *N. P. Banks,* due today, has
not arrived yet with the mail for this Post. I wish it would
hurry up.

Thursday, April 7th. I received a letter from [school
teacher in Kalida], and one from ["Lide" Wilcox], dated
March 15th.; also, one from [Elizabeth Swiggart], dated
22nd of March. All interesting but one. Don't think I will answer the Former's letter, as it wasn't interesting. Can't answer "disinteresting" letters.

Friday, April 8th. Have passed the day in cleaning up quarters. Company engaged in draining the camp. Mailed a letter
to ["Lide" Wilcox], Eddyville, Iowa. All quiet in camp. I
have almost the notion to take the blues. My nature requires
more excitement than is manifest in our present situation. The
streets of the City in the evening present a gay and lively appearance.

Saturday, April 9th. The U.S. Q.M. Steamer *Thomas* arrived direct from Cairo with a full cargo of supplies for this
post. Also, the *Nathaniel P. Banks,* a regular passenger and
mail steamer, left for N.O. about noon. The *Albert Pearce*
also arrived from Cairo. No late Northern dates.

[33] A book by this title, by Frederick W. Robinson, was published by R. M.
DeWitt, New York City, in 1869. This may have been an earlier edition.

Sunday, April 10th. Again on picket on the Highland road, with one corporal and eight men. The weather most beautiful. Natives passing constantly. Lieut. Moody, officer of the picket guard, stays at this post. General Cook is expecting an attack, But his gay boys are not easy "skeared."

Monday, April 11th. After returning to camp, found two letters for me: one from [Yourtee], dated 27th March; the other from ["Lide" Wilcox], dated the 25th. The Brigade was formed in line of battle this morning at 3 o'clock, expecting an attack, but no enemy appeared. Dress parade at 5 o'clock.

Tuesday, April 12th. The Regiment was again in line of battle this morning at 3 o'clock, and remained until sun up. The day has been a long one, warm, and coats and vests are of no use until evening, when the weather grows cool. Jim and I took a stroll over the city this eve.

Wednesday, April 13th. The U.S. transport *Laurel Hill* passed with sick and wounded from the Red River district, bound for General Hospital, New Orleans. The 24th Indiana Vol. Infantry landed here, and report says more reenforcements are coming. I have a letter from [shield] [34] containing considerable news.

Thursday, April 14th. A heavy rain fell last night and up to 10 o'clock; it still continues to fall in occasional showers. Further particulars of the fight up Red River reached here today, and it seems our loss in killed and wounded is extremely heavy; that of the enemy is much greater. Our forces drove the Rebels in the last day's Battle.

Friday, April 15th. Company K was out on skirmish drill at 9 o'clock. Also, dress parade at five. More troops have been landed, and tonight a report is current perporting a move from here in some direction. Our Brigade will probably be called into the field. "Che Sara, Sara," or, in plain English: "What must be, must be."

[34] His sister, Jemima (Hopkins) Wilcox, mother of "Lide."

Saturday, April 16th. I rec'd a letter from [Julia Allison], dated April 3rd. This correspondant's letters hereafter will be unanswered, as I and her will now play quits. I am anxiously expecting a letter from [Mary Knapp], who is my best and favorite scribbler. Had Brigade inspection at 2 P.M.

Sunday, April 17th. Like a good boy (as I am), I attended Methodist church tonight and enjoyed myself finely. The night is a beautiful one, but the white fleecy clouds, which ever and anon drift ghostly across the bright visage of the Queen of Night, forebode a rainy day tomorrow.

Monday, April 18th. A still more credited report is current that the Third Brigade is under marching orders; suppose that our destination is Red River. River rising slowly and full of boats, mostly from northern ports. Rumor has it that the enemy still hold Fort Pillow.[35]

Tuesday, April 19th. Col. Sheldon was present at our dress parade tonight. Had the Flag of the Union tattooed on my right arm. Calm is the firmament. A clear bright moon is peering down upon our camp, lending its presence to lone sentinels as a companion for the night.

Wednesday, April 20th. On Picket as reserve, with 20 men and two corporals, on the road east of the City. The mail arrived per Steamer *N. P. Banks,* but I rec'd nothing—quite provoking to disappoint me, when I was looking so anxiously for at least one letter. Weather very pleasant, of course.

Thursday, April 21st. Relieved by a detail from 42nd. O.V.I., commanded by Lieut. A. L. Bowman. Weather extremely warm. Capt. T. L. Hutchins returned for duty today. Has been home. Received orders to be ready to embark on first boats for Alexandria, to reenforce Banks.

Friday, April 22nd. The Regiments were furnished with uniform coats yesterday, and the 42nd looks like a regiment of

[35] The capture and massacre of the Union forces at Fort Pillow, Tennessee, took place on April 12, 1864.

"Come-latelies." We are still quietly occupying our camp without further orders up to 4 P.M. The day closes, and we are still on the ground.

Saturday, April 23rd. The Eighteenth Indiana arrived, and are encamped near us. Reports are conflicting and as numerous as bees in May. Private Hugh Underwood returned for duty today from Marine Hospital, New Orleans; has been home on furlough. A perfect deluge of rain fell during the day, and mud is soggy.

Sunday, April 24th. A portion of the mail arrived today, but I did not receive a letter or any mail whatever. Tonight, me and Jim Whitsel went to church, but were too late; the House was crowded to overflowing, and so we took a stroll over the City. And went to bed half-past nine.

Monday, April 25th. Has been one of extreme quiet in camp. No more signs of our leaving soon are manifest. The Tenth Ohio Volunteers passed here en route for Red River. Business in the City dull in the extreme, as greenbacks are not so plenty,—which is the result of long absence of the Paymaster.

Tuesday, April 26th. The Regiment was paraded through the principal streets of the City at 5 P.M., making a display for the multitude of spectators on the verandas and the street corners. No news from the North. I believe, though, I have kept closely to quarters owing to the high state of the murcury, it being very high.

Wednesday, April 27th. No change in the programme. All quiet in Baton Rouge. The Twenty-second Kentucky Volunteers left today for Alexandria. Jim is on Camp Guard and sleeps at the Guard House tonight with his Relief. Am not very well today, but managed to hide a flavorous dish of beans at dinner.

Thursday, April 28th. Amusements of the day as follows: Reflecting the bright rays of the sun, by the aid of a small mirror, into eyes of passers by our camp. Evening: a Heenan & Sayers[36] fight between two juvenile "Intelligent contraband," lasting an hour and finally resulting in the defeat of "Cuffy." Do you know *him?*

Friday, April 29th. If we are going to leave for the field, I should like to be off. Such uncertainty is unendurable. Not so! Soldiers can endure anything! No news from the North. All quiet in Baton Rouge. Guerrillas are still hovering near our lines, but doing no damage to us except harassing pickets.

Saturday, April 30th. Regiment mustered for pay, according to orders from "war department." Lieut.-Col. Don A. Pardee takes command of the 42nd. We are all glad to see him, after being honorably acquitted by General Court Martial in behalf of the United States.

Sunday, May 1st. Cool and pleasant. Attended a Temperance Meeting tonight at the Methodist Church. The 120th O.V.I. of our Brigade left for Red River per Steamer *City Belle.* Our turn may come next. Am expecting mail by the next post. Have not heard from home lately.

Monday, May 2nd. We rec'd orders about 4 P.M. to be ready in light marching order for a tramp, and at half-past four the Eighteenth Indiana Volunteers took the advance, followed by the Twenty-seventh Kentucky and Twenty-fourth Indiana Vets, the rear guard composed of the Forty-second Ohio with the 18th New York battery, also the ———— Indiana battery of brass twelve-pounders; Col. Sheldon in command. Marched 18 miles, and encamped about 11 o'clock P.M.

Tuesday, May 3rd. Five o'clock this morning found us again on the road. Seven A.M., began skirmishing with the

[36] The last great prize fight to be fought with bare fists, before the adoption of the Marquess of Queensberry rules put an end to the practice, was between Tom Sayers, an Englishman, and J. C. Heenan, the American champion, and took place at Farnborough, England, in April, 1860. It was a shockingly brutal match and it ended in a draw.

enemy. Eight o'clock, Companies K and B were deployed as skirmishers, and drove the Rebels until 2 P.M., when they sought their works across Clinch River, after destroying the bridge. Three P.M., started back toward Baton Rouge: a "day's work." Marched 38 miles in 24 hours, and fought 7 hours. Encamped in the swamp.

Wednesday, May 4th. Marched again toward the City, a distance of 11 miles from our last night's rendezvous. Arrived at camp about 10 A.M., tired and worn out. Our loss is two men killed and six wounded, also two missing. The Colonel of the Fourth Illinois Cavalry was killed instantly. I was near him when he fell. The Rebel loss supposed to be heavy. We have four prisoners.

Thursday, May 5th. Commenced a long letter to Brother in Toledo, Ohio. The Boys are still sore footed, and not yet recovered from our late "raid" on Clinton. The expedition was a success. This evening, attended a meeting convened to draft resolutions in regard to the late Colonel Boardman's death. Killed near Clinton.

Friday, May 6th. Nine of the 120th Ohio arrived today from Red River; report the majority of the Regiment captured and Col. Spiegle killed, two Gunboats sunk, and two transports destroyed by the Rebels secreted behind the Levee.[37] Enemy show no quarters. The whole affair is a sad dispensation of War's decree. Mailed a letter to Yourtee.

Saturday, May 7th. Orders today are to clean quarters and make no more preparation to move. Have a letter from Yourtee, Toledo. Only yesterday wrote a letter to him giving particulars of our fight near Clinton on the 3rd. inst, and other scraps of news such as is afloat.

Sunday, May 8th. Calm and pleasant, with no further news from the front. We have New Orleans papers of the 7th.

[37] In the aftermath of General Banks's ill-fated expedition against Shreveport and the disastrous retreat of the Union forces to Alexandria.

Took a quiet stroll over the City. Rec'd a letter from [Mary Knapp], but have not time to answer it until tomorrow.

Monday, May 9th. Wrote and mailed a letter to [Mary Knapp] today; sent all the news that's going. Our landing is active, and business brisk. Several arrivals from below and one from the north. It appears that Steele has been whipped badly. Particulars yet unknown.[38]

Tuesday, May 10th. A bill has passed in Congress increasing the pay of soldiers as follows: Privates, $16; Corporals, $18; Sergeants, $20; Orderly Sergeants, $24; and Sergeant Majors, $28. This is very welcome news to us, especially since prices have increased so rapidly in the past years.

Wednesday, May 11th. The mail arrived with late dates from below, also New York papers, but no news in particular. I have a letter from [Jemima Wilcox], dated 29th April. Capt. Hutchins is unwell. The 42nd were out target firing to-day, and had altogether a very pleasant time. Company G are first best, and ours [K] next.

Thursday, May 12th. This P.M., wrote a short letter to [Jemima Wilcox] of Eddyville, Iowa, and mailed it. Have Cincinnati, Chicago, and Memphis papers of recent date, none of which contains news of importance more than that offensive and defensive operations have commenced on the Potomac. Welcome, shades of night!

Friday, May 13th. This has been an "orful" lonesome day, and a warm one. Jim has gone to a temperance *lecture* in the camp of the Fourth Wisconsin Cavalry. I was too lazy to go. The work of Temperance works well in Baton Rouge. I have not yet signed the pledge. Couldn't see it.

Saturday, May 14th. An *Extra* from the Baton Rouge press gives an account of the recent movements of Grant

[38] The expedition which General Steele had led out from Little Rock toward Shreveport had met with disaster at Pine Bluffs, and had been forced to retreat to its starting point, thus restoring two-thirds of Arkansas to the Confederacy.

across the Rapidan, and his battle with Lee. Our loss in the
three days' Battle is nearly 7,000. Rebel loss far exceeds ours.
They left their dead and dieing on the field. Received mail; I
have a Cincinnati paper of late date.

Sunday, Mary 15th. We have orders tonight to be ready to
move in the morning at 6 o'clock, with Camp and Garrison
equipage and one day's rations. Destination not made known,
—to we Soldiers, at least. To take Camp and Garrison equipage, one would judge that we were only going to some minor
point on the river.

Monday, May 16th. On board Steamer *Iberville.* The Regiment embarked on the Steamer *Iberville* at 10 A.M., and
started up the river. Dark still finds us running up Stream.
The Seventh Kentucky is astern of us on the *Sallie Robinson.*
We are bound for Red River.

Tuesday, May 17th. Daylight finds us tied up opposite the
mouth of Red River. 10 A.M.—we ascend Red River three
miles and turn into Old River; landed and cooked breakfast.
Up stream again 14 miles, and again land on the left Bank
and bivouac for the night.

Wednesday, May 18th. Bivouac on Old River, La., or
Simmesport. We are building a bridge composed of 16 transports, to cross Bank's immense Wagon train. The whole army
is retiring from Alexandria. The hardships endured by this
army in the present campaign are without a parallel during
the War.

Thursday, May 19th. Wagons, ambulances, Cavalry, Infantry, Prisoners, and Negroes still crowding across the
Bridge. It is a scene of wild excitement and commotion. By
the morrow, we may start for the Mississippi again,—a distance of more than 30 miles from Simmesport.

Friday, May 20th. By 4 P.M. all are across, and the Pontoon is broken up. We start back for the river. March in the

rear of the train all night. Daylight finds us near the river. Still we march, and at last reach the landing on the Mississippi where all our transports are tied up. We embark on the *Iberville*.

Saturday, May 21st. Still on board the *Iberville*. The 16th and 17th Corps will be sent to Sherman. Exciting reports are constantly coming to us from the Potomac. Grant's movements affect the world and the future destiny of our Country.

The following entries were made at Camp No. 1, Morganza Bend, Louisiana: [39]

Sunday, May 22nd. Regiment encamped at Morganza's Bend, near the river. Will probably remain here for some time, or at least until transports can be sent in sufficient numbers to carry us to New Orleans. Read a letter from Mother, dated 9th inst.; all well, etc., etc. No particular news.

Monday, May 23rd. Our tents have been unloaded, and late this evening we have laid out our camp and pitched tents. Took an old swim in the river this evening. Didn't see any Aligators. No more news from the Potomac, though I sincerely hope all is well with Our Old Leader, Ulysus.

Tuesday, May 24th. Today, the 42nd were on a scout, and a heavy rain overtook us, and tonight, when we arrived in camp, we were as wet as drowned rats. The rain poured in torrents. We brot in several hundred cords of wood on the wagons for the boats.

Wednesday, May 25th. The Regiment was paid off this morning. I rec'd $68 of Uncle Sam's Greenbacks, and sent $60 to Mother; also wrote a letter to the same, giving all the news. The cry again is "On to Richmond!",—and Grant is moving on to Richmond.

[39] "No further military operations of importance were destined to take place during the war in the Department of the Gulf. Our Brigade, the Second and Third Division of the Thirteenth Corps, continued at Morganza after the Nineteenth Corps was ordered to the Department of the East, embarking in July, 1864. The remainder of the Thirteenth Corps here rested and recuperated after the toilsome campaign on the Red River, drilling and preparing for orders sending us to a more active Department."—C(MS).

Thursday, May 26th. All is quiet at Morganza's Bend. The atmosphere at night is damp and chilly and often bitter cold. At noon-day, the heat is oppressive, and again at night, the thermometer sinks below zero. Such is the Southern *clime!* We should have had mail today, but were disappointed.

Friday, May 27th. The day has passed without change of general routine of camp life. This is a very tiresome place, and I will be glad when the order comes to leave. The Major's resignation was not accepted, and he consequently again takes command of the Regiment. Yours Truly, Owen J. Hopkins.

Saturday, May 28th. Troops are leaving constantly for below. We still get no news from Grant, but entertain no fears for Ulyssus. One year ago today, we were popping Vicksburg with lead and hardware; four months more in the United States service, and we are "civillians." Bully for the four months and the Citizen!

The following entries were made in Camp No. 2, Morganza, Louisiana:

Sunday, May 29th. We moved our camp today two miles down the river; find a better situation nearer water. The *Ed. Walsh* loaded with troops and wagons and mules left for N.O. Tonight, have orders to be ready to move at a moment's notice, with two days' cooked rations. Can't say where we are bound for now. The weather is mild. Dust is trump.

Monday, May 30th. According to orders issued last night, we were on the march this morning at half-past four, on the road to Grosse Tete. The heat of the sun is intolerable, and scarcity of water makes us suffer for the want of it. We halt at 10 o'clock at night, and bivouac on Grosse Tete,[40] 28 miles from Morganza.

Tuesday, May 31st. Early this morning, after a breakfast of coffee and crackers, we are in line at 4:30 A.M., and ready

[40] An error for Bayou Grossette.

for marching. Were on the road at 5 o'clock for a movement
on our way back, having accomplished but little more than the
destruction of the Rebel's camp at Grosse Tete by our Cavalry. Halt near Achafalaya for the night.

Wednesday, June 1st. Was out on picket last night with 2
corporals and 28 men from the 42nd. It rained a tremendous
shower, accompanied by thunder and lightning. This morning,
relieved after the column was in motion, and had some hard
marching to overtake them. We rest for the night at the crossing of the Grosse Tete and Achafalaya Roads, having advanced only two miles. A letter from [Mary Knapp].

Thursday, June 2nd. We remain in bivouac on Bayou Foe-
daio until 4 P.M., when it began to rain, and we are put in
motion toward camp at Morganza, distant 8 miles, where we
arrive tired, wet, and hungry, at 9 at night, it having rained
on us for two hours. We stretch our weary limbs and sleep.

Friday, June 3rd. The day has been stormy, but notwithstanding the rain and my tired limbs, I wrote a letter to Bro.
at Sandusky, Ohio, from whom I rec'd one yesterday. Also,
2 Cincinnati papers. Fired off our guns, and cleaned up arms
and quarters in the afternoon. At night, the rain fell in torrents.

Saturday, June 4th. The Elements all day have made attempts to storm, and at different times came very near to succeeding. A report is current tonight that Richmond has suc-
combed to Grant, *but wise Soldiers shake their heads and
smoke their pipes and say nothing.* Morganza is lonesome and
devoid of amusement of any kind.

Sunday, June 5th. The company was inspected this morning
in full uniform—arms and equipment—at 9 A.M. The outdoor
elements not yet in the best of humor. An expedition, secret in
its nature, left here tonight, composed of the 16th., 114th.
and 120th. Ohio Volunteer Infantry.

Monday, June 6th. Brings no change in the dull routine of camp life. Time hangs heavy with men who have no more to do than eat, drink, and sleep, with hardly enough exercise to develop our physical powers, and when we *are* furnished with exercise, it is not the proper kind to benefit health or nerve.

Tuesday, June 7th. What more can be said of today than we have already said of yesterday: a few old Northern papers to peruse for the one hundredth time, not omitting the advertisements and miscellaneous matter, and finally fall asleep over a review of "Grant's Supposed Plans for the Capture of Richmond." Verily, Verily, I say unto thee: "These are dull times!"

Wednesday, June 8th. Rained all day, but not very hard. Several boats are up from below, bringing N.O. dates to the 6th. Affairs on the Potomac are again assuming an active feature. River falling slowly at this point, yet plenty of water for navigation from St. Louis down.

Thursday, June 9th. The mail arrived, but with no late Northern dates. I am minus mail matter this time. Jim is on picket. Every soldier has turned sutler or huxter, and the cry is: "Here's your ice-cold lemonade!" "Here's your Good cigars!" (tobacco, candy, etc.) This is an evil which should be looked to by the commanding officer of the regiment.

Friday, June 10th. This afternoon, the Major commanding issued an order forbidding any soldier selling articles in camp, such as lemonade, candy, tobacco, and cheese, and all other produce of this nature. The order is a good one, as we cannot practice too strictly the Sanitary rules laid down in this unhealthy camp.

Saturday, June 11th. The 13th. and 19th. Army Corps were reviewed by General Emery this afternoon in a heavy storm of rain. So far, it has rained every day this month. The health of the troops at Morganza is good, as a general thing, taking into consideration the low nature of the land and the mass of filth scattered here and there by the butchering of beef for both Corps.

Sunday, June 12th. One of the heaviest rains of the Season fell this afternoon, covering the ground with one vast sheet of water, which, owing to the level condition of the land, could not be drained but [must be] left to evaporate in the heat of the sun, or sink into the ground.

Monday, June 13th. The orderly Sergeant left yesterday morning for the North on a 60-day furlough. His father is reported as being quite sick. I rec'd two letters this morning: one from ["Lide" Wilcox], and one from [Mother]. The former, a very interesting and encouraging one, altho the latter contained much news. I answered and mailed the former tonight.

Tuesday, June 14th. I am 20 years old today. Celebrated it by marching with the Regiment about 8 miles into the interior after cotton, and returning this P.M. with 60 bales of the staple article. For once, it did not rain, though threatening clouds overcast the sky. The author was shelling Vicksburg one year ago today.

Wednesday, June 15th. Early this morning, the order came to pack up and be ready to move immediately, and in an hour we were marching up the river. Only went about one and one-half miles, when we halted and pitched our tents in a very pleasant spot of earth, where grass grows green, and all promises a fine camp. Wrote to [Mother].

The following entries were made at Camp No. 3, Morganza, Louisiana.

Thursday, June 16th. The regiments of the First Brigade were mustered for inspection at 3 P.M. The greater portion of the day was spent in improving camp and erecting shades in front of tents. Weather calm and pleasant until this evening, when dark clouds appeared in the west, and ere dark a fierce gale blew from that direction, and now the flapping of tents is mingled with the low growling thunder, and ever and anon sharp jagged lightning flashes athwart the horizon.

Friday, June 17th. Was in the woods all day with a detail of 100 men, under charge of Capt. Starr, to cut brush for the purpose of making bowers in front of the tents; sent about 40 wagon loads to camp, and then returned ourselves. The weather is extremely hot, and the direct rays of the sun cannot be endured for any length of time. Tom Armstrong returned to duty from Baton Rouge.

Saturday, June 18th. The mail arrived, and I am one of the fortunate. Have a letter from ["Lide" Wilcox], dated as far back as April 24th, having by some chance been miscarried off its proper route. Captain Potter commands the regiment, Major having gone to Baton Rouge. Murcury high.

Sunday, June 19th. This forenoon I improved in answering the last letter from ["Lide" Wilcox] : the answer was a long one, as I was in a writing humor. We have had no late papers, Northern or Southern, since Friday. *Then,* the news from Grant was cheering. A boat has arrived from below, and perhaps we will have later dates. (Je finirai.)

Monday, June 20. Private Daniel Sickman reported for duty from Parole Camp, New Orleans. Was taken prisoner last fall on the Teche by Rebels under Gen. Green, and paroled shortly after and sent to New Orleans with E. A. Kreider of Company K and several others of the 42nd. They are now exchanged, and reported for duty.

Tuesday, June 21st. Wrote and mailed a letter to [Elizabeth Swiggart], Attica, Indiana. Have been busy writing all day today. The weather dry and warm until tonight. Rain is slowly falling. We have no news of Grant; last reports have him on the north bank of the Chickahominy, while Lee was on the south side.

Wednesday, June 22nd. Foster's Fourth Wisconsin Battery left for New Orleans today. Have N.O. papers of the 21st. A portion of Grant's army is south of the Chickahominy and marching toward the James River. Fort Darling is reported captured. Orders came for a grand Review tomorrow at one o'clock.

Thursday, June 23rd. A small mail arrived in the forenoon, but, as fortune would have it, I am without letters of any kind. The weather is exceedingly pleasant. The Review which we expected today, did not come off. Very few boats have passed since yesterday evening. River quite low, but on the rise. No late news.

Friday, June 24th. On Picket reserve with 18 men. Lieut. Cole of the Seventh Infantry Volunteers is with us, and commands this section of the line. He is a "gay and festive cuss," and we are having lots of fun. From our post we saw the Forty-second go out on dress parade tonight. Oh, the mosquitoes, how they bite!

Saturday, June 25th. At 4 o'clock this morning, we were surprised to hear the beating of the Reveille, and knew at once that something was up. We smelt a review, and sure enough! the whole army marched in Grand review before noon. We were glad we were not in camp. Was not relieved until 2 P.M., when we returned to camp with our mosquito pierced hides.

Sunday, June 26th. Inspection of arms and accoutrements of company at 9 A.M., and dress parade at 6:30 P.M. The weather very sultry. Adjutant George C. Pardee, having been commissioned as Captain, will report to Company D to take command of that company by order of Major Williams, Commanding Regiment.

Monday, June 27th. The Thirty-fifth Wisconsin arrived here from Port Hudson, and was assigned to our Brigade. The Thirteenth Corps having been discontinued by orders from the War Department, we are assigned to the Nineteenth Army Corps, the organization of the brigade to be the same, except it will be commanded by Brig. Gen. A. L. Lee. Have been at work on muster rolls in A.M.

Tuesday, June 28th. We expected to get some news from the north, but were disappointed. If any boats arrived, we did not see them. Will probably have mail tomorrow. The atmosphere was suffocating. I noticed in the *Chicago Times* an article stating that the 130th Ohio National Guard have gone to the front, and are *now* at White House, Virginia. I've a brother in that Regiment.[41]

Wednesday, June 29th. Orders were read at dress parade tonight for all the Overcoats and dress coats of the brigade to be turned over to Quartermaster to be stored at some point until needed; also, requisitions to be made out for shelter tents for all of this command who have not already got them. By command of A. L. Lee, Brig. Gen. Commanding First Brigade.

Thursday, June 30th. Have been busy all day making out muster rolls. We will be paid soon. The mail arrived, but I did not hear from home as I expected. I rec'd a Cincinnati paper from some unknown friend. The weather warm and promising rain. We have most western dates to the 28th, and southern dates to the 29th. Mustered today.

Friday, July 1st. The day is calm and beautiful, but very warm. Troops are leaving constantly; we expect to go soon. No later news from the north. All quiet at Morganza, except an occasional fierce Battle with Mosquitoes, generally ending in the enemies favor and our defeat. Popular sentiment: "Old Abe" for our next President.

Saturday, July 2nd. The mail brought me a letter from [Mother], dated the 19th of June, stating that Yourt was with Butler at Bermuda Hundred. Orderly Douglas arrived

[41] Livingston Yourtee Hopkins.

in Bellefontaine on the 19th ultimo: a safe and quick trip. The troops have left Morganza, all except the Third Division (ours); they are going to Brashear City. We will move our camp soon.

The following entries were made at Camp No. 4, Morganza, Louisiana.

Sunday, July 3rd. Mailed a letter to [Mother] in the A.M., and about 10 o'clock moved from our pleasant camp nearly two miles further down the river, and near the boat landing. We did not finish our "fixing up" on account of the frequent showers of rain that fell in the afternoon.

Monday, July 4th. Except a slight indulge on the part of the *Officers* in "the flowing bowl," the day has not been different from the 365 others of the year. I was on duty at Gen. Lawler's Headquarters with 20 men in the P.M. The *John J. Roe* passed down, loaded with Government supplies. The *Pearce* passed up. Memphis papers of the 29th of June.

Tuesday, July 5th. The noise of stake-driving and pitching of tents has ceased, and things in camp begin to assume a quiet feature. This evening, we had a very pleasant battalion drill. Tonight, a pleasant breeze is stirring, and mosquitoes are scarce, thank goodness! This is a miserable pen.

Wednesday, July 6th. A grand prize drill was held this morning by the champion companies of each regiment in the Brigade, the judges being the Colonels of the Twenty-third Iowa, Seventh Kentucky, and Thirty-seventh Illinois Volunteers. The premium was awarded to the Forty-second Ohio, and tomorrow will drill against the best in the Division. Col. Sheldon takes command of the Regiment.

Thursday, July 7th. A small mail arrived, and I have a letter from [Mary Knapp], which I answered this morning; also wrote to [Julia Allison]. A very fine rain fell about 6 P.M.

and lasted several hours, the ground drinking up the water as fast as it fell. Several boats have passed since morning, both up and down. No late news from the front.

The following is the letter to Julia Allison:

CAMP OF THE 42ND. O.V.I., MORGANZA, LA.
[Postmarked July 10, 1864]

FRIEND JULIA,

I have long been in doubt as to the true cause of your protracted silence, and at last have concluded to ask the reason. I answered your last letter promptly, and have waited in vain for a reply.[42] At last a letter came from Mary; said you had been looking for a letter from me. This seemed strange, and thinking my letter would certainly reach its destination in time, I did not write again. A recent letter from Mary says you are very angry because I do not write. This frightened me, and I commence *tout de suite.*

I, who have faced Vicksburg's frowning batteries, would gladly face them *again* rather than meet the storm of a woman's anger. Grape and canister, shrapnel, Hotchkiss and Case shot, minnie balls, swords and bayonets,—all are nowhere in comparison! Remember, there is a certain class of individuals who congregate on the Mississippi and make it their business of breaking open the U.S. mail and reading the letters of gents and Ladies,—withal, a very *mean* habit!

I have a letter from Yourtee.[43] He is at Bermuda Hundred with General Butler; his regiment (the 130th. O.N.G.) are principally all doctors and lawyers, commanded by Charles W. Hill, ex-A.G.O. Bro wants to know whether I corresponded with Miss [Allison] yet; told him . . . none of his business!

Weather here is not quite as cold as Greenland, But We, Us & Co. manage to live, assisted by the thought that our term of service will soon expire, and we can rest for a while in some cool, shady spot in our old Buckeye State. The Fourth, which we celebrated so extensively last year, was unmarked by anything of interest. A few Shoulder-straps made merry

[42] See the entry for Saturday, April 16.
[43] Yourtee enlisted when he was seventeen, as his brother had done.

over a few bottles of Catawba,[44] but raised no excitement in camp, and the sun shone down as hot as on the other days of the month. A portion of our Corps embarked on Gulf steamers a few days ago for ———, and we are waiting for orders to follow.

A grand prize drill was held on the 6th, and the 42nd. Ohio took the prize from every regiment in the First Brigade. Our regiment will drill tonight before General Lawler against the champion regiment of the Third Division. Think we can beat them. Every item of news is interesting from Grant and Sherman, and we feel confident in the two commanders' ultimate success.

The term of service of the Forty-second expires in September; want plenty of refreshments at the depot when we land in Bellefontaine. Don't think I will remain a citizen long, if the war lasts; like General Grant, I propose to fight it out on this line. When you write, tell me the date of your last letter. Give my love to Mary, and keep what share you please—all, if you want it. I have left a kiss of reconciliation on the first page; if you find it, it is for you and no other. Perhaps 'tis near the flag.[45] Write soon; send your letters on the fastest train and Steamboat. My pen acts like it had been out on a long campaign and wants to rest; guess I will dismiss it from the service. Excuse brevity, for "'tis the soul of wit," and again: answer without delay.

Yours again, as ever,
JOHNS.

Friday, July 8th. Tonight, another prize drill was held to decide who was best in the Division. Night put a stop to the proceedings before we were half through, and the assembly adjourned until 7 A.M. tomorrow. Am pretty confident that the 42nd. will be the champion regiment.

Saturday, July 9th. The drill was continued this morning at 7 o'clock, the 42nd. taking the lead. Great enthusiasm was

[44] A light-colored wine made from the Catawba grape.
[45] There is a drawing of the American flag in the upper left corner of the first page of the letter.

displayed by spectators, and popular opinion is in our favor, though the decision of the Judges is (up to 1 o'clock) unknown. (*Later*) : The 42nd. is the champion of the Third Division.

Sunday, July 10th. Wrote a letter to Brother at Bermuda Hundred. Also rec'd a Cincinnati paper of the 29th. June, per mail. Jim is on picket, and I will be on tomorrow. Received orders to be ready to move at a moment's notice, but the tattoo has beat, and still we are in camp. Think we will join our Corps at New Orleans.

Monday, July 11th. Dawns bright and clear, but we are still at Morganza. I was roused out of bed before daylight, and detailed to take charge of 45 men to unload siege guns off the Steamer *Universe.* I took off five heavy 42-pounders and three mortars; the job was a heavy one.

Tuesday, July 12th. Nine o'clock P.M., the order came to be ready to embark at daylight tomorrow morning. The boats are here ready for us. Our destination is supposed to be some point on the White River, Arkansas. It seems the entire Brigade is going, with Camp and Garrison Equipage.

Wednesday, July 13th. The Regiment embarked early this morning on the Steamer *Polar Star,* and at one o'clock proceeded up the river. The Seventh Kentucky Volunteers are also with the expedition, on the *Col. Colburn.* The Twenty-third Iowa Volunteers are on the Gulf boat *Kate Dale,* and the Thirty-fifth Wisconsin on the *Universe.* Our boat carries the Head Quarters flag, with Gen. Lee on board. Reached Natchez about 12 o'clock night.

Thursday, July 14th. En route on board the *Polar Star.* When we woke from our beds on the Hurricane deck this morning, we found our boat tied up at Natchez, Miss., having reached that place about 2 o'clock last night. We disembarked for the purpose of cooking, and cleaning up the boat. At 11 A.M., we proceeded again up the river. The heat of the sun on the Hurricane deck is intense.

Friday, July 15th. Arrived at Vicksburg about 9 A.M., having passed Grand Gulf last night and Warrenton this morning, at daylight. Disembarked at Vicksburg, while the boats loaded with provisions and coal. This has been the warmest day of the year. Nine P.M., again proceeded up the river after a hot day on shore.

Saturday, July 16th. The fleet ran all last night, and this morning, at 9 o'clock, passed Millikens Bend, but did not touch at that point. Also passed Goodrich's Landing, half-past 2 P.M. Twilight still finds us on the route toward White River,—our supposed destination. Today, passed one Northern packet, but did not speak her or enquire for news, as usual.

Sunday, July 17th. The fleet steamed toward the North Pole all night and under a full head of steam. We are still going this morning. Met and passed the Northern packet *Leviathan* on her way to N.O. Very few boats are on the river at the present time. Oh! the heat of the sun is suffocating, and rations scarce.

The following entries were made at the mouth of the White River in Arkansas.

Monday, July 18th. We passed Napoleon, Ark. at daylight and reached the mouth of the White River about 8 A.M. We have disembarked, and up to this time are laying in the woods on the right bank of the Mississippi, waiting further orders. In the evening, we unloaded our tents and pitched them on the river bank, and tonight we can sleep free from the evils of a Hurricane Deck and its flying cinders.

Tuesday, July 19th. Our camp is just at the mouth of the White River, on the right bank of that stream. Head-Quarters has not yet disembarked; this looks like another move, perhaps toward Little Rock, Ark. The St. Louis and White River packet *M.S. Mepham* is now lying at the landing, just from St. Louis. She has Western dates to the 15th and 16th, But no interesting news.

Wednesday, July 20th. The expedition which left here last night returned, having secured a number of prisoners and a good stock of forage. Tonight, we have orders to pack up and carry our Knapsacks on board the Steamer *Venus,* and be ready to embark early in the morning.

In C(MS), Hopkins describes an amusing episode that took place during this foray.

Late in the evening, the Forty-second crossed the Mississippi, and proceeded in an easterly direction on a scout. When some miles back in the country, we surprised a small detachment of McGruder's Cavalry at a plantation house, and captured six of them, including a commanding officer,—a Rebel Major. The latter was placed under the charge of a private soldier in Company K, and in the darkness of the night effected his escape in a somewhat novel manner.

The Major, becoming very loquacious, began telling ghost stories, finally relating his own experiences as a "see-er" of ghosts, and after a while relating anecdotes of his bear hunts on the "Arkansaw"; by degrees working his attentive auditor up to a pitch of excitement, and watching his opportunity, he suddenly startled the guard by the exclamation: "My God! There is one now!" This had the effect to frighten the poor fellow completely, who on the instant glanced behind him, only to find a clump of bushes. The wily Major was sharp, and had darted away before the guard could recover presence of mind enough to cry "Halt!", or fire at the receding form in the pitchy darkness.

That soldier should receive a promotion without an hour's delay.

Thursday, July 21st. In accordance with last night's order, we embark on the Steamer *Venus* at early dawn, and about 11 A.M., left for St. Charles, Ark. in company with a fleet of 8 transports, five of which were loaded with troops, and convoyed by two Gun boats of the tin clad squadron. Tied up for the night 40 miles from the mouth of White River.

Friday, July 22nd. Did not leave our landing until 11 A.M., when the fleet steamed up the river towards St. Charles.

The river is very narrow, and often our boat rubs the banks, while the boys jump ashore and run along the bank. The channel is only 5 feet deep; often only 4 feet. At night, the *Venus* shipped her helm and had to tie up, after blowing a signal of distress.

Saturday, July 23rd. We were on the route again by 3 A.M., and without any accident arrived at St. Charles and disembarked about 9 A.M. and proceeded to arrange camp. I was detailed by General Orders to report to Captain Hutchins for special duty as assistant on fortifications.[46] We laid out the groundwork of three forts, and a heavy detachment of men were put to work immediately.

The following entries were made in St. Charles, Arkansas.

Sunday, July 24th. Before daylight this morning, I was out on the line laying out the ground for another heavy "work." In the afternoon, was busy drafting the position of the picket lines and ascertaining position of ground, etc., etc., with Major Williams, Officer of the Day. I was on horse back.

Monday, July 25th. Was engaged all day in the work of construction of breastworks, or rather staking off the ground work of fortifications. Rations are growing scarce, the bill of fare reduced to "coffee and hardtack," with a variation at intervals of a meagre allowance of fresh beef (boned). But we are expecting the arrival of more supplies tonight or in the morning.

Tuesday, July 26th. The greater portion of the day was spent in superintending the construction of an *abbatis* in front of the line of defense. A detail from the 23rd. Iowa were engaged on this duty. Four hundred of the Ninth Iowa Cav-

---

[46] "Soon after landing, the writer was, by general orders from Gen. Lee's Headquarters, detailed as Assistant Engineer on fortifications, and furnished with a horse to ride, which, in comparison with the writer's usual mode of locomotion, was quite an advantage and one highly appreciated. Furnished with a 'pass' through the picket guards, I made frequent explorations into the country after 'Geographical knowledge,' and generally returned with several baskets full, and often three or four squalling 'knowledges' on either side of the saddle." —C(MS).

alry arrived from Duval's Bluff, and will be assigned to duty at this Post. Days pleasant, but nights very cold.

Wednesday, July 27th. The day has been waning slowly. Not a breath of air is stirring, and the river which flows past our camp looks like a sea of glass. The sun has at length suddenly disappeared behind a black cloud which lays extended the whole length of the horizon—a token of rain.

Thursday, July 28th. This morning, a few large drops of rain fell, but not in sufficient quantities to lay the dust. This P.M. was busy in making profiles for dressing and giving proper shape and faces to the parapets now in course of construction. A scouting party left camp at about 4 P.M. toward Arkansas Post.

Friday, July 29th. This has been a busy day on the works. Large details are engaged. A cavalry courier came into camp and reported the force that left here yesterday about 15 miles out, and will not return until tomorrow. Two boats arrived tonight.

Saturday, July 30th. Early this morning, I was up and mounted, and sent out into the country after lumber with 3 teams and a guard of 25 men. When I returned to camp, found four letters for me: one from [Elizabeth Swiggart] and another from [Mother]; the other from "Columbus, Ohio"; also one from [Jemima Wilcox]; dated respectively July 11th., 19th., 1st., and 14th.

Sunday, July 31st. Wrote two letters: one to [Jemima Wilcox] and the other to [Elizabeth Swiggart] in answer to those which I received yesterday. The weather quite warm, with a slight rain in the afternoon. Night has at last spread her sable mantle over the last day of July, and I retire to my downy couch to wake with the first of August.

Monday, August 1st. I was outside of the Pickets all day with a detail of men after Gabions and Fascines for the works.

It rained (to use the language of the natives) "a right smart shower." The Sixth Michigan Regiment of heavy artillery left this morning for down the river.

Tuesday, August 2nd. It is reported pretty currently that we will soon leave here to return to Morganza, a report which I sincerely hope has no foundation whatever, yet I fear it is so. I was out in the country in the forenoon with a detachment after Fascines for Sally-porte of Fort. Our regiment goes on the works tomorrow.

Wednesday, August 3rd. I gave some instructions to a few men on the works in regard to reveting interior of Sally-porte of fort No. 6, and they accordingly went to work and finished one side. We have plenty of green corn and some vegetables from the country, and a bakery is in process of construction, and as soon as finished, we will have plenty of soft bread.

Thursday, August 4th. I wrote a long letter to ["Lyde" Thompson], Toledo, O., but as the mail is very irregular here, there is no telling when I can send it. The climate here is almost as warm as Louisiana, for all the apparent difference. We have despaired of ever hearing from the north again.

Friday, August 5th. Nothing new has disturbed the usual quiet of the camp. At noon, I issued whiskey to men on the works. Over one-third of the Seventh Kentucky detail refused to drink, as they stated for a reason that the regiment were nearly one half of them Sons of Temperance, having taken the pledge at Baton Rouge.

Saturday, August 6th. The mail arrived from the north and I have a letter from [Jemima Wilcox], dated April 29th.; also one from [Yourtee], dated July 9th. At night, we rec'd orders to be ready to embark at a moment's notice. That notice came at dark, and by ten o'clock at night we were all on board the *Venus*. The troops that relieved us are one brigade of A. J. Smith's Division of the Seventeenth Army Corps from Memphis, Tenn.

The following entries were made on board the steamer "Venus."

Sunday, August 7th. After taking on some ordnance stores at the lower landing, we found ourselves steaming rapidly down the White River, our regiment leading the advance. Brigade Headquarters are on the *White Cloud.* The *Venus* left the fleet far astern, and landed at the mouth of White River about dark, where she coaled up.

Monday, August 8th. The regiment moved off the boat and bivouacked on shore. Companies E and K were ordered on again to guard the steamer up White River, to lighten the *White Cloud,* which had run aground. Found her about 50 miles above, but she had crossed the bar, and we returned again to the mouth.

Tuesday, August 9th. We left the mouth of White River about 3 P.M., and the fleet which but a month before cruised in these very waters, upward bound, was now gliding rapidly through the muddy tide of the Mississippi, with nothing of interest to break the monotony of the voyage. At dark, as we make our downy beds for the night, we are still running.

Wednesday, August 10th. Without delay during the night, we find the distance between us and our destination rapidly diminishing. We reached Vicksburg at 5 o'clock in the evening, but guards were stationed and no one were allowed to land. We only stopped a few minutes. I was Sergeant of the Guard today.

Thursday, August 11th. On . . . On . . . the fleet Steams past transport and coal barge, deserted plantations and forests of magnolias, only hailed occasionally by the enquiry for news from some grim old iron-clad or monitor as it lays at anchor in the channel. Passed Natchez, and arrived at Morganza half-past three in the afternoon.

The following entries were made at Camp No. 5, Morganza, Louisiana:

Friday, August 12th. At Tattoo, we are still at Morganza. And hardly think we will proceed farther down until morning. Rain has been falling since one P.M. at short intervals. The *Starlight* passed us en route for New Orleans. In all probability, we will go from here to Herron's command, now operating at Mobile, Alabama. Farragut has captured Fort Gaines and 800 prisoners; also four other Forts in the harbor.

Saturday, August 13th. About noon, we disembarked at the southern extremity of the Bend, and on the right of the Brigade. Part of Company K is quartered in a house. We do not expect to stay here but a few days at least, until we receive further orders from N.O. and a fresh supply of coal for boats.

Sunday, August 14th. The mail brought me a letter from ["Lide" Wilcox], dated 4th., and one from Cousin Mag H——,[47] dated 1st. I answered former this P.M.; also answered [Mother's] of 19th July. I also have a Cincinnati paper of late date. The weather is pleasant, with an occasional shower of rain. Col. Sheldon commands the brigade.

Monday, August 15th. The news reached us last night of the fall of Atlanta, but the report is not confirmed by the dispatches of New Orleans papers. Our loss is said to be heavy, and the enemy is represented as losing 27,000 prisoners, besides a heavy loss in killed and wounded. We are anxious to hear the correct report, which we expect tonight.

Tuesday, August 16th. This is the most lonesome place[48] that it has ever been my bad fortune to be stationed. Endless cotton fields extend around us, and the prospect is void of interest to the eye of a soldier. So far, it has rained every day since we landed on the 13th., and the ground is soft.

[47] Margaret Hopkins, daughter of his uncle, Harris Hopkins.
[48] "In the rear of our camp stretches almost boundless fields, where once King Cotton reared his luxuriant head. A deserted plantation with the old mansion and slave quarters, the former deserted and the latter still occupied by a dirty vagabond crew of negroes.
"Far in the distance is seen a boundary line of cypress trees growing in a black swampy loam, at night made hideous by the millions of frogs and other reptiles that infest a Louisiana swamp. To add to the cheerful aspect, a continual drizzling rain. . . ."—C(MS).

Wednesday, August 17th. General Douglas returned from home today, and brings lots of Bellefontaine news. The mail arrived and I have a letter from [Mary Knapp], dated August 8th, which I answered tonight, but dated ahead to the 20th. A tremendous shower of rain fell in the fore part of the day, but tonight it has cleared up beautifully.

Thursday, August 18th. Today, I received a letter from my Brother at Bermuda Hundred, Va., dated 31st of July, and also have a very "sound, sensible" one from [Julia Allison], Bellefontaine, dated August 1st., which I will answer soon, and which will be my last letter to that individual for some time. I mailed one to [Mary Knapp] this morning. Rec'd a very gay present in [Julia's] letter: a flag (the old stars and stripes).

In connection with Yourtee's letter, see Owen Johnston's to Julia Allison, page 110. Obviously, the brothers had a sense of humor in common; it was to make Yourtee one of the foremost caricaturists of his time.

BERMUDA HUNDRED,
July 25, 1864.

DEAR BRO,

Your letter of June 26th came to hand while I was out on picket day before yesterday. I was highly elevated in spirits after its perusal, and felt just as though I could raise a muss by firing on the enemy pickets. The *Chicago Times* was in error, if it stated that Gen. Hill was our colonel. That gentleman is not, nor has not been, our Colonel, thank fortune! He is now on Johnson's Island,—colonel of the 128th O.V.I. I know something of his "style," however, and whatever you think of him, I as well as the majority have a rather poor opinion of him; that we requested to go to the front, is also a mistake. We all wanted to leave the Island, as it was a perfect prison, but when we were ordered to the front, shoulder-straps began to talk of "resignation," "physical disability," etc. I, for myself, didn't care a "tinker's cuss" where they sent us, only on mother's account, who I knew would be on nettles all the time.

I have just been on three days of picket duty. I was on a Vidette post and was stationed behind a big tree.[49] It was rather uncomfortable, however, as the tree was on a side hill, which made standing behind it very tiresome. I could not go to sleep on account of musquitos, which I think go far ahead of Louisiana Musquitos still. Their bills were like bayonets, their eyes like a hundred pound shell and were frightful to behold. These make a frightful humming with their wings and their bite is "wuss nor orful." I had to draw a new suit of clothes—straps, cartridge-belt, and all—on my return to camp, as my old rig was so perforated as to be entirely useless. They didn't leave their bills in the wound . . . not they!

You wished to know if I ever wrote to Lide Wilcox. I do not, and don't think it would be proper, as I have not the pleasure of her acquaintance, and to open a correspondence with one whom I never had seen, I should call little better than Impertinence. Think she writes a very good letter indeed, to Judge by "sample sheet."

You would like to see how I look behind a hardtack, would you? Then turn over the leaf. Well, here is the hardtack [drawing of a hardtack with two feet protruding at bottom], but where am I? Oh, I am behind and you will have to go round on the other side to see me . . . . The recipe for preparing hardtack I will not take this time, as my time is so near out it will not be of much benefit to me, but if I reenlist, you may depend upon me as a customer. I think the price very reasonable. I suppose, of course, you pay the postage. This will probably be the last letter from this place that I shall write you, as I start home in two weeks.

I was not much surprised to hear that you had dropped Correspondence with Miss Julia, as you had hinted as much in a former letter.[50] Now, Johns, I must say I don't altogether approve of the course you have taken, as you allowed the correspondence to run on so long I may venture to say that you might have broken it too abruptly. If I had been you, I should

[49] He cartooned the incident in his *Comic History of the United States* (New York: American Book Exchange, 1880), p. 177.

[50] See the diary entry of Saturday, April 16. He wrote to her again, however, on July 7.

have made serious inquiries what were her motives in writing; at the same time I should have told her mine, how a correspondence between two parties may have either good results or bad results, depending upon the way in which it may be conducted. Perhaps yours was too ardent and not formal enough, and a female is apt to hang upon the least point in which she may imagine there is the least sign of love—but, of course, of that you are the better Judge. But if I were you, I would not break up the correspondence altogether; though only in the guise of a friend, tell her your circumstances. However, she must know them by this time. If I had to choose between Mary Knapp and her, I should certainly choose the latter, but every man to his choice. I believe with you that there are a great many good fish in the sea waiting for a worm, and will be for some time yet. I don't *begin* to think about marrying yet, and shall *never* until I can get good accomodations for a family and can afford the *wind* . . . .

Only about half of our company are fit (or said to be fit) for duty, which makes the duty of we well ones double. I was detailed for picket . . . out for three days and have just returned. I had a bully time. The Rebs and we are on good terms, and when there are no officers about, we send over good-humored remarks, and even trade papers with them. They seem, or pretend to be, very sick of fighting, and express a desire to desert; in fact, deserters are coming in almost every day. They give very melancholy accounts of the condition of their army; in a pecuniary point of view, those in this army are the hardest looking cusses I have ever seen since the days of Messrs. Isaiah Marriott, Alick Emberlain, etc. Their style of conversation is equally elegant; they use such expressions as "you-uns," "we-uns," etc., but you, no doubt, have seen Rebs as well as I have, if you are but a "three months man" . . . Pardon me, I was just giving illustrations of *our* Johnnies, but another night finds this letter unfinished, so Goodnight, I shall see you tomorrow . . . .

I am very glad you did not reenlist. You escaped it very narrowly. You have, I believe, about or nearly two months more. I start home in fifteen days. I wish you could be there. Don't send any more letters to this address . . . .

I got a letter from Jemima [51] a day or two ago. She had to do her own harvesting, as "hands" were scarce. Received a letter from home a short time ago: Almon was making money faster than ever. I wonder if we will ever be so fortunate as he has been.

We are daily looking for an attack. Every night or two, we are called up behind the breastworks, but nothing has transpired so far. Lee still holds Petersburg. All quiet today; no fighting . . . .

I see Doc Thompson and John Hopkins about every day. Take good care of yourself, and Believe me

Your Affectionate Bro,
—L. Y. HOPKINS

Friday, August 19th. The mail left for up the river with my letter to [Mary Knapp]. I wrote one to [Julia Allison], dated it the 20th., and commenced one to Bro, which I shall send to Toledo, as his term of service will have expired by the time it can reach him. I was on my way home one year ago today!

The letter to Julia Allison:

CAMP OF FORTY-SECOND OHIO
VOLUNTEER INFANTRY, U.S.A. MORGANZA, LA.
August 21, 1864.

FRIEND JULIA,

I received yours of the 1st. this forenoon, and as I feel in the mood for writing—which is seldom the case—I will proceed to reply, "briefly," of course. You know all my letters are brief. The fact is, a soldier never has much to say, on paper or in conversation, and you must not blame me if my letters are "short."

First, I will acknowledge the receipt of the little bit of *bunting* you were so kind to send me. I shall indeed guard it with my life, if only for the sake of the *giver.*

Now, a question: are those beautiful scarlet envelopes all the go, or was it a whim of your own that you sent it? It was the second one I received, and the other was from a country

---

[51] Their sister Jemima was the wife of Major Wilcox of the Seventh Iowa Cavalry. She lived on a farm at Eddyville, Iowa.

girl who, I suppose, thinks them *beautiful*. Why! the boys are beginning to mistrust me and accuse me of being in league with some *Banditti*, or holding a correspondence with some lodge of the K. G. C.'s.[52]

Yes, I am glad our time is out in September; want to go home so bad to see Ma and them, and especially to see my friends in Bellefontaine,—if I have any, which is doubtful. I'll bet you my cap against your right-hand glove that I am not glad to go home. Mary will hold the *stakes*. Your cousins must be real Heroes. One cannot be a real Hero unless he is taken prisoner once or twice. I never was so fortunate as to fall into the hands of the Johnnies, but perhaps you know the reason. I was always remarkably active on foot.

So you wish me always to tell you where to direct your letters? As I have so long to stay in the service, I will just say that it only requires the name, company, and regiment, *via Cairo*. This is all that is required. Some of my letters have more on the envelope than the letter itself contains.

The Forty-second took the prize at the drill, and now has the honor of the *Belt*. No, I don't correspond with Miss J—— [M—— J——]; she did not answer my last letter for some reason. Yes, she wrote very interesting letters. Why do you ask? Of course, I always thought her a very good girl, and do yet.

There is but very little news to write, as everything is so quiet at this camp of ours, which, to say the least of it, is the most lonesome place that we were ever at. The following language of a certain traveler is applicable to us:

"He could not deny that, looking round upon the dreary region and seeing nothing but bleak fields and naked trees, hills obscured by fogs, and flats covered with inundations, he did for some time suffer melancholy to prevail upon him, and wished himself again safe at home."

I got Mary's letter yesterday and answered it last night after midnight, as I was on duty and had to be up half the night, and my "pard" was writing to . . . Sallie.[53] I shall

[52] The Knights of the Golden Circle, a secret society in the North that espoused the cause of the South and slavery.

[53] Sally Lawrence, daughter of Judge Lawrence of Bellefontaine, a close girlhood friend of Julia Allison, and her schoolmate at College Hill.

not send a kiss this time, as you take so little trouble to find them, nor will I send love, only to Mary, since you care nothing for my regards. You naughty girl, I shall have my revenge when I get to Bellefontaine. No, I forget—I will not halt at your old town, but continue on the march until the tall spires of my beautiful city—Toledo—are in sight. Then, for Iowa! Suppose you have not forgotten that, have you? What if I remind you of that plan of ours?[54] I believe Mary would back out. But I must close for tonight, though it is yet early, and I'll wager a bunch of cartridges or a hardtack that you are looking at the bright moon at this minute, for who could help it, if they are not afraid of the night air. Its face is so very bright tonight. I *may* write more tomorrow.

Good night, Julia.

(One day later)—All quiet along the lines; no fighting up to 10 o'clock A.M. The enemy attacked on our right late last night, but were repulsed; with what loss, is unknown. (Mosquitoes). You need not turn Copperhead just because I have. I never *was* in favor of the war; hate Abolitionists! I will refer to my Diary and see what I was doing the day you mailed your letter; here it is: "St. Charles, Ark., Aug. 1, 1864. Was out in the country seven or eight miles today with a detachment of men as a guard for 5 wagons; sent out by Gen. Lee to procure lumber for the fortifications (platforms for guns). After loading the train with lumber, the boys went for the poultry and other luxuries of the country, and at night reached camp well loaded with apples, peaches, chickens, and pigs,—enough to last a week. Turned them over to the cooks for a famous dinner tomorrow. Issued a ration of whiskey to the men on the works at dark, and dismissed them until 12 o'clock tonight, when our entire regiment will go on duty and work until daylight, etc."

To explain the above, I would just tell you that I have been studying for an engineer the past two years, and as there was no regular engineer with us at the time of landing at St. Charles, Capt. Hutchins and myself were detailed by Special Order to act in that capacity, and as the Captain and myself

---

[54] A plan to emigrate to Iowa.

had had considerable experience at Plaquemine under instructions from Capt. J. T. Baker of U.S.A., then and there in charge of work, we managed to lay out the ground work of six separate Fortifications, "so near military" that Gen. Bailey afterward pronounced them "very effective; very good, indeed." Don't you think we ought to be made Brigadier Generals at once?

Guess I won't vote for Fremont, or old Abe, either, for about ten months. If I *had* a vote, it should be for Pierce; hope they will nominate him.[55]

Oh, yes! the Photos: where would I get them taken? There are so many places here! I did not lose yours through neglect. I would rather have lost my musket. Have grieved more than a little over the accident. I have forgotten now how you look; can't you send me a copy of your personal appearance, and trust me 'till we get to America, where Photographs can be procured? I shall take as good care of it as of my Mother's picture. Your little Flag shall accompany me everywhere,—through the camp, the march, and "in the deadly strife." But here is the end of the last chapter, and I must close. Excuse careless writing and bad spelling and all the other mistakes, and in soldier's uniform or Citizen's garb, Believe me,

Yours Truly,

O. J. H.

About a week after writing the letter to Sergeant Hopkins that elicited the above reply, Julia Allison received a note from another admirer, William Kernan, who enclosed a wilted flower. The flag had evidently triumphed over the rose.

BELLEFONTAINE, OHIO
August 9, 1864.

MISS AILUJ,[56]

'Twill be just one month ago tonight; and, as you perceive by the enclosed, I have fulfilled my promise then made—a

[55] In his address at Concord, New Hampshire, in 1863, former President Pierce had sponsored the Peace Party (the Copperheads). General Fremont was the presidential nominee of a "Radical" convention held in Cleveland in May, 1864. In June, the Republican convention in Baltimore chose Lincoln.
[56] "Ailuj" is "Julia" spelled backward.

habit I have accustomed myself to—not, however, in person, as I had *hoped* to do and as I still *would* do, did not urgent business require my presence in Urbana for a day or two, on the way to which I shall probably be e'er this reaches you.

It is unnecessary for me to comment on the enclosed, the occasion or cause which prompted it, or the subsequent events that have transpired and effected the great *misunderstanding* that has existed between us.

I do not, cannot, blame you, for what has occurred I anticipated as something that would inevitably take place. Let me assure you, also, that my original esteem for you has undergone no change. And, as we are not likely to be any *nearer in relationship,* let us, at least, remain friends.

With sincerest regards,
GULIELMUS.[57]

P.S.—The enclosed, wilted and dead as it is, is perhaps emblematic of your "phelinks"; but should it not be the case, and you should desire to, send me a fresh and living one to replace it. Nothing would be more acceptable. G——.

Saturday, August 20th. Coffee is a mocker, and Salt-junk is raging! Hardtack is trumps, and I hold a full hand! I mailed Brother's letter and one to [Julia Allison]. A heavy rain fell last night, and continued to pour down after daylight. I *recon* it's mighty dull times now. The Old Wheel moves slow.

Sunday, August 21st. Today, I received a letter from [Sarah Eliza Thompson], dated Aug. 10th. We had Company Inspection at 10 A.M. and Dress parade at 5 P.M. We have N.O. papers of yesterday, but no news. All quiet at Mobile. There was no rain fell since yesterday. Adjutant-General Thomas left here a few days ago for Washington with a detail from the 42nd. as bodyguard.

Monday, August 22nd. The Regiment was out on Brigade inspection at 3 P.M. and Dress parade at half-past six. We are drawing very poor rations now. The Salt-Junk is tainted and unfit for use. The Hardtack is inhabited by millions of bugs

[57] Latin for "William."

and worms, but thanks to Q. M. Lewis, we will have soft bread from this out. (Maybe!)

Tuesday, August 23rd. Lieut. Col. Pardee has returned to the Regiment and will take command. He has been relieved from duty as Provost Marshal of Baton Rouge, and returned to duty as commander of the 42nd. Ohio in the absence of Col. Sheldon, Commanding Brigade. The weather very pleasant, etc., etc.

Wednesday, August 24th. Again I open this book, but what to write? Am at a loss to decide, as times are so dull, and nothing transpires to change the dull routine of life in camp. Well, here's a subject: A detail has come for a certain number of men to go north on detached service as guard for something or somebody. They take Descriptive Lists and everything, and will not be back again.

Thursday, August 25th. This morning, went to work and wrote a letter in answer to [Sarah Thompson], which I rec'd on the 21st. Our five days' rations gave out last night and we had to *fast* today. Had nothing but bread and coffee for breakfast and dinner. I am detailed for duty tomorrow as guard for forage train.

Friday, August 26th. This evening, I am quite fatigued, having marched about 8 miles with a detail of men numbering 100 after wood for Hospital and Head-Quarters. Returned to Camp about 2 P.M. Another detail was made to clean up a new camp above here, near the fort, and we will probably move tomorrow.

The following entries were made at Camp No. 6, Morganza, Louisiana.

Saturday, August 27th. Sheldon's Brigade moved camp today about two and one-half miles up the river in order to shorten our lines, as one division of troops left for Baton Rouge. We had to carry our beds and baggage and everything except tents. This has been the warmest day of the season. Just one month from this date I am free; my time expires on the 27th of September, 1864. I have Bellefontaine *Republicans* of the 5th and 15th. [Julia Allison]

Sunday, August 28th. Our new camp promises to be a pleasant one; at least, I think we can stand it one month. Have reasons to believe it is the last time we will *drive stakes* in this Regiment. The general belief is that we will be mustered out here, giving twelve days to go home in from the tenth of next month. This will be satisfactory to us, of course.

Monday, August 29th. One of the heaviest rains that I have ever witnessed fell last night, delugeing the earth in floods. Our tents were but poor protection against the storm, and my blankets this morning were saturated with water. Tonight, however, the ground is almost as dry as ever; the air is cooler, and a pleasant breeze is stirring.

Tuesday, August 30th. The mail has been due for several days, but has not come yet. When it does come, I look for news from home. We have some exciting reports of the capture of Memphis by Forrest, but I guess he did not occupy the city long, nor carry it off with him when he left.[58] No boats have arrived from above for the last 3 or 4 days, inducing the belief that the river is blockaded at some point between here and Cairo.

Wednesday, August 31st. Orders came early this morning to be ready to march at a moment's notice. But whether it was to embark or march, is not yet ascertained by the "rank and file." At 5 P.M., the regiment was mustered in the rain by Col. Pardee, but we don't expect to be paid off until we are mustered out of the U.S. service. Adieu, August!

Thursday, September 1st. The atmosphere was pleasant, and probably made so by a refreshing breeze that was stirring

---

[58] While an expedition from Memphis, under General A. J. Smith, was out looking for the forces commanded by General Forrest, the latter made a sudden rush on the city, occupied it for a few hours, and then retreated into Mississippi.

from the N.W. Our minds, also, were invigorated by receiving a liberal mail from the north, which brought me a letter from *Home*. All were well and doing fine. Have Memphis papers giving details of Forrest's recent raid into that city. It seems that that "Gentleman" was the greatest loser.

Friday, September 2nd. Dark and sombre clouds, ever and anon illumining by vivid flashes of lightning, are approaching from the east, and if I am any prophet in such matters, we will catch it before morning. No papers have come during the day, and all is quiet. Every artifice is resorted to in order to kill time, which drags slowly. I improved one hour in writing to a Cousin, [Margaret Hopkins], residing in the old Buckeye State.

Saturday, September 3rd. Last night, an order came to be ready to embark at 6 o'clock this morning, and accordingly we struck tents at that time, and all was in readiness by 3 P.M., at which time we marched on board the Steamer *Ohio Belle*, a "side-wheeler" Government Transport. At dark, both Brigades were aboard and ready to start early in the morning.

The following entries were made while en route for White River, Arkansas.

Sunday, September 4th. The fleet left Morganza at 4 A.M. and passed Fort Adams in the forenoon, and arrived at Natchez at sun-down, where we again had a sight at the thousands of refugees congregated; the reflections they caused us were not of the most pleasant nature, but brought vividly to mind the evils of war. Left Natchez and proceeded on our route. 11 P.M.

Monday, September 5th. Our flotilla ran without stopping throughout the night and all day today, and arrived at the scene of former glory [Vicksburg] at 5 P.M. I was Sergeant of the Guard, which was composed of 20 men; orders were to allow *no* soldier to go up into the city. After cleaning off the boats, the regiment again marched on board, and up to Tattoo we are still tied up at the landing.

Tuesday, September 6th. Left Vicksburg early this morning after taking on Commissary stores, and proceeded at a good speed up the river; touched at several points in the afternoon, and waited for the Steamer *Kentucky* with the Seventh Kentucky Volunteers on board. General Daney commands the fleet; Col. Sheldon, the First Brigade. We are ordered to White River.

Wednesday, September 7th. Our Fleet ran all night and made pretty good time, though the night was dark. Was delayed several hours this P.M. by our convoy, *Gunboat No. 14*, breaking her wheel, which caused the boats to tie up and wait until it could be repaired. Again, in the evening, moored on passing Columbia, and while far below Napoleon, Ark. we are still running (8:45 P.M.).

Thursday, September 8th. Before daylight, we reached Mouth White River, where the troops disembarked and encamped on the bank of the river. The 42nd. occupied the same ground it did in July last. It is thought we will be ordered up the White River in a few days. The steamer *Julia* passed en route to N.O., after leaving a small mail with us. I have a Cincinnati paper of August 31st.

Friday, September 9th. The day was passed as usual by the 42nd. boys making themselves comfortable and taking things easy generally. The Steamboat *Kentucky* left for Memphis with the sick and afflicted of this Command. In the afternoon, I wrote a letter home and mailed it, and shortly after the *Dove* left for the north with the mail. The weather is very fine, and our present situation is quite agreeable.

Saturday, September 10th. Perfect quiet reigns in the camp of the 42nd. The others are tearing up again and leaving for Duval's Bluff to reenforce Gen. Steele. Two Regiments left this morning, and others are embarking as I write, and will leave in the morning. A small mail arrived from Morganza, but I did not hear from home as expected. I wrote a short letter to Niece in Iowa ["Lide" Wilcox]. The weather is extremely sultry and the season unhealthy.

The following entries were made at the mouth of the White River in Arkansas.

Sunday, September 11th. Arrivals and departures of boats are of very frequent occurrence, the majority of them out of White River, and continue on north, after taking on coal at this point. Troops are constantly going out of service from Steele's Department;[59] one regiment went home today, and several detachments yesterday left to be mustered out. I wrote a short business letter to [Julia Allison] this A.M., giving a brief summary of news from our part of Dixie and our move here.

The following is the "business letter" to Julia Allison.

HEAD-QUARTERS, 42ND. OHIO, CAMP
AT MOUTH OF WHITE RIVER, ARK.
September 11, 1864.

DEAR FRIEND,

You may be a little surprised to get this from me, as I wrote last, but I now intend to discard formalities and write whenever the notion strikes me, and if my friends are too busy to read my letters, or too *much* absorbed in the cares of life to pay attention to their contents, they have only to cast them aside. But placing full reliance on you as a soldier's friend, I can venture to scribble the following.

The First Brigade (Sheldon's) left Morganza on the 4th., in company with two others of the Second Division. Our fleet numbered nine transports under convoy of *Tin-clad No. 14,* and arrived at this point daylight of the 8th. and pitched our tents on the river bank to wait further orders and transportation to reenforce Steele at Little Rock. It is reported that Marmaduke has been playing smash with our communi-

[59] Department of the Missouri.

cations from Duval's Bluff to the above place, and destroyed
20 miles of R.R. Old Marmaduke is a mean old sneak and a
Gorrilla, and we are going up to "git him."

By our move to this Department, we find ourselves nearly
600 miles nearer America, and if nothing happens of more
importance than an earthquake, we hope to see that "land of
the free" before many days. Will probably start for home
about the 20th. I have just 16 days before my time is out. Only
13 men of Capt. Gardner's old company will go home at this
time. Another party goes out in October and November 26th.
Our brigade is composed of old regiments, whose term of
service will expire between this and November. The Forty-
second is the only Ohio regiment.

Have received Chicago Platform and particulars, proceedings, etc. of the Convention.[60] "Mac" will get a few votes in
the army, but Abraham is uppermost in the minds of the mass
of soldiers. Those who vote for the "Chickahominy racer"
are Hospital shirks, play-offs, men sick of the service, tired of
the arduous though honorable duties of Campaign. For my
part, I take things as they come, and laugh at the political
discussions of my comrades. You know it is best to think
much and say nothing. The Boys have been trying to ascertain
my views, but I flatter myself that they are as much in the
dark when they are done questioning me as they were in the
beginning. Either way, I am not a dangerous Copperhead,
or a radical Lincoln man, not being a voter by a few months.
I tell them that my politics are to crush rebellion and restore
the Union. In fact, politics are discussed but little in the army,
though we cannot but feel the importance of the coming Presidential Election, where the interests of our Government are at
stake and so much depends upon promptness of action and
unity of sentiment.

I received the *Republicans* you were so kind to send me,
and I thank you for the favor; we are always glad to get papers of any kind, and especially the Bellefontaine *Republican.*

[60] On August 29, at the Democratic convention in Chicago, General McClellan
received the presidential nomination. In the November election, he carried three
states—Delaware, New Jersey, and Kentucky. Lincoln carried the rest with a
plurality of nearly half a million votes.

On the opposite page are the names of our company whose time will be out on the 27th September. My compliments to Mary, and best wishes for Julia.

As ever,
JOHNS.

P.S.—It is uncertain whether we will take the boats for Little Rock, or embark for home. The other troops are all leaving. Our Brigade only is left.

Monday, September 12th. I mailed what I expect the last letter to ["Lide" Wilcox] while I am in service. The whole talk in camp is about being mustered out and the fine times we will have when we go home. We learned several days ago the proceeding of the Chicago Convention, and are not a little surprised at the nomination of Gen. McClellan by the Democracy.

Tuesday, September 13th. The departure of a foraging expedition from our camp was all that disturbed the quiet of the place. Some rumors are afloat that our Brigade will go back to Morganza before long, but I can't see it yet. Would sooner go up the river. Another Cincinnati paper came for me tonight. Who from?

Wednesday, September 14th. The Steamer *Paragon* touched here this morning on her way to Cairo. She had a good list of passengers, beside a number of soldiers "on the Homeward bound." We also hope to go north about the 21st., as our time will be out on the 27th. I wrote a business letter to [Mary Knapp] last night and sent it today by the *Paragon*. A slow rain is falling as I write.

Thursday, September 15th. This day has been a day of perplexity and disappointment, for we learn that four companies of the Forty-second are to be mustered out on the 27th., while the rest will have to stay until the 26th. November, whose time is out at the same time, only a difference in muster. This is all owing to the infernal *Red Tape* system in which army affairs are now conducted. Col. Sheldon left for

Ohio today, and the four companies will go on the first boat. Wrote to Almon.

Friday, September 16th. I was appointed Quarter Master Sergeant today by Col. Pardee, the appointment to date from the 14th. John C. Van Voorhis was promoted to Sergeant to fill vacancy so occasioned. I was Sergeant of the Guard when the order came, but was not long in turning over gun and accoutrements. The Regiment, or detachment, will leave for home on the first boat. They have turned over arms and rig complete.

Saturday, September 17th. Entered upon my official duties as Q.M. Serg't of 42nd. Ohio. Cyrus A Rickard, Co. K, 42nd., was appointed Commissary Sergeant at the same time as my advancement. I received two papers from [Julia Allison] last night, and wrote a letter to Brother Al[mon]. The mustered out men of the Regiment (four companies) left at 10 o'clock this morning on Steamer *Julia* for Cairo; thence, home.[61] The remaining six companies are good for two months longer, from all appearances.

Sunday, September 18th. Everything is extremely quiet since the departure of the first detachment. Perhaps a slight depression of spirit on account thereof causes it among the remaining few.[62] No mail has arrived since yesterday. The days are warm and sultry, and nights the very opposite—cold and chilling. Col. Pardee takes command of the First Brigade in absence of Sheldon.

Monday, September 19th. I have not heard from home since the 19th August, perhaps because they expect us home the

---

[61] "A safe passage to their happy firesides! It seems like parting with a portion of one's family to say farewell to our late comrades."—C(MS).

[62] "To be thus idle whilst others of our comrades were dealing blows at the hydra-headed monster Rebellion, was galling in the extreme, and many longed for an opportunity of reenlisting in some command that had work to do. I had made up my mind to remain in the army until the war was ended, or lay down my life in the cause, and much for this reason I longed for home, from whence I could start anew into some fresh regiment of Volunteers who were about to take the field."—D(MS).

last of this month. Everything at this point is extremely quiet, and very few boats going up or down. The mail for the 42nd. comes in small parcels of ten or fifteen letters, etc. Have not rec'd a full mail since leaving Morganza. Nights growing colder. Wrote Yourtee.

Tuesday, September 20th. This morning, wrote a short letter to [Mary Knapp] to inform that person of our detention for two months longer in the service. We have ten days provisions on hand, and will issue tomorrow or next day to the regiment. The *Olive Branch* arrived from the north en route to N.O. Capt. Pardee and Staff Lieutenants Wilson and Rodecker will leave on her for that place, having been ordered there for duty.

Wednesday, September 21st. There is some prospect of drawing clothing soon, and we are preparing requisitions for the amount wanted per Regiment. The Post Quarter-Master will go to Memphis for a supply. The weather is quite pleasant, and last night was warmer than usual. Very little is being done in the way of active business at this point, and no military operations whatever to stir up our minds.

Thursday, September 22nd. The *Venango* arrived from White River and reports all quiet at Little Rock. The day has been unusually pleasant, and a refreshing Autumn breeze has stirred since morning. I wrote to Sis in Iowa;[63] also made out requisitions for clothing and handed in to Lieut. Dyer, R.Q.M., 42nd. Ohio, who expects to go to Memphis soon for clothing. Adieu.

Friday, September 23rd. Several boats have arrived from up river, and a small mail for the 42nd. The time drags heavily and every day seems a week. How I long for the 24th. of November to come, since that is the time now set for our *deliverance* from the two months of conscription, but, like martyrs, we will wait and watch over the borders, like the *Great Vallandigham,* whose name I should not have disgraced these pages with.

[63] Jane Knox.

Saturday, September 24th. Still all quiet at the Mouth. No news to raise the siege of monotony now in power. The river is falling rapidly and very low. Si [64] and I were busy this P.M. making trunks for our personal property and clothing, as we have turned over our knapsacks to Capt. Tom Hutchins. The air is much cooler tonight and the musquitoes are played out.

Sunday, September 25th. Three years ago today, I enlisted as a private in Capt. A. Gardner's Capital Company K of the 42nd. Regiment Infantry, Ohio Volunteers, in the service of the United States for the period of three years, and went into camp at the Fair grounds in Bellefontaine, where the Company drilled until the 26th. September. It has been a long time to us. The weather is beautiful. A National Salute was fired in honor of the Great Victory in Western Virginia. [65]

Monday, September 26th. Three years ago, entered Camp Chase, Ohio, as a new recruit. Since then I have fought in fourteen battles and four engagements without ever being wounded or taking 50 cents worth of medicine. I consider myself among the fortunate ones of the War. Could hardly go through it all again without accident. Have just two months from today, which will make three years and two months. Hired a colored George to cook for mess. [66]

Tuesday, September 27th. This is the third anniversary of my life as a soldier of *Uncle Sam,* and the day that I should have been out of the army and at home, instead of being down here in the Mississippi Lowlands fighting mosquitoes and everything else but Rebels. Several boats from the north have arrived with a small mail for us. Wrote to Yourt.

[64] Commissary Sergeant Cyrus Rickard, of Company K.
[65] Sheridan's victory in the Shenandoah Valley.
[66] "In my new position as Quarter Master Sergeant I fared a trifle better than when on duty with my company. With some hard work, we arranged our two tents to suit us, and were furnished with a man to cook our meals, and together Commissary Sergeant Rickard and myself managed to while away the dull hours with some degree of comfort, and in the long sultry days (for October there was sultry) we beguiled the time in reading, or playing cards, or listlessly watching the passing steamers gliding by our quarters, until the 4th. of October, when orders came to muster out the non-commissioned staff." —D(MS).

Wednesday, September 28th. A very heavy rain fell last night, and today the ground is soft as *mud* can be. I have had nothing to do since morning, and the time passes slow. The *Hannibal* and *Gladiator* arrived from the north and bring northern dates to the 4th., and news of the gradual decline of gold. This is a good sign, and I hope it will last.

Thursday, September 29th. Today, was rejoiced to get a good, long, interesting letter from [Julia Allison], dated 17th. and mailed 20th.; been just 9 days on the route. Think it is time I was getting a letter from home. The weather threatening rain. We have no late news from the north, and all is quiet in this Department. Procured transportation today for five men to go north: time out.

Friday, September 30th. Having been busy all day making out Clothing, Camp and Garrison Equipage invoices, I am a little tired of writing this evening, but as I make it a practice of posting my Diary every night, I will manage to fill this space, I guess. Our Cook is sick today, and Harry had to get supper for us. Raining ever since morning.

Saturday, October 1st. Mailed my letter to [Julia Allison] this morning. The first of October came in rather cloudy, and a double rainbow extended across the horizon. Have finished up my Special Requisitions No. 40, and feel like laying aside the pen. Tonight, the weather looks a little more promising, and I think the rain is over; will hope so, at least.

The following is the letter to Julia Allison:

CAMP OF 42ND. OHIO, IN THE FIELD.
October 1, 1864.

Your good, long, interesting letter came safely after being nine days on the route, and as you say, I will take a few hours to myself amid the cares of life to answer, though my cares are very light, and the only trouble at present is the fact that I am drafted for two months longer than my original term of service, owing to the evil machinations of Red Tape and Bad Management combined. But you have no doubt heard

the particulars ere this. It is enough that we are *done con-
scripted* 'til the 26th. of November. I would not care so much,
only I expected to go home and become, in a measure, *accli-
mated,* before cold weather actually set in. Now, I have concluded to go home and *settle up,* and come back to Vicksburg,
or Memphis, and get into business, where I shall spend the
winter. This is my present plan for the future, but can't tell
what may happen. I am sure I never could stand the cold at
home after being in this warm climate so long. I don't know
what my *Friends* at home—Mother, especially—will say
to this arrangement. I'd rather enlist three years longer *as a
private* than stay in the north this winter. Oh! I didn't think
about our Iowa trip! What shall we do? Better postpone it,
hadn't we? What say you?

We are still occupying our dull old camp at the mouth of
White River, the place being a kind of secondary base of supplies for Steele's Army. Brig. Gen. Dennis is in command of
the Post. The White and Arkansas Rivers form a kind of island, separated from the mainland by the Cut-off which we
found of so much service in January 1863, in operating
against Arkansas Post. No town here, but a range of negro
huts built of logs extending a quarter of a mile up and down
the right bank of the river, white tents enough for six or seven
regiments, a number of coal and government barges with a
monitor at anchor in the river, mark the ugly old place from
which your friend writes this rainy morning. "Nothing con-
ceivable is more disagreable" than a storm in this "wooden"
country. Not satisfied with converting the earth into one
dense frog-pond, it comes in all the fury of a tornado, upset-
ting tents and tarpaulins, lifting roofs of houses and barns,
and raising *ned* generally.

Last night, a storm of this kind came up about 1 o'clock,
and just lifted everything. Over two-thirds of the tents up in
the regiment were lying flat this morning, and the Boys were
wet through; just *caving* [67] now, not swearing a bit, though.
Our tent would have blown off the ground, had it not been
pitched under the hill near the water's edge (the bank slopes
gradually down), and the Commissary Sergeant, Cyrus A.

[67] A colloquialism meaning "giving in," "submitting."

Rickard (who lives with me) and myself got up and held it by the poles until the gale was over. All the Barges and flat-boats, transports, and coal-crafts broke loose from their moorings and floated down toward New Orleans, and the Gunboats are busy towing them up this morning. 'Tis quite a different thing to read of soldiers lying out in the rain, and the actual experience itself, and as you, or no one else that has never visited an army camp can fully appreciate the luxury, I will not attempt to describe it. I know from actual experience how the boys feel this morning.

You most certainly have my sincere admiration for the very earnest manner in which you defend the good Cause, and I am no soldier did I not hope that such untiring loyalty would meet its reward in all the blessings a grateful country can af-ford. Julia, you shall ever have my good wishes, if not more, for your success and prosperity in all the walks of life.

If you have *such eyes* as those ladies give you credit for, it were a pity that some others I know hadn't the same kind, especially the contemptible Peace hyenas. I know it to be a fact that they cannot meet the steady gaze of a soldier, or even look up when a loyal man meets them face to face. Though only twenty, I profess to be a good judge of human nature, having paid some attention to that subject since entering the Army, and I have learned that the eyes are, in a measure, the windows of the inner man, and so long as you can look the contemptible, sneaking, back-biting, cowardly Copperheads out of countenance, you require none of the eyes of a ————, but the conscience of doing right,—which is a power in itself. Here is my private opinion of "eyes," *publicly expressed,* and I hope in sufficient brevity to suit all anxious inquiries after the same.

I saw three of the prettiest girls yesterday on the *Olive Branch* I have ever looked at since leaving home. They were from New Orleans; belonged to Aid Society; waved their handkerchiefs at Cy and I when the boat left the landing. Don't often get to see white folks down here—only travelers on packets. All boats have to stop here and report; land close to my tent. I always get the news from the North. The steamer *Julia* is my favorite boat. I have got a sketch of her, taken at Morganza. I have quit drawing, and that is my last production. Still raining. Let it rain! Who cares?

I wasn't looking for a letter from you until you got the news of our detention until November. Wrote to Mary informing her of the fact; she has my letter before this time. Haven't had a letter from home since 19th. of August; don't know whether Brother is home or not. George Douglas' time will be out the 25th. of this month; Jack Wilson's, not 'til November. I sent you the names of those only who ought to have gone out in September.

I meant just what I said when I told you that *Mac* would get a *few* votes in the Army (this part of it). I have no doubt the Potomac Army will poll a large vote for the Chickahominy Hero, but as your Friends in the Army of the Cumberland say, the race will be a light one. The Peace democracy of the North will have all the work to do, if they elect George. I'm afraid Abraham will hold Washington four years longer, if we Copperheads don't look out.

I sent Dick's Photo home from Baton Rouge. Thought you didn't want it, as you did not write for so long, or at least I couldn't get your letters. Where is the one I was to have? I shan't ask *you* again.

Give my love to *Jennie*,[68] and tell her not to look for me this winter. I should like to have been at the show you mentioned; know I should have admired the first performance. Always did like Country girls best! They are more common, like myself. Admire yellow Calico dresses,—short-sleeved and low neck is my style; don't like the kissing part, though. That looks so ugly, if not real green. I never was guilty of the sin. A railroader can't be any worse than a soldier, certainly. If they *are,* I pity the traveling community, for their lives and pocketbooks are in imminent danger constantly.

Who is Sallie L——?[69] Am not acquainted. Believe, too, I have seen her once or twice. Ain't she the lady who passed a corporal (an old schoolmate) on the street in Bellefontaine about one year ago, and didn't speak? If it is the same Sallie, give her not my regards and compliments, but my love. Effie,

[68] Julia's cousin, Virginia Seevers, who lived in Oskaloosa, Iowa.
[69] Sally Lawrence, daughter of Judge Lawrence, in Bellefontaine.

too.[70] I will send love to Mary [Knapp] when I write to her. I received the papers, and was glad to get them.

How did the reception come off? Seems to me they make considerable fuss over a few *Hundred-Day men*.[71] Poor fellows! How they must have suffered away from home almost a *fourth of a year!* I'll bet they were glad to get back. I read a letter not long since from one of them, stating that they marched one whole day with nothing to eat but Hardtack and river water. O, horrors! Has our government come to that! When the *brave men* of its army must suffer that way! Why! I remember, when on the march from Cumberland Gap, of offering ten dollars (all the money I had) for one single tack. But the lucky owner refused to part with it, and we marched on fifteen days without even a hardtack, living on parched corn and corn meal, but "them days" are over now, and I should think Uncle Sam could furnish better for the National Guard.

Oh! what a lucky Soger I am! The Steamer *Luminary* just brought me a letter from one of the sweetest, *goodest* little girls that ever was.[72] Please excuse me while I break it open and read. I know just who it is from: postmarked Mount Pleasant, Iowa, September 20th.

(Half-hour later). My letter wasn't as long as yours; therefore, not so interesting, and most too *formal,* though containing some good news. Said I was most probably enjoying the blessings of home in Ohio, etc. Can't see the home; can you, Julia? I guess my letters will come fast enough after they find I'm not coming home quite so soon. I bet you will have fun reading *this* letter,[73] but what's the use sending one unless it *is* a letter? I hate short ones, and hardly ever like to take the trouble to read them. So be careful and always fill your paper, if you wish to interest one of Uncle Sam's boys.

I was in Bellefontaine one year ago from the date of your letter, I think; am not certain. I must stop writing soon, or I

[70] Effie Price, daughter of lawyer John Price, in Bellefontaine. Both Judge Lawrence and John Price are well known in Logan County, Ohio, history.

[71] The Governors of Ohio, Illinois, Indiana, Iowa, and Wisconsin had authorized the formation of companies of volunteers to serve for a hundred days.

[72] His sister, Jane Knox, in Eddyville.

[73] He filled four foolscap pages and all the margins, then inverted the first page and wrote between the lines.

will not have room to sign my name. Cy says you never can read this. When I get to writing to my friends, don't know when to stop; seems like talking to them. Wish I could see you. Have enough to tell to last two months. Have you got your new "flag" yet? What style of hats do the girls wear now? Please answer soon, and tell me all the news.

Yours, as ever,
JOHNS.

Sunday, October 2nd. An old mail arrived from Morganza, and I have two letters from [Julia Allison], dated Sept. 1st. and 2nd. Was down this evening to see Captain Hopkins of General Dennis' Staff. No news from either way, except the report of a decided decline of gold in New York. The river is very low and still falling, and it's quite a difficult matter to land boats close enough to shore to run out a plank, and hard to get water without wading in mud.

Monday, October 3rd. Answered [Julia Allison's] letters of 1st. and 2nd. September, giving that chap perfect fits for some of his slang in the last two letters; hope it won't make *him* mad. The clothing came today, and I issued overcoats and blankets to Regiment; will issue other things in the morning. The weather is cool tonight, and one feels like putting on an overcoat. Heard some good news tonight.

The following is the letter to Julia Allison.

HEADQUARTERS 42ND. OHIO, MOUTH
WHITE RIVER, ARKANSAS. October 3, 1864.
FRIEND JULIA,

Capt. Tom Hutchins has just brought me two letters from you, dated Sept. 1st and 2nd., directed to Morganza, La. Only answered one of the 17th. Sept. day before yesterday, but as there is so much going on here, I have plenty of news to make up a letter any time, so here goes for the answer for both.

Am always ready to quarrel,—especially with Ladies; never with Gents. They sometimes retaliate too severely. I wouldn't bet anything against your right hand! If I should win it, 'twould be worse than an old Cop[perhead] . . . would box

my ears the first time anything went wrong. Don't like kisses?
Well, don't believe you will ever get them, if everybody is like
————. If I sent *love,* it must have been when I was asleep,
or in one of those sentimental moods which make fools of
everyone. It's an article not in my Calendar. Never knew what
it was, except for a good cup of . . . Coffee! Think it is
pretty hard to spoil condemned bacon. Good, true, honest
friends are scarce in this republic; generally, their friendship
is as deep as mud on a brick walk, or goes as far as a man's
friendship for the D————.

You're too hard on the poor National Guards; I think
they deserve more credit than three-year boys. You don't do
them justice. Poor boys have been away from Mothers so
long! Just think! Three months on hardtack and pork! Why
are you down on us Copperheads so? We have never harmed
you.

No, Dick will not go to Bellefontaine; he belongs to Company G from Bedford, Ohio. Sent his photo home; thought
you didn't want it, as you didn't say so. Oh, do send me
yours! I can't live without it. Bad luck to the day I lost the
other! Haven't seen a happy moment since; its presence was
enough to inspire any soldier to heroic deeds of valor. And
then the eyes . . . were so beautiful . . . hair, also, fault-
less and done up, too . . . latest style . . . no, that's so you
will never again have justice done you.

Partial to Lieutenants? Glad to hear that! Think I am
safe, then. Yes, *Sergeant* sets off my name, or any other soldier's name, if his stripes are merited. By the way, if you
don't like the "Sergeant," just leave it off. I never told anyone to use it in directing. I like the common way of directing
best.

I believe I've quarreled long enough *now,* and if you are satisfied, I will acknowledge myself *worsted.* Wait, though;
here's something about "soft-soap" and a "broomstick."
"Them's" articles I don't deal in; will make all allowances,
as they are the "native elements" of women, and sound better
when their sweet lips pronounce the word. What is "sentimental"? "Star-gazing," I suppose. If *that's* so, I am more than
sentimental and three or four times over, for I've laid many

a night with nothing over me but my blanket and the stars, and didn't grow sentimental and love-sick and all that kind of stuff either. All soft-soap! Do for chickens and babies!

I think engineering will be a pretty good business in Iowa, —on the C.B. & Q. R.R.[74] You say you like R.R. engineers: glad to hear it! Alas! my memory is too good; don't wish to recruit it—not me! That's why I don't wish to stop in Belle-fontaine. I have turned over my gun and knapsack to Capt. Hutchins and have no place to keep *love*, unless I put it in the desk, and then Cy would steal it. Used to keep it in my knapsack, but that played out. Kept *one love* in my musket with a corn-cob in the end of it, but coming up from Mor-ganza, I shot Corn-cob, Love, and all away at a "sandy-hill crane."

Now for a circumstance. Lieut. Pete Miller was up at Du-val's Bluff last week, and coming back on the Steamer *Mattie*, he happened to be talking to a party of officers when, passing St. Charles and in the course of their conversation, Pete men-tioned my name, and a Captain on Gen. Dennis Staff enquired where I was from, etc., and finally came to the conclusion that I was some relation; upon landing, he came to see me, and sure enough he found a Cousin. I never knew he was in the Army; hadn't seen him for years. He is from Medina Co., Ohio, but hasn't been at home for some time. I was down to see him tonight.

Your two letters of the 30th August and 1st September have been to Morganza and back. Some of my letters directed to the 19th Corps have been to Sheridan's Army.

Let me see; I have nothing else to write, I believe. Wish I *could* be sentimental! I'll try. How I would like to be in old Bellefontaine tonight! Wouldn't I go straight to ———, and wouldn't I more than ———! (I forgot what I was go-ing to do. Memory fails one tonight; don't remember a thing about what happened there when I was last there!) Oh, yes, I do, too. Something I've laughed at a thousand times since: do you want to know? When you send me that dear little pho-tograph, I'll tell you. If I only had your *facsimile*, the next two months would be but one day. Then, can you deny a sol-

[74] Chicago, Burlington, & Quincy Railroad.

dier this one favor? Send me one, and I'll never ask but one other favor of you. You may back out of that emigrating arrangement, if you want to, but Mary knows better.

You always mention Fannie R——'s [Riddle] name; who is she? just like you? Also, Mary K——[Knapp]; who is she? Is it "We, Us & Co.": J—— A——, F—— R——, and M—— K——? Quite a confederacy you have formed and seceded from us Cops! Why! you ought to be strong enough for quite a resistance in case of civil war, but you had better not say anything; *we are armed,* you know!

I believe Company K are all well. One of the boys (Jim R——) was in this evening; also Capt. Hutchins, just before dark. Thinks he will be mustered out with the Company.

If I thought such a thing as *Love* really ever existed, I would send it to you. But as it is, I must keep all my regards, good wishes, and all that, for Mary. Hoping to hear from you as often as the spirit moves you, I remain, as ever,

Your Army Copperhead,
JOHNS.

[Marginal notes] We heard day before yesterday of the great decline of gold; hope it will stay declined. The river is very low here, but rising above. One or two Bellefontaine boys by some means have found out who I get letters from in B——. Wonder what they'll do about it? Dick Bailey said to send his love when I wrote to that "Bellefontaine girl." I am going into Quarter Master's Dept. at Vicksburg this winter. Will go home first. Perhaps stop in Bellefontaine—can't tell; won't, if it is in the night.—O.J.H.

Tuesday, October 4th. An order came tonight to muster out the following members of the Non-Commissioned staff and Band, viz. Horace S. Clark, Sergeant Major and Acting Adjutant; Owen J. Hopkins, Quarter-Master Sergeant; and John Parry, Chief Musician. We will start for HOME about the 7th., or as soon as descriptive rolls are made out. All is quiet here. Issued clothing to Regiment this morning.

Wednesday, October 5th. Have everything packed up ready to start on the first boat, which I think will be along tonight. Hope it will not come until morning, as weather is too cool to

get up in the night. Clark and I have packed up a box of provender to take along. Transportation will be furnished to
Memphis, and from there to Cairo. Now for perhaps the last
night in camp.

Thursday, October 6th. The Regiment is ordered to be
ready to embark in the morning, at daylight, for Duval's
Bluff, Ark. The Steamer *Delaware* is landed near my tent,
and we have all the wagons and Commissary goods put aboard
of her tonight. I am still anxiously waiting for my means of
going north.

Friday, October 7th. The Forty-second Ohio, Seventh Kentucky, Thirty-seventh and Forty-sixth Illinois left for upper
White River,[75] and we are left here to wait for a boat going
to Memphis. The mail arrived on the *Benjamin Stickney,* with
one letter from home. All are well. About dark, embarked
on the Steamer *Dunleith* for home and (Domesday ?).

*The day before he left the camp for home, he wrote his last
letter to Julia Allison from the headquarters of the Forty-
second at the mouth of the White River.*

October 6, 1864.

FRIEND JULIA,

As a "friend of mine" leaves for God's country by the first
boat going north, I have concluded to scratch a few lines to
send by him. The 42nd. Ohio, 37th. and 46th. Illinois, and 7th.
Kentucky Volunteers are ordered to Duval's Bluff, Ark., and
will embark on the *Sallie List* at daybreak, in the morning.
We are loading our Corn Stores tonight. The Regiments will
only take one tent to the company, five days' rations, and leave
all who are not able to march. The boys are not quite so willing to go as I have seen them, as most of them have served
over three years now and think the *hereafter* in the service is
all extra. May see hard service yet—don't know. Could tell
you of certain operations in Arkansas, if I dared, but contraband is contraband.

---

[75] "We waved them a regretful adieu as they steamed up the White River,
leaving our party on the shore to await the arrival of an upward boat. . . .
Thus we parted forever from the Old Regiment, whose name and fame is
written in the bright pages of Ohio's history, and whose tattered flag aids to
decorate the walls of the State House at Columbus. . . ."—D(MS).

I have something good to tell all who are concerned in my welfare, but choose to keep it to myself for the present. I have not heard from home yet, and don't know what has happened in the last two months; don't know whether Yourtee is at home, or not; and if at home, safe and well.

The nights are very cold, and my Overcoat, especially this evening, is my best friend. The Mississippi is very low and so is the White River; the troops will embark on the smallest boats, or those of light draught. Even then, it will be a difficult matter to ascend as shallow and crooked a river as the White. I can't say I am enjoying the best of health, but the Bellefontaine boys are prospering as finely as Old Soldiers *only* know how. I received two Cincinnati papers you sent, and am much obliged; any kind of paper or letter is a welcome visitor to us, and their contents are read until they are indelibly stamped in memory. Yes, send papers and letters to the soldiers, and you are sure of their gratitude, if no more. The 42nd. Ohio is raising Ned tonight. Don't believe there will be much sleeping done.

(10 P.M.)—Have at last got all the Wagons and Ammunition, Commissary Stores, and Head Quarters Baggage on board, and I had better finish before a boat comes to take my "chum" and this letter home—"north," I should say.

Several of the officers are on a tare tonight, and have already pulled down Lieut. Hubbell's tent, and also Capt. T. L. Hutchins'; tried mine, but the Commissary Sergeant and myself caught them at it. They have gone up to Brigade Headquarters now, and I hear them routing out Quartermaster Dyer. But I must close, for the night is so cold I can hardly write. The days are warmer.

Tell the friends of the 42nd.—K Co. and Bellefontaine boys, especially—that they are O.K. Don't write to me until you hear from me again. Please give my sincere regards, love, and all else to Mary, and tell her not to write until "further orders."

By Command of O.J.H.

P.S.—Mr. J.L.M. will mail this at some convenient point North. Yours,—Q.M.S'GT.

The following entries were made while he was homeward bound.

Saturday, October 8th. Reached Helena in the morning, and after a short delay, proceeded on up the river, with no signs of enemies. The river is very low, but rising. I have met a friend from Toledo, Mr. Foulkes. The *Dunleith* is a small, slow, side-wheeler, and a short craft generally.

Sunday, October 9th. Reached Memphis and got transportation to Cairo, and also three days' rations. Embarked on the *City of Alton;* left at 5 o'clock. Our craft is a fast and splendid boat, and we are sure of making port tomorrow.

Monday, October 10th. Arrived at Cairo and secured transportation to Columbus, Ohio, and laid at the depot until train time. The train will be full, as there is a number of troops going east by the Illinois Central. Boys are feeling pretty good since landing.

Tuesday, October 11th. Took train last night at 2 o'clock, and started toward home. Changed cars at Mattoon for Indianapolis, and at dark dashed into that city. I was here separated from the boys, and continued on to Cumberland; then ran back to Indianapolis, but didn't find a man.

Wednesday, October 12th. Took 5 o'clock train for Columbus without the rest of the boys; am in hopes they have gone on before. Reached Columbus about 2 P.M. and ensconced my baggage at the Soldiers' Home, and myself in the I & C Depot to watch for the boys to come,—but they didn't.

Thursday, October 13th. The Sergeant Major and the rest of the party arrived on the train early this morning, and we have put them into Columbus Barracks until they can be discharged. We made out their papers, and they will be mustered out tomorrow.

Friday, October 14th. Today, I was mustered out the service of the U.S., and paid off. Will leave for home by the first train in the morning; I understand there is one going at 5 A.M. I will be at home tomorrow night, if nothing happens. My health is poor.

The following entries were made in Toledo, Ohio.

Saturday, October 15th. Embarked on board the 5 o'clock train this morning, and arrived at Urbana 7:30 A.M.; changed cars and passed through Bellefontaine about 11:00 A.M.; saw some of my old acquaintances at the depot, but I didn't stop to talk with them long. Reached home 7:30 P.M.

Sunday, October 16th. Finds me at home again after an absence of one year. Everything looks comfortable, and I shall soon feel at home. Went to Church at 10 A.M. and night also, but went to sleep at night and came home before it was out.

Monday, October 17th. Was recommended by the Military Board and Colonel Morton for the position of Lieutenant and Regimental Quarter Master, 182nd. O.V.I. The Adjutant General will answer tonight; have not answered all questions yet, but expect to by next week. The gold market closed tonight at $2.20. War news not so good.

Tuesday, October 18th. Almon and I started for Columbus at 4:30 P.M. on business concerning my commission. Changed cars at Monroeville and Shelby, and rattled on toward the Capital of the State of Ohio, my hopes and fears varying with every motion of the cars.

Wednesday, October 19th. Arrived at Columbus 2:30 A.M. and went up to see the Adjutant General, and learned that my chances for the position of Quarter Master were rather slim. Took dinner with A. Gardner and settled bill with "Neil House," and embarked for Bellefontaine, where I arrived 10:40 P.M. Put up at "Fontaine House."

Thursday, October 20th. Run around over town all day, and at night was at a *party* 'till after twelve o'clock. Bellefontaine has changed very much, and one can hardly recognize the old Place.

Friday, October 21st. Started for home at 11:30 A.M., and arrived 7:45 P.M. Found the following telegram: "You will be appointed Quarter Master of 182nd. O.V.I. Come with the Regiment on Monday next. (signed) B. R. Cowen, Adj. Gen., Ohio."

Saturday, October 22nd. Busy all day making preparations to leave.

Sunday, October 23rd. Didn't go to Church today as requested by all the folks, but went with Lide [Thompson] and Mother over to dinner at Almon's.

That evening, he wrote a short letter to Julia Allison, the first of a new series resulting from his stopover in Bellefontaine three days before.

TOLEDO, OHIO.
October 23, 1864.

DEAR JULIA,

I wrote you a short letter Friday night, but was in such a hurry that I don't believe it could have been much of a letter, so have retired from the noisy chat of family to the quiet of my own room to write at leisure.

My brother-in-law is here from Indianapolis, Eliza and her "old man";[76] my "Coz"[77] and another visitor are of the circle, and you may guess how many questions I have to answer. Last night, I told them "my story": marches made and battles fought, and almost everything connected with my three years' experience.

Of course, I omitted the scene of my *first* confession. Never shall let them know it. I hold that as too sacred for outsiders. Julia, you made this old Soldier's heart lighter that night than it had ever been, and you shall never regret that you *trusted*, at least, your most sincere admirer. (The term is too cold for expression.) You were blind indeed, did you not see that I *loved* you from first acquaintance, and though too young in the eyes of the world to possess that sentiment in its true light, the Cherished image of my first affection was ever before me.

[76] Sarah Eliza ("Lyde") and her husband, Dr. Thompson.
[77] Margaret ("Mag"), daughter of Harris Hopkins.

Whether on the battle field, or in quiet camp, my Mother's and my Julia's names were dearer than life, and always prevented me from joining in the profane revelries of rough companions.

I have been through the world, perhaps more than half the young men of my age, and always an attentive observer, but never have found the girl that came half-way up to my ideal of a perfect woman until I happily became acquainted with you . . . .

We leave for Columbus tomorrow at noon; expect there will be some tall crying at the depot. Sorry you are not here to cry for me, but if you can manage to shed a few tears about 12 o'clock tomorrow, don't know but what it would be just as well. Am going to have some Photos taken at Columbus; will send you one. Perhaps bring it myself. Your letter containing *your* Photo hasn't come yet; did you put the Regiment on it? If you *did,* it has gone down to Little Rock. Expected to find it at home when I came, but was disappointed. Sister and "Coz" say I must go to Church tonight, and I must get ready to go with the troublesome teasers. What troublesome things women are! Answer soon—to Columbus. My sincere comps. to Mary and Miss P——[Price].

YOUR JOHNS.

Monday, October 24th. Left with my Regiment (the 182nd.) for Columbus at 1:35 P.M. A large multitude was collected at the depot to see us off. The train started at the above hour, and the 182nd. was off to the Wars!

Tuesday, October 25th. Arrived in Columbus at daybreak, and went to camp. I remained in the City, and was Commissioned and mustered as Quarter Master, 182nd. O.V.I., to date from today. Went down to camp and issued a few things to the Regiment, such as Camp Equipage.

He also wrote a letter to Julia.

HEAD QUARTERS 182ND. O.V.I.
CAMP CHASE, OHIO. October 25, 1864.

DEAREST JULIA,

We left Toledo yesterday at 1:30 P.M. and arrived here this morning at daybreak. Regiment marched to Camp from

Columbus, and was assigned to quarters. I returned to the City and was Commissioned and Mustered in as Quarter Master. Fear I shall not be able to see my "heart's most precious treasure" before we march to the field, that time being set Thursday next, but I don't believe we will get off so soon, as I have arms and accoutrements, Camp and Garrison Equipage to issue yet,—which will take some time.

We have just the gayest Regiment that ever left the State: officers all young men—beardless youths—like myself, and so far as I am acquainted, I like them better than those of the 42nd. Major Butler of the 67th. is Colonel, and a fine man. All the *field officers* have seen service, and a majority of the Company officers. Will have over 1,000 men when organized.

If I don't get to see you before we leave for the front, shall be sadly disappointed, though perhaps can get leave of absence this winter. Don't think I would go straight through Bellefontaine next time. Have too much interest in a certain young lady there. I am not going to write so much nonsense this term of service as did before; shall confine my correspondence to narrower limits.

How foolish a fellow is when in love! Why! I was not the possessor of enough moral courage that night to tell you the true state of my heart. Won't it be best to mention it here: that you are *all* to me, and I could never see a single accomplishment in another woman, if I should live 200 years. That's so! Julia, don't you laugh at me! I'm Quarter Master now; have left off foolishness.

Haven't had a letter from you yet—photo, or anything else. Am going to send you mine before I leave, if you want it. Write soon, and don't fail to tell me if I occupy at least a remote corner of your affections, and you will make happy your

Sincere Soldier,
JOHNS.
1st. Lieut. and R.Q.M., 182nd. O.V.I.

P.S.—Comps. to Mary and friends. Direct to Columbus. Time for leaving has been postponed to Friday 28th.—OJH.

Wednesday, October 26th. Tonight, issued clothing to the Regiment; also made requisition for additional stores.

Thursday, October 27th. Was extremely busy all day. Everybody running to me for everything, and all is confusion. The Regiment has orders to leave, and they are not equipped yet.

Friday, October 28th. Issued arms and accoutrements to Regiment in the morning, and two days' rations. They left at 2 P.M. I remained behind to turn over Government property.

Saturday, October 29th. Run up to Bellefontaine to see my ———. Saw her and had a gay time; will stay over to-morrow, when I will go back to Columbus, and then to the Front.

Sunday, October 30th. Was up late last night. Left Belle-fontaine at 11:30 A.M. for Columbus, and arrived at 3:45 P.M. Put up at the "American."

On the 28th., in his hotel room in Columbus, following the departure of the regiment, he wrote another letter.

COLUMBUS, OHIO
October 28, 1864.

DEAREST OF WOMEN AND MY OWN "WIFE,"

Your very welcome letter came to me yesterday while busy issuing clothing and arms to the regiment, but I wasn't long in leaving everything in my Sergeant's hands and excusing my-self long enough to read it. What a Host of happy feelings the dear missive awakened! And bewildered by the thought that one so far above me in everything to be esteemed, could condescend to love a rough soldier, used to nothing that the world calls refinement, and with but very little more of a leg-acy than a rough exterior, though—God knows!—an honest heart and a will to *do,* and a determination to perform what I once undertake. Unlike you, I possess nothing like the fiery temper you mention, but am slow to anger and not full of re-sentment until once beyond certain bounds; *then,* my anger is as great as that of man can be, and not only *this,* but as last-ing as eternity. I was never known to forgive when fully aroused. Such is the difference in our natures. Can any bad re-sults spring for our engagement? I hope not. I am certain when a man once loves a woman as I love my Julia, he can't be capable of one unkind thought toward his wife, and if the sentiment is reciprocal, happiness in its true sense will ever dwell in that household. What say you?

If you had seen the amount of work I have done lately, you wouldn't blame me for the brevity of my letters. My Q.M. Sergeant just arrived today, and the Clerks are all green hands, and I have everything, in a word, to do myself. Will have more leisure now, as all camp and garrison equipage has been issued, and shall have more time before long to hold sweet communion with my Dearest, sweetest little "wife." [78] Julia, I am sure that God in Heaven will smile and approve a love so pure and holy as ours. I seem like a new man since you gave me the three happy words: *I love you.* My aim in life hereafter will be loftier. My every act, word, and bearing shall bring me nearer that level which will place me a happy husband by your side.

You fear for my faults, do you? Point them out to me, and (God willing!) I will rectify them. If you say so, I will promise you upon the honor of a soldier, that I will never touch a card without direct permission from you as long as I live. My comrades for the past three years can certify that I never indulged to any extent, and was always opposed to whiskey-sellers as much as anyone. Nothing shall be left undone for your sake, if I can help it, and if knowing that you are loved by "Johns" is the least source of happiness for you, remember that his whole heart is yours, and don't despise the gift, for a truer one never loved before.

My Regiment has left for Nashville; left here today at 6:30 P.M. I was compelled to remain behind to settle with the Government for Arms and Equipage. Am stopping at the "American" tonight, up on the third story, writing to my *Jewel,* the "girl I left behind me."

Bought a horse today: large, iron-gray,—regular war horse. Will leave her tomorrow and go on to the Regiment. You had better state the case to your father. If I am not mis-

---

[78] For the writer, though not yet married, "wife" is a frequent and very special term of endearment in his letters to Julia Allison. She remonstrated, but he continued the practice.

taken, he is a man of sense, and who has a right to separate two joined already by the laws of Heaven. I told my young brother. He said I always *was* a lucky fellow! Better tell Claude you only esteem him as a brother, if you think anything more than friendship is his excuse. I will trust you, and you can associate with whom you please. But, Julia, never assume the air of a coquette in my presence, for I hate them. What would I think if you should prove one to me! No! the thought wrongs you. How can you ever be other than my sweet "wife" now?

I must close, as it is very late and I am tired; tired of arduous duties, but never of you. Write soon.

YOUR JOHNS.

Sunday, back in Columbus, overwhelmed by his great good fortune, he scribbled a hasty note to Julia, thinking that he would leave in the evening. He was delayed until past midnight, so he penned a second and longer letter and dated it Monday.

COLUMBUS, OHIO.
October 30, 1864.

JULIA, MY OWN,

Arrived safely at 2:25 P.M. today, and will leave 7:20 tonight. Are you sleepy today, I wonder? It was only one o'clock when I went to bed last eve. Received your letter, but this isn't the answer. Hope I will soon have time to write long letters to my Julia and hold sweet communion with the idol of my heart. I go back to the Army a happier man, since I have the assurance that my more than idolatrous love is returned by the only woman I could ever admire. Sweetest, dearest, best, and most perfect of women, you are all to me. Believe me true to the end, and remember that you are the only Girl that ever turned the head of Your

SOLDIER JOHNS.

COLUMBUS, OHIO.
October 31, 1864.

EVER PRESENT JULIA,

I believe I promised to answer the letter received from your own hands yesterday, and as it is my rule to never make a promise without fulfilling it, I am going to take my time and answer tonight. Wrote to you today; only a few lines, though. Also sent my photo. Isn't it gay? Had to have it taken with blouse; my valise was at Camp Chase when I took a notion to have the photo taken. I didn't fix up any. You know I never do. Ain't proud enough.

This time last night, you were wasting my smoking tobacco. Did you notice that girl that sat just back of us, or back of you, rather, on the seat to your right? How she eyed us? Thought at first she was looking at me only, but she finally rested her ugly eyes on you. Then the sermon interested me so: couldn't help it! Had nothing to disturb me from listening to every word of it! I came away, and forgot to call on Mary. What will she say? Will be sure to mistrust something.

Claude was at the Depot when I left. Shook hands and said good-bye. You are right: Claude is a perfect gentleman and a fine looking fellow. Don't know whether it's best for you to go with him, or not; suppose if you both behave yourselves, nobody would find fault. Believe you said I could trust you. So use your own judgement and govern your own conduct; of course, it isn't for me to do. I only have a right to interfere when I see there is danger of losing my Gem. You are mine already in the sight of God, and only there remains the ceremony of man's law to make us one in the sight of the world.

I used to argue that *Love* was an article not to be found in this Orb of ours, or, if it really did exist, 'twas only in the hearts of shallow, moon-struck school girls and boys, but recent experience, especially the past two years, has taught me differently, and I have the facts fully represented in my own case, and have found that the rough and tough, though honest, soldier can love as well as school-boys and girls. I was impressed seriously with your appearance the first time I ever saw you, and a feeling very strange to one of my then-disposition gradually came over me until, by the time I joined the Army, I knew that it was nothing short of deep and Holy love that I entertained for you. What frightened me, was the firm belief that I could never be to you more than a friend, for what could a plain, unpretending, young fellow like myself hope for in my then-situation? Over a year went round, during which time my love for you far from diminished, though now softened down to a quiet reverence for your memory. A something—so strange were my feelings—that 'tis out of my power to describe.

In our fierce battles at Vicksburg, while Rebel balls were flying like bees, *you* were in my thoughts, and when our military operation had subsided into a siege, I found time to think, so I mustered courage enough at the proposition (I must admit) of Sergeant Hi Allmon (though I never mentioned your name to him). I sent the sketch to you.[79] You answered, but I didn't get it until just before I started home from Vicksburg. Saw you at home, and was surprised at the change in your appearance, and all for the better. You then looked so beautiful, so far above me—the rough, unpolished soldier—that I could have worshipped you. Our correspondence commenced, and in none of your letters could I catch a glimmer of hope for me, so cold were they all, so matter-of-fact like—as you say—that I believed I was only one of the hundred of your deluded admirers, and so tempered my own letters to correspond with circumstances. How often I was tempted to tell you *all,* the Being above only knows; but I feared such a course would deprive me entirely of your dear letters, and even of your friendship. I only wrote to Mary to "fill up space." Her letters, of course, were always full of interest, but how different from those penned by the dear familiar hand of my first *love.* The writing itself was a source of pleasure, for you know as well as I that the contents of your letters were never very encouraging to my suit, and I derived all the pleasure from the presence alone of your handwriting.

I came home safely from the dangers of a three-years' campaign, and the sight of you again revived my former love, and the night you asked my opinion of you, I told you *all,* and was blessed with the knowledge that you could return my affection. Happy moment! The happiness of a lifetime consolidated into one second of thought, for the very woman I had so often thought of on the battle field and bivouac, in camp and on

[79] The pencil sketch of Black River Bridge which he sent with his first letter to her, June 20, 1863. See page 71.

the march, says she loves me—*me,* Johns Hopkins! What have I done to deserve it? I don't; but will, or else never rob my Julia's father of one of the best girls in Christendom.

I had my horse put on the cars this evening and sent to Cincinnati; will start, myself and man, in the morning at 2 :35. Expected to go tonight, but couldn't get off. I am writing at the same table I answered your last letter from. The fire is going out, and my fingers are getting cold.

Am going to send you a Photo for Jennie, if you think she isn't too mad. If she doesn't want it, give it to Sis. Powell,[80] —Mrs., I mean. I will have a better picture taken—different style—for you, when I have time. Had been busy making invoices of Camp and Garrison Equipage when I had this taken; don't you see an invoice in my pocket, the right-hand one? Looks like I was going some place.

Don't fail to send yours. Don't send any other kind but like the one Mrs. Powell has. I was real proud of that one, but wasn't going to say so before you, by any means. Always hated flattery and compliments, and seldom pay comps. to anyone. Was real proud of you (as you say) last night in Church; shall be more so when you stand by my side,—my own dear wife forever. Don't delay to answer, please, and write long letters. Comps. and love to no one but my sweet "Wife."

Yours to Love,—and Death to Rebs!
LIEUT.

Monday, October 31st. Left Columbus at 2 :35 A.M. for Cincinnati; arrived 8 :20 A.M. Put up at the "Broadway." Left Cinti again at 6 :20 P.M. for Jeffersonville.

Tuesday, November 1st. Arrived at Jeffersonville some time in the night; don't know when. Put up at the "National," a dirty hotel for a first class. Remained all day.

Monday, November 7th. Left Jeffersonville, Indiana, and crossed over to Louisville on my way to the Regiment.

Tuesday, November 8th. Arrived in Nashville, Tenn., and put up at the "Commercial."

[80] Mrs. Powell was a neighbor, and not a relative. The writer referred humorously to her as "Sis," since she was of the Methodist faith.

Wednesday, November 9th. Went out to camp and assumed the duties of my office again.

Here ends his "Diary" for 1864. His further experiences as Lieutenant and Regimental Quartermaster of the One Hundred Eighty-second, O.V.I., garrisoned at Nashville, Tennessee, are revealed in his letters addressed to Julia Allison, in Bellefontaine, and in certain other private correspondence.

One cannot properly go on to this new chapter in the life of Sergeant Hopkins without a final word on the last days of his beloved Forty-second, O.V.I.

On September 17, four companies (A, B, C, D) left camp at the mouth of the White River on the steamer "Julia," bound for home. They arrived on the twenty-third at the whitewashed barracks of Camp Chase, which they had left thirty months before. On the thirtieth, the veterans became civilians once more. The remaining companies embarked for Duval's Bluffs, Arkansas, on October 7, the day Sergeant Hopkins and a few non-commissioned officers sailed on the "Dunleith" for home. On November 10, companies E and F returned to Camp Chase and were mustered out.

While at Duval's Bluffs, the men who had enlisted in the various companies in 1862 (Portland recruits) were reorganized into a company under the command of Captain Campbell (Company G) and sent to aid General Edward R. S. Canby in the siege and capture of Mobile. The remaining companies of the Regiment were mustered out at Camp Chase on the second of December, 1864.

Only once did Sergeant Hopkins hear from his old comrades in Company K while they were still in service: he received a letter from his "buddy" Jim Whitsell.

DUVALL'S BLUFFS, ARK.
November 5th, 1864.

ESTEEMED FRIEND,

Yours of recent date came to my observation last evening, and respect due you prompts me to reply immediately.

Allow me to congratulate you upon the honorable position you hold. I am proud to know that you, my messmate, have not forgotten our parting requests. I was somewhat astonished at hearing of your going into the Service again so soon, but no life is any [more] honorable than that of a soldier. You now will have the advantage of the campaign before you, while on the other hand, the three years that have expired, you were surrounded with many disadvantages. The worst wish I have in store for you, is that you may prosper and be credited with a name among the heros of our Country's Cause. Jo[h]ns, you have my warmest friendship and sincere regards, and I will only add that we are in winter quarters, have built huts with large fireplaces in them, which is quite comfortable.

Capt. Hutch[ins] has bin engineering, but has bin relieved. Gen. Andrews is in command, and the duty is hard, the corpls. coming on duty every other day. Companys E and F have started home; we will start in about 12 days. I should be happy to meet you at Columbus, Ohio. Mr. Baley [Dick Bailey, Co. G] has bin very sick, but has about recovered, and sends his best wishes to you. Capt. Campbell remains with the Portland recruits. A new promotion in Co. G of Corp'ls. Durgey (only Lieut.), Rotherie, Collens are said corporels in Co. G, 42nd Ohio.

I will conclude, hoping to avail myself competent to Interest you next time.

Remain your confidential Friend,
CORP'L JIM.

P.S.—Address Limaville, Stark Co., Ohio.

Perhaps you would have no objections to here the Gossiping in Co. K at hearing of your promotion:

1st. B. F. Myers—"D——nd if I would like to belong to the 182nd."

2nd. The Hon. J. R. Whitsell—"I am glad he merits his position."

3rd. Orderly Geo. Douglass—"It was through his brother's influence."

4th. Ezra J. Allmon—Neutral.

5th. Thos. C. Hunt—"Bulley for Hopkins! Ha! Ha! Ha!"

6th. Geo. M. Wallis—"I allways liked Hop."

7th. Wm. H. Leister—"Pretty Good! I can't go it again."

8th. Capt. Hutchins—"Capt. Campbell, you know Hopkins?" "Yes, certainly." "He has excepted the commishion of R.Q.M., 182nd. That is a pretty good thing fur Hop."

9th. All the rest is quiet.

This is the deposition of the Witnesses, and I give a Verdict of 7 to 2 for your Wellfair.

Perhaps you think this not prudent. If so, excuse my Ignorance.

IV

LETTERS FROM NASHVILLE
1864–65

LOUISVILLE, KENTUCKY
November 3, 1864

DEAREST, THOUGH DISTANT, JULIA,

Thy name's a charm to me to keep me from sinning against my Maker, for who that loves as I, can for a moment forget the loveliness of God's work as represented in yourself? No, I am too thankful that He has given me such a gift to cherish as my life; as you say, I fear I will forget my duty to Him by permitting my Love for you to attain the nature of Idolatry. I have but to remove my thoughts from the immediate surrounding objects, to have them rest in calm and sweet reflections on the beauties, graces and accomplishments of my sweetest of Julias. The very *name* is music. Then, your nobleness of soul. Yes, you are too far above me in that, and I feel a momentary sadness when I think how little I deserve even your admiration. Still, I have all the assurance necessary— your word—that you indeed love me, and what more elicits my gratitude is the fact that you sent me willingly the second time to serve my country in her hour of peril. May God bless you for the act, if it was any sacrifice on your part, and though not placed in a position to serve the flag quite so directly as before, I shall never disgrace the name of Soldier by one action or deed of dishonesty. Your name shall be a talisman to guide my future career.

You see, Julia, I am a regular Lovesick soldier,—a creature I once reviled and despised, though I see now it is to one's advantage to have someone or something to think of and keep us out of mischief. At nearly every House we stopped since leaving Bellefontaine, I've been invited to drink, but how vividly the promise I gave to you came to my aid, and I no longer thought it indecorous to refuse to drink with a friend, even a brother officer.[1] It was always a degrading sight to me to see a young man call for whiskey, and though sometimes almost compelled to taste the miserable stuff, I inwardly loathed it. My promise to you is as good as a temperance pledge, and my vows of fidelity as binding, I was going to say, as the oath of Allegiance, but the comparison is nowhere, for there are too many who daily break that oath.

I left Columbus for the front Tuesday morning, and am only this far on my route. It is so very difficult to get along, as there is such an immense travel on the railroad of soldiers going to and from the army. I am waiting for the six o'clock freight with my horse; won't get away from here until morning, but hope that another night will find me far on my way toward Atlanta. Shall expect to find some letters there for me, and that Photo of Yours. I am afraid you'll forget it. I've found a place to keep all the love I get. Not afraid but that it will hold all you send.

How are you succeeding with your father? Does he mistrust yet? What did Mary say because I did not call? Can't help but think of what you told me that night in regard to her. She must have been dreaming! I guarded as strictly against creating a wrong impression through my letters to her, as I did in concealing from you my then-hopeless devotion. She hasn't answered my letter yet, I guess. Somehow, can't help but hope she won't. Don't believe it would be right to correspond so extensively now. What do you think of it? I have no love or pleasure in writing to any but You and Home.

I sometimes wish my place in the service was where I could win a name for myself, and prove myself worthy of the sweetest girl that ever sang the "Star Spangled Banner." I'm not very brave, but don't believe I could stand and see a bat-

---

[1] The members of the Allison family were strong temperance advocates, and Julia was reared in a belief in total abstinence. An address on the legal aspects of selling and drinking liquor, which her father delivered before the Temperance Society in the Bellefontaine Courthouse, August 21, 1861, was printed in the *Logan County Gazette* (August 30, 1861).

tle without pitching in. General Ransom's [2] remains passed through here today en route home for interment, with a funeral escort. He died at Rome, Georgia.

Then you think the time will fly rapidly to me and slow to you? Quite likely, as I will have so many pleasures and comforts to cheat time of its dullness. I anticipate a happy time down in Georgia, [3] such a fine country! No, in earnest, Julia, the hours will be days to me; and the days, weeks. But then, the pleasure of meeting again will repay for all deprivations, and you as mine, all my own, will be the only reward I'll ask for my four and one-half years of service.

But Julia, are we not dreaming? Let us nerve ourselves and grow strong, that we may be prepared for what may come. Have you not taken a thought that your kind Father might refuse his consent to our marriage? What then? The idea makes me sick at heart. No, I will not anticipate calamities. It's enough to endure them when they come, and you remember that "faint heart never won fair lady." I shall make your father be proud to give his blessing, or . . . I won't say what I intended to.

The Copperheads have it here today that Sherman has evacuated Atlanta, but I bet my commission it's all a Butternut falsehood. They are grouped together on the street corners, talking over the anticipated rise in gold, etc., etc. Believe I've told you all the news I have, and wrote down my very sentiments soberly, without joking, so will close. Write as often as the spirit moves you, and tell me your every thought. How sweet it is to hear you say you love me!

Believe me your ever-faithful "Lieut."; and now may the blessings of Johns rest and abide with you, now and forever. Fare thee well.

[2] General Ransom was a volunteer officer in command of a brigade of McArthur's Division of the Seventeenth Corps, under Sherman, at Big Black, Vicksburg, and Natchez. He later shared with Osterhaus the command of the right wing of Sherman's army at the start of its march through Georgia.
[3] He anticipated service in the Georgia campaign.

HEADQUARTERS, 182ND. O.V.I.
NASHVILLE, TENN.
November 9, 1864.

EVER DEAREST AND BEST OF ALL JULIAS,

Yours of the 2nd. came to me this morning, and tonight, since the crowd has left my tent and all is quiet except the Sergeant who is very anxious to know "who that white envelope was from today," I have seated myself to answer, or rather, to have a talk with my *sweetheart*.

I only had half a dozen of the ugly things taken (photos). Tell Mrs. Powell I sent them out to my numerous friends as soon as I could, but they didn't go round. Let Carrie [4] have that one, if she is really in earnest about wanting it. Yes, I ought to have a good character and a good name, but of course *I* am not the judge. If loving one's country as his life, and willing to sacrifice it for the good of that country, is Patriotism, then I am surely a patriot, for my God, my Julia, and my Country are all that calls me to live and be a soldier under my Country's banner.

I have a very fine young man from Toledo acting Q.M. Sergeant,—only on trial. Haven't made any appointment yet of either Q.M. or Commissary sergeants. So far, I like the two I have on trial, and think I will have them appointed tomorrow, perhaps.

Yes, I am sure you are the only girl I ever loved. Thought I loved one once before, but it was only a boyish affection and didn't last long—nothing like the calm and sweet abiding love now, of so much pleasure to me.

Why should I have called on Mary? Can't have any pleasure or real happiness in any one's society except yours. Tell that United States Army officer that I have a perfect right to "U.S." on my cap. If it is necessary to furnish convincing proofs, refer him to "Revised Army Regulations." As to Staff only being entitled to the wreath and "U.S.," I beg leave to differ. Doesn't he know that in the organization of a regiment there is always a "Field and Staff"? Company officers, such as Captains, First and Second Lieutenants, wear the bugle

---

[4] In 1865 Carrie McClure married Lieutenant John Price, whose father, John Price, Sr., was in the law office of Stanton and Allison in Bellefontaine.

with the number of the regiment. But enough of this! Don't you think that Claude is prejudiced for *certain reasons?* You know, he is a *regular Officer*. They, you know, have always felt themselves above those of the Volunteer Army. I'll tell you why I'm not jealous: because I trust you and know that you will be true, for you have said so. That is enough. I, for this reason, couldn't object to your going with who you see fit to deserve the pleasure of your lively and dear society. I would only say: *Amusez-vous, mais ne negligez point votre devoir.* There I have you! How do you like French?

Tell Carrie I could see very well if the hall *was* dark! I thought she was real pretty, though she must not blame me, if I place her second to Julia in that part. No one can come up to *her!* Oh! I am always making mistakes! I wasn't to say anything about your personal appearance again! Excuse me this time; suppose I must keep my opinion to myself. Very well, all right!

I have a letter from Sister in Toledo. She said she heard of my "church going" in Bellefontaine . . . "thought" brother Al and I certainly admired the name of "Julia." [5] How do you think they know so much? I have never told them yet that I was even acquainted with you, except Yourtee, and he would rather lose his head than tell any of my secrets. I shall surprise them *all* some day.

Yourtee is running on the Rail Road Express: messenger between Cincinnati and Indianapolis, I believe. Don't like the idea of his going into such business so young,[6] as he will be exposed not only to danger of accident, but to all the evils of a not over-refined set of men, roughs and scoundrels, and—as you say of railroaders, generally—men without character. I hope the same God who has watched over me through three years of danger, will also guard him from wicked influences.

It has rained here constantly for the last week, and the mud is extremely bad. The river is rising rapidly, and it is thought will overflow the banks in a short time. You have read descriptions enough of Nashville, both in private letters and papers, and I will only add that it is a *gay, dashing place.*

[5] Almon had married Julia Phillips, of Toledo.
[6] Yourtee was eighteen years old.

We may stay here all winter; can't tell. There are quite a number of Ohio regiments besides ours stationed about the city for garrison duty. I was very glad to get back to the Regiment, but found quite work enough to keep me busy for weeks to come, though, for green hands, my sergeants kept things pretty straight.

I came across a man at Jeffersonville, Indiana, by the name of O. J. Hopkins; he was Captain and A.C.S.,[7] U.S.A., stationed at Indianapolis, I think, or some town in Indiana. We tried to scrape up a relationship, but didn't succeed. Was introduced to several Hoosier girls while in Jeffersonville, but they all looked green, as Hoosier gals generally do! I stayed one night at the house of Gen. Jeff Davis, or rather, of his father. The old man is a regular Copperhead. He and I had it up and down!

The election went off quietly yesterday in the rain, and in a few days you will hear a VOICE from the Army more horrifying to Rebels than musketry. How proud it will make you of your favorites, the soldiers; won't it, Julia?

Your letters are written just as you talk; that's why I like them. Don't like letters written with so much "style." Isn't this letter long enough? If not, I will send it out by the morning mail and write another one tomorrow night. Write often, I beg of you, and cheer the long hours of camp life.

YOUR EVER TRUE JOHNS.

P.S. Direct to Nashville, and for goodness sake don't forget the Photo!

HEADQUARTERS 182ND. O.V.I., NASHVILLE
November 11, 1864.

MY OWN,

After a very busy day I had seated my weary self for rest in my tent, when the chaplain brought me a letter from you, dated the 3rd. inst. What a welcome was the dear old hand! And what a reward for a day's hard labor! Labor, I say, but some wouldn't call it that. I have been in the saddle ever since eight o'clock this morning, going from Camp to City and

[7] Acting Commissary of Subsistence. His full name was Orlando J. Hopkins.

from Office to Office. The red tape course of doing business is enough to try the patience of one more amply endowed with that article than this Quarter Master. I am very near through issuing Clothing, Camp and Garrison Equipage, and you may be sure I am not sorry. My requisitions have to go through five or six different offices, all situated in separate and remote parts of the city, and in a place like Nashville, it requires *riding* to make the rounds.

The Regiment is encamped about two miles south-east of the city, but I, as yet, have had no leisure to look at scenery, much less to sketch it. What is more, I have given up sketching, as an occupation fit only for school boys and girls, or some worthless *loafing* man. And what is more against me, I have no talent,—and therefore make no professions.

So you haven't talked with your father yet? When I used to read novels (I have quit it now.), I read one which suits our case exactly, and when you say you fear "he will dash all our hopes to the ground," it made me remember my novel. "Never will marry without his will. Know you wouldn't want me to."—How curious you write sometimes! I hardly know how to take you. In fact, I don't believe I should try to *take you* at all, without I had full right to; so rest easy on that score. I am not one to rush matters to such extremes, and without the full blessings of parents, I could not hope to make you my wife. How sad even to ruminate upon! Though it would still be a source of consolation to know that I had ever been loved by Julia Allison, and yet how sad to be without you! To be deprived of your cheering society, and even lose the pleasure your letters give me. Do you know what I should do? I would enter the *regular army* for life. My Country owes me a commission in that, and I might pass away the weary years, better separated from the hollow mocking ceremonies of Home society, and what woman's smile is equal to . . . (Excuse me, Julia, I had forgotten!). Why, I almost hate every woman but you because they fall so far short of my . . . estimate of a perfect woman. Pshaw! Julia, we are foolish, childish, to look at the dark side of affairs. "While there is life, there is hope" is my maxim, and I have succeeded *so far* in all my undertakings in life, and so long as my "lucky

star" continues to shine . . . . No, that is sacrilege. It can be
no other than a just and merciful Providence that brought
me safely through so many battles, gave me my life, allowed
me to live while the heart's blood of dear comrades flowed
freely at my right and left—to live to see the hour when Julia
promised to be mine. Yes, He gave you to me, and what man
dares to forbid us to *love,* even if he *has* the power to separate
us in the sight of the world? I love you as I could never love
another, and even if your fears were well founded and an explosion should take place, I promise you *now,* not by word of
mouth, but by what is more binding: my own signature, *never
to marry other than Julia Allison.*

The remark concerning coquetry which I made in a former
letter, had entirely slipped my memory, and I hardly know
what to say. What should I do, if you proved one to me?
Why, you remember what I told you with regard to disposition, temper, etc., etc., and that I said that I would never get
angry at you? I fear I should have to back down on that,
though there is only one way in which the mighty change could
be brought about, and that by your *Proving false* to your
promise and vows when last we met.

I am no sentimentalist or one to magnify dangers and admire things by moonlight only. I love too well the broad and
noble light of day, when things are seen in their proper light.
And am somewhat of a moralizer and believe that God or-
dained everything for the best, or to work harmoniously for
some future good, and that it is the duty of man to abide without a murmure to his decrees. Let us hope that our affairs
are working that way, and that all will end well.

My prospects in life are as promising as I could wish, almost, and by proper management will be able to enter business with my Brother in Toledo,[8] who promises to take me in
as a pardner in a very remunerative branch of Commerce. I
tell you these things, Julia, believing that you have a right
to know the prospects of the man you have chosen as "the
only one in a thousand." My friends, though making no pre-

---

[8] Almon was a member of the firm of Hopkins and Griffith, grain and produce commission merchants, in Toledo. After the close of the war, he employed
his brother in the office for a while, but did not make him a partner as he had
promised.

tensions to wealth, are by no means below the standard in what is called "riches," though, for many reasons, my family has ever been reserved,—so much so that few know today their true circumstances. Trust me, Julia, though some think me not wealthy, and you shall *Never* repent the hour you gave your Heart and Hand to him who values the gift beyond his life. He would suffer anything rather than cause you one moment of pain.

The Soldier boy that will ever be true to Julia, your own devoted

JOHNS.

P.S.—I wrote to you last night. Your Photo wasn't in the letter; did you really send it? The envelope had the appearance of being broken open, and was sealed again with sealing wax. What does it mean? Love to Julia and Comps. to Carrie. Will write a long letter soon. We are going to remain here some time. Dispense with form and customs and write often.—R.Q.M.

HEADQUARTERS 182ND OHIO,
NASHVILLE, TENN. November 13, 1864.
MY LIFE, MY ALL,

Yours with the Photograph came yesterday, and as this is Sunday I will lay aside business and "devote the hours to thee." I kissed the Photo until I fear I have spoiled it; don't think I will burn it this time.

As you can't bear flattery—not flattery, but to hear the truth!—I shall not tell you my opinion of it. So you are deceitful? Well, as long as you are not so with me, I shall not find fault, but my own sweetest, if you should prove to be a double actor (actress, I mean) toward me, I . . . I beg your pardon, Julia, for the injustice the very thought does you. I trust you too implicitly for that. Am perfectly well satisfied that Claude's is not a brotherly friendship, but that he actually loves you, perhaps as much as *I* do, and your accomplishments have impressed *him* as deeply as they have me. Are you confident that you *have* a sufficient "shield" against falling in love with him, as you say? I hope so, at least.

Do you ever show my letters to Carrie, or any one else?

You must not show them to any one; not that I believe you *do,* for I know you have more judgement than that. No one has a right to see them but my own, my dearest, my truest and best Julia of all Julias. You must not work too hard. It makes your hands rough. I hate to see a Lady's hands so. *My* wife won't have to work. Hate to see a man's wife in the kitchen, except on business with the Kitchen girl.

Tell me why you are not happy, Julia. Don't forget it. I want to know why, so I can help you if possible. You said in a former letter you didn't think, or rather, you had a *presentiment* that I would never be yours. I don't believe in such stuff; so much like an old maid's talk! We never know beforehand what may happen tomorrow, of course, and to be forewarned of any approaching good or evil is all "moonshine." That's my public opinion, privately expressed.

I should so like to see you today, looking as well as you did another Sunday I know of. Hope your cold is better. You must take better care of yourself, or I will scold you. Might as well begin now as hereafter, hadn't I? Next to your last letter had been opened, and sealed up again with sealing wax. Did you do it?

Wouldn't you rather I would accept the position of Captain of a company? That would place me in the way of military preferment and promotion. Would be sure to rise, for I am well versed in the tactics, and in a new regiment like this, the chances are good for one with experience. I shall leave you to decide.

Tell Claude I don't wear the wreath and "U.S." *now.* Have a hat with a bugle and "182" on it. Sometimes wear the cap and wreath yet. Used to wear the "U.S." through ignorance; haven't been in the service long enough to know who is entitled to "U.S." He must make some allowance for raw *recruits.* Volunteers, especially! *They* are always green.

Old Company K of the 42nd. must be on their way home by this time. When they come, give them a hearty welcome. I love them all as brothers,—*all,* I said. No, not *all!* I hate one man in that company: not the man you think it is, though. I'm perfectly indifferent to E—— A——, for he is not worthy of notice . . . . Captain Hutchins is an especial friend of mine, and if my character is ever assailed by A——'s malignity,

I would refer you to the Captain, or any of the Boys, for the truth. Still, aside from all these, I have an enemy, though not a willing enemy on his part, there. I hate him and always shall, and if he again crosses my path, or in any way interferes with me and mine, he or I will suffer. I am, as I have said, Julia, slow to anger, but lasting in hate. It's my nature in spite of myself, and God will not hold me responsible. This is one of my faults, and I hope the greatest one. I am not deceitful, either. Will soon give a man to understand if I dislike him by my very manner and bearing toward him. You will become acquainted with me in course of time, my Dearest. But you have my greatest faults before you; all the minor ones, perhaps your influence will reform.

My greatest press of business is over, thanks to the aid of my very energetic Sergeant and the assistance of a good clerk, and I began to breathe more freely. I was obliged to order my Commissary Sergeant to his Company and to take another one on trial. He seems to understand his business better. I have had very poor health since being with the regiment; barely able to perform my official duties; sometimes in the saddle when I should be in quarters under care of the Surgeon.[9] But my affairs are such that I can't trust them in the hands of these *new men,* and consequently I have had my hands full. Capt. J. Burke just came in and says: "Our Q.M. is writing to his dearly beloved." That's so, but I am trying to make him believe it is to my sister, because I have selected this large sheet. I told the Adjutant I was making out a requisition for *Stationery.* He said he was well aware of it, but it would be some time before it came, and *then* it wouldn't be *blanks* from the looks of the letter I got last night. What is it to him if I don't draw "blanks"?

This is a beautiful day, so warm and nice. More like June than November, but tonight it will be as cold as ever. I don't care, though: have a good stove in Quarters. I ought to have called on Mary, but neglected it. Hardly know why. Wasn't because I had anything against her. I think as much of Mary

[9] He had received a hernia while assisting in moving a heavy piece of ordnance at the siege of Vicksburg. His regimental Surgeon offered him a discharge at the time, but he begged to remain in service. The Surgeon supplied him with a truss, and promised to say nothing about it. Sergeant Hopkins kept his injury a secret from everyone.

as ever. Think she is a real pretty and a very good Girl. No, she hasn't answered my letter yet, nor have I written to her. When you write, tell me all the news as usual, and write a short letter like *this*. I hadn't time to write more, so have to send you these few lines. Give my highest comps. to Carrie: I like the name; it's real pretty. Also, regards to Effie.

As ever, Yours to love or deceive,
JOHNS.

The references to Claude in this and other letters betray Lieutenant Hopkins' concern lest he be a serious rival for Julia Allison's affections. It is a natural concern that plagues every soldier at the front who has left a sweetheart behind. Whether Lieutenant Hopkins was justified or not, whether Julia Allison did have the "sufficient shield," may be surmised from the following letter from Claude to her, dated from Chattanooga ten days later than the above note. The letter also illustrates the problem of drinking for the civilian who has recently become a soldier, a subject on which Lieutenant Hopkins has so much to say.

LOOKOUT MOUNTAIN,
November 23rd, 1864.

DEAR FRIEND,

It affords me great pleasure to write those two words, for *true* friends are not found every day, and I believe you are one of the very few friends I have; there are many who profess to be true, but I believe them not, for I know that when they are tested, they are found wanting.

You I trust, and place confidence in you, knowing it will not be betrayed. You will find me a *strange* man, and I beg you to bear with me in my inconsistencies. My letters will be written according to the *mood* I am in at the time. But you will know the *heart* is right. If anything is written you do not like, do not take offense, but tell me of it, that I may make amends for the transgression.

I have turned a new leaf in the chapter of my life, and I want your help; will you help me?

I have never lived with any object in view, but have taken the world as it came, being content to make the best of it for the time being. Lately, I have seen the errors of my life, and henceforth I will live with a view of making myself worthy of the respect, if not the love, of those few who are dear to me. I am indebted to you for this change. You have not hesitated to point out to me my faults, and told me that you were pained to see them. You will not have cause to say the same again. The first step has been taken, and my army friends are surprised. I hope those that are at home now and those that are going away, may all come back with the same hatred for the intoxicating bowl that I have. It is the curse of the Army, and I will steer clear of it in future. Never again shall the demon have a hold on me.

Do you believe me? Oh! do not doubt me, for I could not bear it; do not deny me your confidence. Have faith, and when I return, none will be ashamed to know me.

I must ask pardon for not writing on Sunday. I was delayed in Chattanooga from Friday morning until Sunday morning, and when I got into camp, I was too sick to do anything, having taken a severe cold. I tried to write, but had to give it up. It was a tiresome and lonely trip, and I am thankful to be in camp once more. Today is very cold; the rain ceased yesterday and turned into snow and ice. It became so cold last night as to deprive us of sleep. In a few days, my quarters will be done, and then I will be comfortable. At present, I am occupying the tent of an absent officer; it is a very dark one, almost impossible to write in daylight. You must excuse me, for I cannot see what I write. The Regiment is out on picket, and Bigham and I are alone, and enjoy ourselves well. B—— is pleased to hear of my new resolutions and says some one North is to blame for the change, and hopes I will "stick to it." He will not tempt me. It will require a strong will to keep clear of all. I *will* do it. I have seen enough since I left home to stop any man who will look the evil in the face.

I expect an early answer. Give my comp's to Effie (cannot give love); did she get the Photo? I did as you wished.

Believe me,
Yours Truly,
—CLAUDE.

Direct: Regular Brigade, Lookout Mountain, Chattanooga, Tenn.

HEADQUARTERS, 182ND. O.V.I.
NASHVILLE, TENN. November 15, 1864.
DEARER THAN ALL,

Another busy day and another *reward* in the way of a good, long, interesting letter from my own Guide Star. How kind you are, Julia, to write such letters to me! It seems as though you were *gifted* for that. I mean letter-writing.

I came up from the City tonight tired and angry, if not hungry, but when the Chaplain handed me your letter with the *old familiar* handwriting, I was better immediately, and everything like fatigue was gone in a second. The Adjutant wished to know who I was "transacting business with in Bellefontaine"; began to suspect that "our Q.M. had something more on his mind than hardtack and rations" by the way I always seemed so eager to open those small white letters written by the "peculiar hand." (They think you write so strange!) The Colonel said he couldn't tell why he didn't get any letters from home, when I got letters every mail. I told him my letters were of an official character, relating to business *only*. He said he "knew it, of course."

We rejoice with the loyal citizens of the North that our country is not to grovel at the feet of Jeff Davis, but is going to fight out her own battles and suppress the rebellion, crush treason and Rebels, North and South, and restore the supremacy of our government, and be a nation free,—or a country lost. Yes, "give us Liberty or death!"

"Tired of you"—what do you mean? I wish I could see you tonight, be where I could gaze at you forever. It's too late to promise: I've already shown your Photo to several of my *intimates*. All call it *splendid*. One young Captain was going to bet he had the prettiest sweetheart of any officer in the regiment. I told him I'd bet my commission against his old boots that he hadn't. Adjutant said he would bet so, too, because he had seen the Quarter Master's *Intended's* photo. Then they all wanted to see it, but I am too selfish to let anyone look even at my Julia's Photograph. I look at it every night before retiring, and would kiss the dear treasure as often, if I wasn't afraid of spoiling it. When the Chaplain handed me the letter containing the picture, he wouldn't leave my quarters until he had seen what was in it, and I won't tell you what he said—you hate flattery so!

A new Adjutant has been appointed for the Regiment. The old one will probably be dismissed the service; was left behind at Louisville, Ky., and never came to us again.

Yes, I have been sick, but am much better now. Am prospering finely, except for a small accident. My horse took fright a few days ago and jumped against a carriage in the street. My foot caught in the spokes and twisted out of place nearly, and has pained me a great deal since, but is getting better. One of the Ladies—two Ladies and a Gent were in the carriage—screamed so nicely, it almost repaid me for the pain I suffered, to hear her. Do you ever make so much fuss, Julia, when accidents happen?

Tell Effie I was harder to entertain *that night* for the reason I had so much to think of, and was really low spirited for a *certain reason*. Will talk more next time, if I don't . . . if nothing happens! I have also felt rather in a melancholy mood every time I have been with *you,* for "vast reasons not now to be made public." I hope, Julia, I shall be happy some day, which is something I have not experienced for several years. The nearest to that state I have been, is in the last month, or since I have learned that Julia loves me. That ought to make me happy indeed, but . . . no, I will never tell anyone.

I am talkative enough when I feel at home, like I do here. Was perfectly at a loss when I was at *Home*. All wanted to know of Mother why Johns was so still since coming home; thought I must have had something on my mind, as I could only talk about the Army and the War. If I answered all of Effie's questions, it was something strange; but, in fact, I thought she was equally backward. Everytime I looked at her, she dropped her eyes and blushed (Don't tell her!); suppose 'twas all on Pat's account.

I would so like to have the Stars and Stripes floating over every town and city, Fort and Harbor, of the land. I wish everyone was as loyal as my own dear Brevet-Lieutenant. Do you wear the badge? If they *were,* the War would have been over before it commenced. To be Loyal is to be loved, so I think. What would I think if my sweetheart—the "Girl I left behind me"—would forget her soger boy and fall dead in love with some man who had never fought for our nation's emblem, the Starry Banner?

"Give Johns my never dying love"—do you think it is *never dying?* Remember life is long sometimes, and who is not subject to change? I have averaged one letter every other day to you since being in Nashville. Always can find time to write to my "little wife" and read and re-read her dear letters, so write whenever you possibly can, and cheer the life of your Johns with those mirthful, lively letters, and I shall be ever grateful and love you the more.

I want to ask a favor of you. Please promise me. Don't let on to care a straw for me to anybody in Bellefontaine. Don't ever mention my name, except when compelled to. It's a strange request, you think, but I have many reasons for it. Please, for my sake, promise me. I assure you, if you do so, *all will be well.* Keep the truth from your parents as long as you can, until I come back from the wars, and I assure you your father will be proud to accept me as his son.

Ain't I a nice little "Pet"—so very little and delicate! A *regular, nice, young man!* Few know it yet. How is Carrie? How is Effie? How is Mary? If you have any love left from that which I send you, divide it between the three, and all the Compliments you hate so, give to them,—especially to Carrie. Can't you tell me who is her Intended? My "Family" has all retired, and I must, too.

Fare thee well, but not forever.

—Q.M.

[Marginal notes] We expect to remain in Nashville all winter. I will try to go home, if we do, about New Year's, so "meet me at the gate." The more I see of the officers of the Regiment, the more I like them; with one or two excepts, they are Gents. One is a Dutchman and doesn't know much; that is all the trouble. Days are getting cold. Col. Butler, Lieut. Col. Chase, and myself mess together. We have jolly times, and set a good table. Can't you and several others come over and take tea with us tomorrow evening? We need only our wives to make our circle complete. Bring your knitting along. —JOHNS.

NASHVILLE, TENN.
November 19, 1864.

DEAR "WIFE,"
   I got yours of the 12th. tonight, and answer immediately, if not sooner. Don't see why you don't get my letters. I write nearly every other day. At least, I answer all your dear, good letters, no difference who says I shan't, or what I am doing. I drop all and answer. Am slightly acquainted with Frank,[10] having served with him; he was a corporal when I was a private. Was it him who told you some of my bad tricks and habits? Wish you wouldn't make any inquiries about me; fear you will find me out,—all my characteristics. Then you won't think so much of your Johns.
   It's the first time I ever knew that "selfishness" was one of my faults. Perhaps it is; I'm not the judge. I am sure of one thing: shall never be selfish with my Julia dear, more than to want her all to myself,—and death to the man who would step between me and her I worship and think of night and day! I believe I am becoming *jealous* of some one; don't know who. There are so many young men at home, and few but are better looking and, I fear, more worthy of Julia Allison, but it would be hard to think of giving you up. Many of them are more free from faults, but I am bound to reform for your sake, and believe I am thriving in my resolve to do better.
   Today, I was out riding in the rain nearly all day, and in the evening called at the Post Q. M. Office. I was perfectly drenched, and Capt. Mills invited me to take a *social glass* with him, but the sweet face of my little "wife" was looking at me earnestly, and I thought of my promise, begged to be excused, thanked them, etc., and came away. It almost insults me now for anyone to ask me to drink—so ruffianly and vulgar. And even the very men who should be the embodiment of a gentleman, the soul of honor (soldiers and especially army

[10] Corporal Franklin S. Kauffman, of Company D (1861–62).

officers) are more intemperate and ruffianly than all the rest
in their habits. True, they are not all so, but I fear that tip-
pling is too much of a habit with my fellow soldiers. I intend
to be a model Lieutenant and one of the "best Q.M's. in the
service," as my Brother in Toledo told me when I left home,
and I shall follow his advice.

Am real sorry you hurt your hand; it hurts me almost as
much to hear of you suffering pain. Do you think the ring had
anything to do with bringing on the accident in question? If
so, you should tell me. I want to know if it is so. Are you still
strong in the faith that I will never be more than a lover to
you? If I thought so . . . I wish Claude would go back to
the regiment! What's he staying there for? Better be at the
front!

How it rains! Been raining ever since morning; have been
to the City twice. Mud was very bad. I was splashed all over.
Wish you could have seen me tonight when I came in. Even my
hat was covered with mud. Nashville for mud, mud, mud, any
day! Our camp is nearly three miles from the City, on the
Hyde Ferry Pike. Regiment is engaged in constructing a large
fort: the duty of Hundred-day men! And they eat all the rations I can get for them. Col. Butler is a splendid man, as well
as officer. Talks all the time and keeps everyone cheerful,—
just what I like.

A letter from Sister says to give Julia her love, and she
expects "a sister's love," from what she can *hear*. I was so
surprised when I read *that,* that I couldn't speak for a while.
All the time, I thought our acquaintance even was a secret
with those at home, for I never mentioned it to any one but
Yourtee, and am sure *he never told.* They all knew I wasn't
going to Bellefontaine "for nothing," and were anxious to
find out my business, and sure enough, they have begun to mistrust. Can you imagine how? I can't. When I was going down-
street one day in Toledo, my Coz stood at the front door
and said: "Bye, bye; give that Bellefontaine girl my bestest
love!" I pretended to be much surprised, but couldn't deceive
her, etc.

I do wish I could see you tonight. Wonder what you are
doing just now? Teasing some one, I bet! We are going to

have *Oysters* tonight, about 8 o'clock, and it's nearly that time now. Yes, Adjutant says they are ready. Can you wait 'til I'm done?

(An hour and a half later.) There! All's right! Oysters, canned peaches, pickles, coffee, cheese, hardtack, and various other good things composed our bill of fare, and I believe the Adjutant has eaten twice as much as I did, I know, and so did the Colonel and the Major. They are all awful eaters. I have a very energetic Sergeant who is a great help to me. Also, the Commissary Sergeant is doing finely. I turned off several teamsters today; they think I am rather hard to please. Don't know but I am; don't know that I am. You may find out some day.

I am sure I'm getting real jealous. Hate to hear you compliment any one. You mustn't look at handsome men; they are dangerous. Sometimes I am glad I'm not handsome, for certain reasons, though I know *looks* goes a great ways with some. Some prefer riches, others want power, tho' the two are the same; while the mass are governed by appearances (outward) and pay more attention to show and dress than they do to their own *morals*. I despise a fop, or anything foppish. How shallow-brained and worthless! If your feminine friends, Julia, would marry, advise them to take a good, honest soldier, one who has smelled gunpowder, if they would escape an insurmountable *evil*.

Give my everlasting devotion to Julia, my never dying love to Carrie, my sweetest smiles to Effie, my Comps. to Mary; and again, all the love of my heart, all the good wishes imaginable, I send to Her who rules my every action, my every expression, my aims in life: the dearest, sweetest, of Carries, Julias, Effies, or Marys, mine now and mine when the cruel war is over.

Yours "Respectfully,"
JOHNS.

P.S.—Capt. Burke says: "Tell her I'm well, with lots of love." I write very often; sorry you don't get my letters; some of them are so interesting. Write often, my Star, and be true to—JOHNS.

CAMP BUTLER, NASHVILLE.
November 20, 1864.

MY EVER DEAREST JULIA,

Where is she tonight, at this very hour? At church, listening to the divine words of the Gospel, while I am talking to her through the pen? Is she thinking of me? While my every thought, my whole soul is devoted to her?

I am writing in my own tent, all alone like a bachelor. A big fire in the stove, my overcoat hung up at one end of the tent, my trunk nearby, several articles of clothing hanging here and there, my "penny pipe" and smoking tobacco close at hand, a good lot of dry wood in the box to make a fire when this burns down, a cot, a writing desk with your *handsome Johns* busy scratching off something to somebody, would meet your eye, could you look in on me tonight. No noisy "Commish" disturbs me, though there is no telling when that mischievous Capt. Burke, or tormenting Lieutenant W——, or Major West, will come in to disturb my very pleasant occupation: writing letters to those I love. It seems so much like talking to them, and I seem to be near my little "Wife" when I sit down to write to her.

Thought sure I would get a letter from you today, but was disappointed; will begin to scold you again, if you don't write oftener. What would you think to see me step in some day, and find you washing dishes, cooking, or some other outlandish work? I'd open the door next time without waiting for you to change dresses. I'll never forget how you looked the last time I was there, when you came down from Mr. Stanton's,[11] and what followed when you came in the room. It was the first . . . *real proof,* I was going to say . . . time I could realize that I was loved by Julia Allison. How truly noble you looked! I loved you again more sincerely than ever. I could worship you for loving the old flag as you do, and for your ever ready defense of our government, when Copperheads and traitors assail it. I believe that was one half of my reasons for loving you in the first place. Your letters were always so full of indignation against Cops. and Rebels. I sometimes read of

[11] Julia Allison's stepmother was the daughter of the Hon. Benjamin Stanton, member of Congress in 1861.

our boys down at the front, enduring the hardships of active campaign fighting the Johnnies, and I wish I had gone as a private, instead of R.Q.M. I could have done my country more good, but again, when I think of the trials of a common soldier's life, am certain I could never undergo one year of it. Hope my Julia will think none the less of me for going this time as a non-combatant. Whenever my services are needed in the front rank, I will go there; or if in the rear, far from the "smoke and din" of battle, I will go *there:* anywhere to serve my country and my Julia.

I have sent a large photo of myself home; when you call at Mrs. H——'s, you will see it, if it ever gets there.

I tell you, we had a good dinner today! I made all of them take off their hats, as it was Sunday. Col. Butler always eats with his hat on, but I made him and Major West both take them off today at dinner. Some of our Company Officers put on more style than Colonels Butler or Chase, especially some second Lieutenants I know of. I hate so much style, but suppose it is according to orders from General Sherman for all officers stationed at Posts or Garrisons to wear full uniform at all times. Some of the 182nd. officers go down town and spread around through town with all the pomp of a Brigadier. I see them crossing the streets and I try to splash them with mud by trotting my horse as near to them as possible. I do it just for mischief, because they are so green and try to pass off for *veterans* and *old soldiers,* when they belong to nothing but a one year's regiment. Wish you could see the airs we 182nd. officers put on, especially Johns Hopkins: see him running races with his big gray horse through the streets with Major West; see the Provost Guard present arms to us! They think we are General Thomas! *Vice versa,* see me with my old slouched "Burnside" on crossways, my pants stuffed in my boots, splashed with mud up to the ears, riding at breakneck speed—and you form some idea of your Soldier boy in "active service"! I always ride fast; have two horses, bay and gray, and ride one while the other rests. The Colonel told me last night I would soon have *no* horses, riding the way I did, but I can't help it. Can't bear to ride slow; haven't the patience.

Have you found out any more of my bad tricks since you

saw Frank? Doesn't it change your notion of my good name when you hear of my faults? By the way, Frank never was a favorite in Co. K; always had the name of a "play-off" or shirk. Some thought that's the way he got out of the service. I certainly admire Effie's judgement, if she calls me handsome. I am of a different opinion, and have a glass to decide in my favor. Was invited to drink three or four times today, but how could I? No, my Sweetest, I will stick to any promise I ever made you. Do you get my letters? I write almost every other day. Please do the same; tell me all the news. Write long letters. My tender regards to Carrie, Effie, and Mary— and the love of a true man to Julia,

—O. J. HOPKINS.

P.S.—Write on a big sheet and write it full and crossways.

NASHVILLE, TENN.
November 23, 1864.

DEAR "WIFE" AND SWEETHEART,

I received two letters from you last night: two good, long, soul-inspiring letters. And tonight will begin the answer to both. It has been snowing all day; ground frozen hard. I made two trips to the city, and believe I have frozen two of my fingers. It was bitter cold. How I pity you poor Northerners!

Had you put off our marriage 13 months?[12] I can't wait that long; no, indeed! You must be the wife of a soldier; and that, too, the 182nd.'s R.Q.M.'s wife! Won't you be up in the world to be a soldier's wife! Splendiferous! To be in dead earnest, my Julia, are we not too light-hearted, too thoughtless about the matter? Only consider: *your father's consent is yet to be gained,* and if he should say *no,* where would be all our light dreams, our plans for the future? Blown to the four winds, exploded as air bubbles; in short, putting an end to the whole affair, for I believe you said: "I never can marry without my father's consent." Let us think of these things, dearest, and form our hearts for whatever change may come. I suppose your father would forbid you to correspond with me. Suppose I was never to see you more? Would you still

---

[12] Until the end of his term of re-enlistment.

love me quietly all to yourself? Would you, in your solitary
moments, pray for the Johns of your heart, still hoping for his
welfare? Or would you, Julia, try to wean your heart from
memory and forget that he loves you now and always?

Poor Carrie! I hope she has heard good news from the
Lieutenant [13] by this time. Can't she spare a little love,—just
a little? She is like me: wants all the love for the one it belongs
to. You shall have all mine, all I can spare from my old
Mother, my Country's flag, and the Right. Always thought I
was proof against jealousy until I learned to worship Julia
Allison. Then, I hated to think of . . . of probabilities.

I have just issued 674 blankets to the regiment tonight,
and as soon as the crowd dispersed from in front of my Quarters, I commenced this letter. The boys will sleep warmer tonight. Poor fellows, I pity them! Out in their shelter tents
such a night! My Quarters are so warm and comfortable. I'm
ashamed to have a private come in on any business; so different
from his cold, comfortless "dog-tent"! I feel for them, because I once was a private and know the hardships they endure. I ought to be one now, where I could be of more service
to the government.

I commenced this letter on a smaller sheet, but come to
turn it over, a piece was torn out of the corner. I was real
provoked after writing one whole page. My Sergeant was in,
and took a good laugh over the mistake. Col. Butler is a
married man; also, Lieut. Col. Chase. Col. Chase was married after leaving home; has a fine looking wife. They are
going to send for their wives this winter to come down on a
visit. "Guess I'll send for mine!" Major West is a very
commonplace man, with no military style or airs, and is a
good-hearted fellow (married). Adjutant Leedom is about
thirty-five; characteristics the same (married). Lieutenant
H—— and the rest of the staff officers are single, I believe.
"A.C.S." means Acting Commissary of Subsistence: generally
a captain of volunteers.

It's most too late to finish this tonight, so I wish you a
happy goodnight, with many sweet kisses. Fare thee well,
—JOHNS.

[13] Lieutenant John Price, whom she later married.

(Wednesday, Nov. 24th.)—This was a beautiful day, but cold. I was up to the city; the ground is hard enough to bear a horse, and some places, as smooth as ice. I sent the Sergeant out five and a half miles with the teams today after wood. He just got back; is tired and hungry, of course. He is an only son of a widow. His mother lives in Norwalk, Ohio. He is a very good, steady boy. His sister died the day the Regiment left Toledo. He was recommended for the position of Q.M., but being a non-veteran, the Adjutant-General refused to commission him, though I guess he would have succeeded, had I not applied when I did. Samuel Morse is the name. So far, he has been faithful to me, and so long as he discharges his duties faithfully, shall have my every good wish and aid for his advancement.

I formed a very favorable opinion of Mrs. Powell; can't believe there is anything wrong, but of course don't know on such short acquaintance. She seemed to be very sociable.

The Colonel, Lieut-Colonel, and Major are Field officers; the Surgeon, his Assistants, and the Adjutant and Quarter-Master are the Staff. The Sergeant-Major, Hospital Steward, Quarter-Master and Commissary Sergeants, and the Chief Musician, are the non-commissioned staff. Captains of Companies are officers of the Line; the Lieutenants, the subordinates; Sergeants, non-commissioned officers, privates, etc.

You must give me some credit. I refuse to *drink* every day, and am training my hair to stay back: trying to do everything you told me. All for the sake of her I love dearer than life. I have been introduced to several ladies here. Am acquainted with two wholesale merchants here: the Heidelbach Brothers, from Toledo. Often go down there; was there to tea twice. Several ladies, nearly all from Ohio, were present. I looked at them all, but how far short they came from what my Julia is, how different in every respect! You will never have cause to be jealous, if you are *black eyed!*

Your eyes, they were the first to turn my brain. I once hated women kind; yes, hated them all, was a real woman-hater—until I saw Julia Allison at school. Do you remember meeting me on the street one day, about three or over three years ago, and presenting a bouquet? That was the first time I ever made any allowance for women. I can date my love for you from that date.[14] Every day has it grown stronger. I often made up my mind to confess all by letter, but changed my mind for want of courage. That night—the 20th. October—I was resolved to tell you that you were worshipped by me, but was sure you would hate me for it. At the door, I mustered courage and told you all, waited for my sentence while you remained silent so long. You spoke at last, and there was happiness in every word. Do you remember what was said, and what followed? I do, and ever shall, my dearest, my *all*.

I wish you would speak to your father about it, and find out how his verdict will side. I don't care how soon my friends know how matters stand; as you say, they may as well know it now as after a while. I shall leave it to you to name *the day,* after the consent of all parties is gained: leave it to your own option whether you will be a *soldier's wife,* or wait until the cruel war is over. I sometimes think it wrong for a soldier to marry, for his life is not his own and safe for one hour, and there are so many widows now in the country. Still, it seems to me that thirteen months will be a long time to wait.

I have splendid property in Toledo, or at least enough there to make us a comfortable, happy home. Mother is going to Iowa to live with my two sisters there. My oldest brother offers me a splendid chance in his firm as Pardner, so you see I am not without some plans for the future. God, I hope, will punish me if I ever take you from your good home to want for the least thing. I will never marry until I see my way through, which I hope to soon, very soon. Then for a long life with my black-eyed Julia.

I shall vanquish the green-eyed monster yet; in fact, have already, for I believe you do love me truly now, for I have the proof, and God bless you for it, my Life, my All. I am bound to be good, too, for your sake: be ever worthy of your trust and confidence, and win for you and me a name far above reproach. How glad to hear you say you're satisfied with your heart and hand in my keeping! Don't call me noble yet. I may

[14] The date seems to coincide with his departure from Bellefontaine in late September, 1861, for Camp Chase.

be some day, but am far from being good or noble now. I suppose you have found out more of my faults by this time. Just tell me what they are, and I will suppress them. I am doing my best to keep my *hair* back, if that will do you any good, but don't succeed very favorably. It's slow work.

Your photo is far from being spoiled; I take too much care of it. Does mine talk any? I hope it's more company than I am. Don't forget to find out your father's views, and report to these Head Quarters. Can't you mention the subject to him? If I was acquainted with him, I would write a letter to satisfy my own curiosity. Let us hope for the future and strengthen ourselves for future events. Accept my love as I gave it to you that evening. My love to Carrie, Effie, and Mary, and worse than that to my own true "Wife,"

—Your Johns.

Head Quarters, 182nd. O.V.I.
Nashville, Tenn.
November 24, 1864.

My own true "Wife,"

How shall I answer your letter which I received tonight? It was dated the 18th. I have been *very,* very sad since. How could I be so thoughtless, so wicked, as to write, to even breathe, one word that would cause you one mite of pain or unhappiness? And yet I *have,* though carelessly. No, dear, I have never doubted that you were true since I looked into your dear, eloquent, soul-stirring eyes, and you breathed the words: "I will be true to you, Johns." *There* was proof enough for me. I have never doubted since. No, not a jealous thought has even entered this heart of mine, nor would the combined evidence of half the world make me believe for a moment that One so good, so loyal, so good a friend and earnest adherent to the old Flag, One so ready to defend the rights of her country's soldiers, could for an instant trifle with the theme of *love,* or a soldier's heart. No, not if you should go with the best and noblest young man in the U.S., and every other person I met would tell me Julia Allison was false to me! I wouldn't be jealous, for I am sure, very sure, you *are true;* and may God ever bless you for it! Now, my sweet one, what do you think about *releasing me?* You should be glad that I do not reproach you for the same sin. But I do not believe but that you love your devoted Johns too well for such a thing. It is well that I trust you now, or I would be unhappy again.

You must not get angry at what is in my letters. I mean no harm to the feelings of my Life, my own dear Julia, sweeter than all the world beside. You can't interpret my letter? Well, I do write strangely sometimes. But I had sufficient cause to make the request I did. I now countermand the request, as a certain change has come over the face of my affairs, and all danger has passed. Yes, indeed, Julia, I had a secret [15] that but few should know, though not a breath of criminality was in it, nothing to mar my reputation, or detract an item of your love for me. Far from it! One of your generous disposition would have loved me better. The danger is passing away, and I begin to grow happy again. You may now tell your friends, your associates—tell the *world*—that you love Johns Hopkins, and defy them to separate us. Speak freely to your father. Tell him you can never love other than Johns. If you know of any good traits in my character, "plead my cause" earnestly, eloquently, and if he loves his daughter as an affectionate father should, you will be successful. I will plead my own cause when I see him; would write now, if I were acquainted.

Yes, Julia, there is a *something*. Am sorry I mentioned it. I am always doing wrong. Please forgive my thoughtlessness. Don't be uneasy or unhappy on account of it. It is *nothing,* I repeat, to make you love me the less; besides, it is almost past.

How I would like to see you tonight, to kiss away that hectic flush! You alarm me, Julia, when you write of anything being the matter with you. Oh, God, spare me my Julia! I won't believe He will take you from me, though I had a brother once, our little Frank; [16] we all loved and idolized him, and God, to punish us for it, took our dear brother from us.

I hope your cold is better; five days,—that is long enough for

[15] His "secret" was probably the hernia received at Vicksburg, which had become aggravated by his constant activity on horseback. He no doubt feared that his injury might cause his discharge if it became known. See page 199 n.

[16] Frank was the youngest in the family. His death, at the age of fourteen, was caused by the explosion of the boiler on a Mississippi river boat.

quite a change. Yes, I hope you are better. When I read: "However, I never will see you again.", imagine my thoughts. If your love equals mine, what would be your feelings, should I say in this letter that we had met for the last time, that I would die on the morrow? But this is too unpleasant a subject for two such youngsters as you and I! Let's drop it! I was joking only when I said I was jealous, or believed I was. When you become better acquainted with me, you will find that jealousy is the least of my composition. "Rid myself of you": banish the thought! Julia, you wrong me *there*. Please take that back for my sake.

We have no Chaplain now. The one that was acting couldn't get mustered, and so went home. I told you last night about the Colonel and Lieut. Colonel. I shall try to go home this winter as soon as I get my affairs under "headway," so that I can leave them in the hands of Sergeant. Must drill him first. I have a clerk nearly all the time, besides the Sergeant, but haven't half the business on my hands I had about two weeks ago.

Yes, you do write good, and just peculiar enough to be interesting. Col. Butler likes your writing, though he has only seen it on the envelope.

"Better come home, if you want to see me a Miss." Please explain! I insist; I demand an explanation. What if I can't come home, then what? I do like the officers in this regiment, but the time will pass slowly, notwithstanding. The Adjutant *is* a married man. "Ain't you sorry?" Now where is your particular reason? "Take care, old girl!" I don't know whether I was thinking of you or not, when you wrote. I am almost always thinking of my dark-eyed Julia, the fairest of the fair, the dearest of them all. No, I don't laugh much when reading such letters as your *last*. I was too sorry to hear that you doubted me, and what was more, to hear you were unwell.

What did you learn about me? What did you hear was the trouble I was undergoing? Tell me, and I will tell you whether it's so or not. Tell me what you heard, and I'll tell you some of my difficulties. Not without! Col. Burke has a letter from home at last; they are all well. His wife is coming to see him this winter. Are you doing right to keep your father's suspicions ever on the alert? Tell him all, at once, and if the worst must come, why not today as tomorrow?

I wrote a foolscap full of foolishness last night to you, and sent it this morning, but when your letter came tonight, I couldn't sleep until I had compromised with my little "wife." Don't you remember promising me not to get angry at anything in my letters? Or have you forgotten it?

My Sergeant rooms with me, but is up to the Colonel's. A lot of noisy officers are in there singing "Mother, I've Come Home to Die," and other such stuff. I'm improving my time better. I look for them all here before long, so must hurry and finish before they come.

Reports have it that Hood is within thirty miles of Nashville with a heavy force, marching this way, and our communications cut off last night between here and Louisville. If that's so, I think we're going to do our best to keep the old gent out of here. Let him come! We are Sherman boys now.

Yes, here is Capt. Coslett, but he didn't come in; saw I was engaged; said "give her my Comps." Of course, that's all they can think of, the "Greenies": new recruits, conscripts, drafted men, forty-dollar men, and all other kind of men, as they are! I met a Lady on the street today—looked very much like Julia, but I didn't fall in love with her. Give my regards to *your* staff—Carrie, Effie, and Mary—and reserve all the love of a soldier's heart for your own dear self. And now may the blessings of Johns rest and abide with you, both now and forever.

—"Farewell."

NASHVILLE, TENN.
November 27, 1864.

MY HEART'S PURE LOVE,

I am happiest when dreaming of thee, and kept in the straight path of duty by the thought that I am loved by the dearest and sweetest of woman-kind. Words can't express the wild, strange devotion of my soul for you, for Julia Allison, the very ideal of all that's perfect. (Your pardon for the above; I forgot that you didn't wish to be called "perfect." If you are not, let me say you come the nearest of any one I ever met.) Am looking anxiously for a letter. When it comes, will you be well, or will you say . . . worse? I have been very uneasy about you ever since your last letter. You really frightened me at first, until I began to think you were only joking about the symptoms of consumption. It isn't often one of so healthy an appearance takes the consumption so suddenly.

This is Sunday. Sunday in camp—how lonesome it is! It has been raining all night, and visitors are tracking mud into my quarters all day. I have some gay times with these green officers. Some of their motions would make you laugh; so awkward in drill, using their swords as awkward as babies. Col. Chase drills them every morning with the musket. I get out before them and make fun. Once in a while, I take a musket and go through the manual, just to make them ashamed of themselves. They often want the Quarter Master to drill them, but I tell them it's "out of my line."

I have the name of being real strict and even *cross,* but I can't find out in what way, unless it was because I turned off three teamsters yesterday for disobeying orders. Also scolded my Clerk last night for spoiling a "Monthly Return" he was making while I was up in the city. He is only 17 years old, has a father in this regiment—a lieutenant in Co. G. Clerk has been to College and is a good book-keeper. So is the Sergeant, but they know very little of a Quarter Master's business, so different from any other. I will have them trained after a while, I think, if I watch them closely. It requires all my attention to keep things "straight," the regiment is so green.

The mail boy comes round every morning after letters. I met him the other day going down to the postoffice with the mail, and asked him if he stopped at my quarters for mail. He said; "Yes, sir, I found a letter in your desk already sealed and took the liberty to take it out. It was to Miss Allison. Did I do right?" I told him it was all right. He brings the mail at half-past two; it is now one. I think I will get a letter from Julia today; won't seal this until I see. Sister has been scolding me for not writing home. I told her I hadn't time. She said I had a curious way of making excuses; found time to write to

Bellefontaine every other day, but could tell *them* I was well only once a month!

My brother-in-law [17] is here; he is a Hospital Steward. Will be Assistant Surgeon; his commission has been forwarded. He sees all my letters before I get them, as the mail is distributed there, and Doc gets them for me. Sends his regards to "Julia." Seems to get knowing once in a while and believes he is aware of how matters stand between us. Have you told your father yet? What does he say?

When my hair gets so it will stay back, I will send you a better photo, but you must destroy the last one; it wasn't good; I hurried the artist too much. I am acquainted with one of the best Photographists in Nashville: Henry M. Hall. [18] He is from Toledo. I am going to have him do *his best* some day. There are several businessmen here from Toledo. They often send us some nice presents. The other day, they sent us a barrel of potatoes and several other necessaries for table use.

Does Mary ever say anything about me? I fear she is out of humor about something. I should have called there before I started; have been ashamed of myself a thousand times since. It was only through neglect that I didn't. I had nothing against Mary, or didn't feel slighted because she treated me so coolly because of that false rumor with regard to my *Politics.* I rather respected her the more for it. It showed plainly she hated Copperheads, and that's recommendation enough for me.

(Evening, 7:20)—I didn't get a letter; don't know why; will look for one tomorrow. The regiment is going to have a dress parade tonight. Won't I laugh at them! Thomas and Hood have been fighting at Columbia, forty miles from here. Reenforcements are going forward. The 183rd. Ohio will leave tonight; they are striking tents now. *We* may be called on next; can't tell. The 182nd. belongs to no brigade as yet; have been ordered on pioneer duty, and are at present work-

---

[17] Dr. Thomas Thompson, his sister Sarah Eliza's husband.
[18] The same photographer who took pictures of Company K of the Forty-second, O.V.I., at Plaquemine, Louisiana, January 17, 1864.

ing on fortifications, and may continue at that work all winter. It matters little to me where I go. My duties are the same. I want to be where I can be of service to the government, ever working for the best interests of the country. This is not idle talk, Julia. I do love my country next to my little "wife." Julia first, my Country next. Never, never will I prove false to either, else Heaven blast me for a traitor! I am going to send you the Photo of my first Commissary Sergeant[19] in some letter not so long as this one. Won't send it now; will make it too large. I excuse all your blots and mistakes; won't you excuse the above? I had too much ink on the pen.

How do you wear your hair now? How does Effie wear hers? Believe if I had never met my Sweetheart and dearest black-eyed Julia, I would have been tempted to fall in love with Effie. She is the next prettiest girl in Bellefontaine, without flattering the least. I called on a friend in Cincinnati, coming down, and told them the next time I came, I would bring my wife. One Lady said she was afraid I never would want to marry, if I stayed in the Army much longer; that old Soldiers hardly ever married, but got to be women haters in course of time. Wasn't that an awful idea? I laughed her out of such nonsense. Told her *I* wasn't in the market, but would bring her an old weather-beaten, sun-tanned Soldier when I came home again. She said she preferred an officer, particularly Captains. I find that's the case everywhere. Shoulder-strapped gents are all the go, while the poor privates haven't half a chance. I will make exceptions, for Julia says she loved me when I was a private in the old 42nd., but she is not like most Ladies. Vast difference,—so I think! Indeed, I do; hope I may die when my turn comes, if I don't!

I have a letter from home of recent date: said Yourtee was at home for a short time, would leave again the next day. He goes home about once a month. Brother Almon is coming down to see me this winter; Mother will probably come with him. I guess they'll find me *at home,* Sundays especially. Don't receive visitors during the hours of business.

We had a splendid dinner today. I couldn't get the Major to take off his hat. There is going to be an oyster supper to-

[19] Sergeant Samuel Morse, of Norwalk, Ohio.

morrow night up at the Sutler's store. All the officers are invited. I shall go, I guess, just for curiosity. Hope there will be nothing there to drink. I almost detest a man that will drink. One (an orderly sergeant) came to my quarters one rainy day, and took the liberty to sit down without invitation. He was intoxicated. I ordered him to leave, which he refused to do. I called a guard, and sent him to Col. Butler's quarters. The Colonel tore the stripes off the gent and sent him to the guard-house. The Colonel is a strict disciplinarian. He was in command of the assaulting column at Wagner; makes the boys here scratch around once in a while. I like his style: very strict, but at the same time, sociable.

Does Carrie hear from Lieutenant as often as you do from me? Do you ever find out the way he commences his letters? What part of the army is he in? I hope he is well by this time. I may get home this winter, but it's rather doubtful. Am going to act as Adjutant on dress parade tonight, as the Adjutant is down town. Will do it just for a change and to please Colonel Butler. Several friends from the city are coming out.

When you write, tell me all the news. Write a long letter. Accept the love of this gay soger boy for Julia, dearest of all.

—JOHNS.

NASHVILLE, TENN.
Sunday, December 4, 1864.

DEAREST OF ALL,—

I received two letters from you yesterday, dated November 21st. and 27th. Was down in the city when they came. Sergeant saw me on the street and told me I had two letters at camp from Bellefontaine. Of course, I hurried up. My horse seemed to understand perfectly that I had news from Julia, and came home dashing. I had been out to the front with a glass, looking at the Rebel line, which is formed within three miles of the city. I could see them very distinctly. Our skirmishers were engaged, and it was a grand sight from where I was on the parapet of Fort Negley, situated on a high piece of ground south of town. Could plainly see the enemy's columns in different parts of the ground or coun-

try lying along the Chattanooga Road. This forenoon, the
Rebs advanced a heavy column on our centre, and a brisk fight
took place, our forces driving the enemy back to his former
position. The 182nd. did not participate in this struggle, being
placed on the extreme *right,* and next to the river.

What Hood is subsisting his army on, is a puzzle to all
military heads here. He is without a base, and it is thought his
movements today were to blind a backward move of his
fatigued and badly used up Soldiery. Prisoners recently captured say they have lived on *corn and whiskey* for three
weeks. I have full confidence in our ability to hold Nashville
against any Rebel force Hood can muster in Tennessee. But
enough of this!

Yes, lieutenants and captains do put on a great deal of unnecessary airs, as a general thing, but I am an exception. I
hate style as bad as anyone. If you could see me, you wouldn't
see much *style* about your Q.M. I wear the full uniform; have
to, under existing orders from General Thomas. They require
all officers to wear the uniform belonging to their rank. I only
obey orders, but leave off all unnecessary *airs.* A certain big
officer in the regiment told another officer that there was more
sound military about "our Q.M." than any or all the other
officers in the 182nd. Our Adjutant, I am sorry to say, is a
rank Copperhead. I was first told so by one of his own towns-
men, a lieutenant in Company G. I told the Colonel about it.
We gave him several severe *rubs* about it last night at supper.
He got red in the face, but didn't say much. I haven't anything personal against the man, but I do hate to sit at the
table with a traitor to his country, for who can support Vallandigham and *gunboat* Mac, and be a friend to the United
States?

How I pity Carrie! I wish she was my sister; I would write
her a sympathizing letter. Don't tell her what I said, but give
her a soldier's regards. The Lieutenant should—and must
—be proud of her. She must be *true.*

Haven't received the *Republicans;* always mention them
when received. I thank you for starting them, at least. Don't
remember your bonnet; hardly ever do notice what a Lady
wears. Always notice her eyes, though, and if they are not

pretty, I won't look at her. I saw a beautiful lady today; she crossed the street just before me. She had splendid eyes,—almost like Julia's. I'm afraid I was a little impertinent, but she didn't seem to care. I tell you, she was beautiful! There are several pretty girls here, though I guess they're all from the North, so far as I can find out. I notice them once in a while, but how different they are from my dear little Julia! I mark the difference, and almost hate all but Julia; I can't help it. If I should travel the world over, I never would find one equal to Julia Allison for all that is my ideal of perfection. Always loved black hair, black eyes, and . . . I won't say the rest!

I often searched your letters last winter and summer for some little word, sentence, or token upon which to base a hope, but all in vain. Had I but known that you cared for me, I would have been happy, at least so far as one in my circumstances could be. I could have made my arrangements sooner, and today you would be all, all mine. I was mustered out of service, came home, with scarcely a plan for the future farther than to re-enter the Army, but in what capacity I knew not. Was at home only four days, when my recommendation was sent to Columbus for the position I now occupy. I went to Columbus myself and received the promise of appointment from Adjutant-General Cowen.

On the way home, I stopped at Bellefontaine on no particular business, as yet I had no hope; saw you, and was doubly impressed that Julia was the only one I could ever make my wife. You asked my opinion of you,—"as a judge of human nature." *I gave it,* and imagine my joy to learn that you at least regarded me as more than a friend. You know what followed, and I only wish I had known it sooner. Suppose, though, it's all my fault, as I never made any advances. It may be all right yet, and you will be my own *forever* before the year of 1865. I shall make use of every means to go home this winter, and then, unless you back out, my little one, you will be Mrs. Julia Hopkins before you are twenty.

I was riding past the Louisville depot the other day while a regiment of the 100th. Ohio was marching down the street. A Lieutenant sprang out of the ranks and sang out: "You Lieutenant, there!" I stopped, looked around, and recognized an old school chum from Toledo. Used to be like brothers. He nearly jerked my arm off, was so glad to see each other. His regiment was in the fight at Franklin and lost heavily. His Company lost its 2nd. Lieutenant and Captain, leaving him in command of the Company. He looked like he had seen hard service. I hardly knew him at first. He went out in 1862, September. I hadn't seen him for four years. He said the uniform changed me a good deal, but he would know Johns Hopkins among a thousand.

Sam [20] sends his regards; says he would like to see the Q.M.'s sweetheart. Below I will give the names of Company officers, or Captains: J. Burke, Co. A; H. C. Roemer, Co. B; A. A. Whissen, Co. C; W. W. Cooke, Co. D; D. A. Terry, Co. E; Wm. Coslett, Co. F; A. M. Lang, Co. G; I. Shelton, Co. H; W. H. Shriver, Co. J; C. A. Wright, Co. K. They are all young like myself and gay and festive. I tell you, we have fun sometimes.

You thought, because I was quiet at Mrs. Knapp's that night, you had a pretty quiet, still, sort of a fellow to deal with, but if you could see me out of company, especially of ladies, you'd change your mind. They call me the liveliest officer in the regiment,—always laughing at some of their motions, and getting them into scrapes. I am sometimes ashamed of myself, but can't help it. Then, too, I have my sober moments when I have much to think of. Thank fortune I am not frivolous; that is, thoughtless. No one thinks or looks more deeply into affairs than I do, when not engaged in making fun. Can take a hearty laugh, and in less than three minutes (as the Major says) look like I had buried my last friend. Such is your Johns: what do you think of him?

That which you beg so for me to tell, will be better as it is. So, if you love me, Julia, don't, for goodness sake, mention it until we are once established in our own home. Then I will tell you, for then it will be all past. It isn't so much, after all; not like it was before I . . . before the 20th of August.

We moved camp yesterday; had to, as a new line of works had to be constructed through the old one.

Should like to step in while you are in some of your deep

[20] Commissary Sergeant Samuel Morse.

studies; think I could "dry your tears," couldn't I? Am going to write to your father, if you think it would do any good. Believe I had better wait until he sees me. What if he says *no?* You would try to forget me, would you! I wouldn't try. What does Jim S—— [21] know about me? We never spoke, as I know of; never was acquainted.

My tent is near a large brick house. I hear a kitchen girl singing some outlandish song. Saw a pretty girl at the window above last night. She watched me mount my horse and ride off, or else I'm awful conceited. Of course, I bowed. Always do! How could I do otherwise? How I wished it was you!

The Regiment is out working on the new Fort Morton; will be out all night. I am alone in my tent, with a good fire, and I am perfectly at home. Are the 42nd boys at home? I have a gent selected for Mary in the 42nd. Am sure she will fall in love with him. Wonder if she's interested in anyone in particular? I hope Mary will get some good fellow: some soldier that served three years.

Have you found any words I spelled wrong in this? Tell me. You don't spell "too" right in the sentence "too large": you had it "to large." Be careful how you criticize me; I will retaliate. How do you intend to have revenge, as you stated in your letter it was in your power to avenge yourself? Your idea of Colonel Burke is very correct; he is a fine looking officer, also very strict. You must keep out of the rain with your cold. I won't have it! You *must!* Go to all the parties you can, but think of me far away. Heaven watch over you tonight and forever.

Fare well, as ever,
—JOHNS.

HEAD QUARTERS, 182ND OHIO, NASHVILLE.
December 8, 1864.

DEAR "WIFE,"

I didn't receive a letter from you today as expected, and concluded to ask why. I think you have fallen from . . . letter-writing! Or perhaps taken the advice of your father not to

[21] James Stanton, brother of Julia Allison's stepmother.

write so often. I don't know, but beg leave to differ with him.
All boys are *not* alike. If you lived to be a hundred, you
wouldn't find another Johns; that is, with the same characteristics, and above all, one who can love as I do. I think more of
the "Julia of my Heart" every letter I get from her, so be
careful and write often.

The enemy is still in plain view; if anything, nearer than
when I wrote you last. Skirmishing is going on continually.
This morning, the Rebels made a movement on our left simul-
taneous with a dash of our cavalry. The Rebs were driven
back with a loss of 200 prisoners. Every attempt on the
part of Hood to cross the river has proven a failure and a loss
of men. That he will yet give us battle, with a view to the
occupation of Nashville, is not doubted by our Generals in
command. Let him come! He'll be a used-up old *hood* when he
takes possession.

I've been very busy the past three days making out my returns for November. I was going to write to you last night,
but Ollie and Sam had possession of the desk and table, making out invoices, receipts, etc., and needed so much telling I
couldn't write. They are willing to do everything I want them
to, but it requires most of my time instructing them and show-
ing *how;* I would save time by doing all the business myself.
Ollie generally spoils one or two blanks before he gets them
right, and Sam isn't much better. Am glad it's only once a
month. I ought to be a good writer by the amount of writing
I do.

Can imagine how cold it is in Bellefontaine tonight. It's
cold, very cold here, though for some time past it has been
like summer. My tent is fastened and a good fire is in the
stove, but I feel chilly. I hate cold weather. Can imagine I
see you in the sitting room by the grate, with one of your own
make of fires. Have you learned how to make fires yet? You
remember you didn't know how when I was there.

Did Claude K—— say anything about me in his letter? Isn't
he in this Department somewhere? General Thomas was out
to see the works day before yesterday. First time I ever saw
him. He is a large, heavy-set man, good-natured appearance,
and looks every inch a soldier. Capt. Burke was in this eve-

ning; wanted to bet he'd get a letter tomorrow and I wouldn't; said I need not expect one, as you had found out what kind of a fellow I was, and wouldn't write any more. Is that so?

I was offered $180 for my horse this morning down street, but I just laughed at the man. I tell you, he's gay! If I were a brigadier-general, could cut a splash, but being only a lieutenant, it wouldn't do. Don't you pity me? Sam has put up his official papers, and by an accidental side-glance I see he has commenced a letter: "My own dear Eva." So you see he isn't without a sweetheart, just like all soldiers; all have left a girl behind them. I am satisfied none can equal *mine* in all that is attractive. I see the photos of some of the officers' *specials* once in a while, but none as yet have equalled Julia; *none have moved this cold heart of mine.* All are without attraction, and my Julia reigns supreme.

If I go home this winter, what time had I better come? You must appoint the happy day, sweet. Guess we had better not have a wedding, though,—just as you say. I hate so much show. Here! what have I been talking about? I forgot. Your father's consent must first be gained. He may talk favorable *now,* but refuse when I write to him. It is hardly to be expected that he will give his daughter to an entire stranger; must see me first. That's why I am anxious to go home this winter.

My affairs about the first of January will be in proper shape to leave in the hands of my Sergeant, who, by that time, will know how to manage, and if the good star of my destiny still shines, I will stand at your side, the proudest husband and soldier in the world, before next summer. My reasons for keeping the fact of our engagement from outsiders were of the best at the time I made the request, but now I don't care who knows it. Did you ever tell Mary? Does she ever say anything about me? I have thought of Carrie often in the last few days; do hope the Lieutenant is recovering. Don't forget to tell me about him every time you write. My health never was better; believe I am getting fleshy. Colonel Chase said "he wished he was as large and stout as the Q.M."

I wonder when I will see you again? How I would like to be with you tonight; would have you sing for me. Do you play, Julia?

I know you can sing. One with a voice like yours always can. I love music when it's good; but if not, I hate it. My little nephew Charlie,[22] at Toledo, is a splendid singer and plays well, understands music: only 13 years old! I am so sorry I couldn't stay home longer; was only there five or six days, altogether. I have another letter from Sis; says I must write home oftener, or she will go to Bellefontaine and find out what kind of a conspiracy I'm in there. They begin to mistrust. Hadn't I better tell them all? I sent your love to Sister; guess that will set them to thinking. Here's the end of the paper, and I've only commenced to write.

If I don't get word from you tomorrow, shall think Captain Burke is right. My letter from home said they hadn't heard from Yourtee for several days. "Dear me!" I wonder. They think it's awful to have him away from home. Me, they think it's a matter of course that I should be away; haven't been home much in the last eight years. Was there longer in Bellefontaine than usual. If I am a *bad* boy, Julia, I can be blamed much; am one of your self-made men, or "out of the depths." What about our going to the West? Are you going, or was it all a joke, or what did you mean?

Give my never decreasing affections to dear little pretty Effie, my tender regards to Mary, compliments of a friend to Fannie,[23] and love of a brother to Carrie, and that of a sincere and devoted lover to Julia of my dreams; and write often and long letters to your own true, though far-away,

—JOHNS.

P.S.—Dont delay the answer; write often, oftener, oftenest. —Q.M.

CAMP OF 182ND O.V.I., NASHVILLE.
December 17, 1864.
FRIEND JULIA, DEARER THAN LIFE,

The battle of Nashville is ended. Hood's demoralized and badly whipped Rebels are flying towards the south. The victory is complete. I sent you a city paper this morning which will tell you all about it. I know it will make you rejoice and

[22] His brother Almon's son.
[23] Fannie Riddle, of Bellefontaine.

thank God for the courage He has given to our army. He is a God of battles, and has again decided with *justice* and the *right.*

It's a sad sight to see our poor wounded boys, but one to excite admiration for the *Federal soldier,* to see how he bears up under the loss of a limb, and how cheerfully he endures the pain of severe wounds. "True hearts have they," and well may the people of the North be grateful for the services rendered by such heroes as Thomas, Steedman, Schofield, and A. J. Smith. Our loss must necessarily be severe, as the enemy posted behind breastworks and in chosen positions were driven from three separate lines of defense, our troops charging in the face of murderous volleys of grape and cannister. Dispatches tonight say our forces are beyond Brentwood, in close pursuit of Hood's columns.

I wrote to Mother this week, telling her all about you and our arrangements; won't it surprise her, though? I promised her once never to marry before I was twenty-five without her consent, but I can make her consent to anything. Have been away from home so much, am the *favorite.* If they knew me better, they wouldn't think so much of me, or you wouldn't, either, Julia. Won't you be disappointed some day when *you find me out?* How my little wife will regret that she ever saw Johns Hopkins! Can't I make you repent of the bargain now? Wish I could. No, I don't either; take it back, quick! All I'm afraid of is that I can't come to Bellefontaine quite so soon, and perhaps not before spring. The very idea of disappointment sickens me, I am so resolved upon going. And you say "now or never"—what mean you? Please explain. Suppose my regiment should start off in pursuit of Hood, and I have to go with it, then my Julia wouldn't wait: is that so? Or did I misunderstand you? Someone must give themselves unnecessary trouble on my account, especially Ez Allmon. I laugh when I think of the little goose; he is too far beneath the notice of a gent. I thought you succeeded admirably at Knapp's that evening, or at least before we left there. I have selected a Lieutenant (of course!) for Mary; he is a splendid looking fellow, wild and gay, about twenty.

Capt. Hutchins' recommendation was quite flattering; something I'm not used to, except from Julia. I wrote to Cap last night; didn't mention the subject of the recommendation, though. Hutch was the best officer in the 42nd. I give him this compliment unasked for, gratis.

If I come, shall I be in full uniform, or in citizen's dress? Will be awkward in the last, as I haven't had anything on of the kind for over three years. Am glad you have concluded not to have a wedding. Always hated so much superfluity. I can imagine how sweet you will look,—and those dear eyes! Expect I will fall on my knees and worship you. Will we have Mary there?

I must close soon, as I have some writing to do yet tonight. Tomorrow is Sunday. What will my Promised Bride be doing? Will she write tomorrow night and answer this one as soon as possible, or convenient? My love to Carrie and Katie,[24] and remember I shall move the hills around Nashville, if I don't get to come at the appointed time. Write soon (once more before I go), and accept the deepest devotion of my heart for the wife of your own true and devoted

—O. J. HOPKINS.

OFFICE AT POST Q.M., NASHVILLE, TENN.
December 25, 1864.

MY DEAREST JULIA,

I have just time before the mail goes out to say that I am disappointed in my expectation of obtaining leave of absence. The final answer came today. I am down in the City on that business, but have failed. If you love me yet, you can imagine my disappointment.

I haven't received a line from you since the 15th, or thereabouts, or an answer from your father.[25] Have expected one these last three days. This makes my fourth one to you, and no answer! What is the cause? I will write you as soon as I get to camp, and explain all. Have only time to send love to Carrie and all the rest.

YOUR DISAPPOINTED JOHNS.

P.S.—Did you get the present I sent by express last Monday? Place my Photo on the first page. Bye-bye.

[24] Julia's stepsister, Kate. She was two years old at this time.
[25] Lieutenant Hopkins had at last written to Mr. Allison, asking for his consent to the marriage.

Q.M. OFFICE, 182ND O.V.I., NASHVILLE, TENN.
January 6, 1865.

DEAREST OF MINE,

I received yours postmarked the 3rd. this evening. After reading it, I answer without delay, as is always the case when I hear from my . . . ; though I wrote last night and gave you all the news, your long interesting letter gives me subject for remark. It was just the kind of letter I like to get, and deserves a better answer than I can send you in return. More scolding for not coming home, and threats of what you will do in case I don't come in three weeks. You ask what I say to playing *quits?* Why, Julia, what in the world do you mean? I will tell you what I *say,* if you only give me proof that you are *sincere* in making such a proposition.

It appears to me, Julia, that in the past three years I have furnished proof of my sincerity in the love I have for you. Never taking advantage of the least opportunity to create a false impression on your mind in regard to my accomplishments and worth. I call Heaven to witness that it has never entered my mind to deceive you in anything, and I am bound by all laws of gentility *now* (if you are deceived in the character of him to whom you have given your hand) to give up all claims, and leave you free to choose from among the hundreds of others who are ever willing to acknowledge virtue and intelligence. Believe not, my dear one, that I could do this without a sacrifice. The deep and pure love I have for you is far from being of so light and frivolous a nature, and should I be compelled to tear your image from my heart, remember what an effort it will be on my part. I am still in hopes that your remark was thoughtlessly made and you were only in sport at the time, yet I can't avoid the belief that some such thought has occurred, or that all is not right. Tell me truly next time, Julia, and I will respect you the more for your candor.

What did your father say, you ask? He said,—but I guess I'll give you a copy of his letter . . . . [The letter from Mr. Allison is given in full following this one.]

What do you think of it? See, you are all mine now, *all mine!* Too late to talk about playing quits!

I will transfer the love sent by Mary to Capt. Burke and take his receipts for it and send them in my next. Captain is Brigade Officer of the Day. I gave him a horse to ride this morning, and I haven't seen him since. I was downtown when your letters arrived; Sam gave me the long one, and kept the envelope with the beautiful pictures enclosed until a few minutes since, when he handed them to me. I waited until he went to supper, when I opened it, and imagine how I laughed! They are splendid. But if that's the way you will look when you grow *old,* I hope you will always *stay young!* Mary makes the best looking *old Lady.* However, I will keep them next to my heart (in my left coat-tail pocket).

Mrs. Butler and Mrs. Chase will be here on the 12th; will stay all winter. The Q.M. of the 142nd Indiana has his wife with him. Guess I'll go after mine, since it's the fashion. We are preparing for them. Have bought a larger table, built a kitchen, and got more dishes. When they come, our family will be quite large. The Major, by the way, starts for home next week. As he is a member of the Legislature, he will probably resign his commission before he returns, or before spring, I should say. I am in great hopes of getting a furlough the first of February. Give my friendly regards to Ez Allmon, Jack Wilson, and all my old comrades who enquire for me; also a soldier's regards to Jim Stanton. I sent you a Photo this morning; did you get it? Wasn't taken the same style as yours and Mary's. I have no notion of letting you off so easy. So you needn't ask me again to play quits. Ain't you a little ashamed of yourself? My love to Carrie, Grandma,[26] and all. Write soon as possible to your own dedicated, devoted, true as steel, and handsome

—JOHNS.

The following letter was addressed to Lieutenant Hopkins by C. W. B. Allison.

BELLEFONTAINE, OHIO
December 25, 1864

DEAR SIR,
Your very important communication was received and its

[26] Juliana Brandon Allison, mother of C. W. B. Allison.

contents considered. From previous information communicated to me by my daughter it was not unexpected. Before its receipt I had made inquiry of Captain Hutchins as to your character and habits. Had I the advantage of a personal acquaintance with you, of course my opinion would be more satisfactory to myself. But the information I have received as to your moral character and habits, and your natural ability and business qualifications, has been creditable to you, and has enabled me to feel respect for you, and to receive your request with favor.

It appears that, from personal intercourse, you have at the most important period of my daughter's life gained her affections, which I believe truly sincere, and I have no reason to doubt equal sincerity on your part. Had I any reason to believe otherwise, I would have interfered before your arrangements had gone as far as they have. For my daughter, I have the strong affection of a father toward his first born, the fervor of which she is scarcely aware of, and you may expect in the future that I will continue to interest myself in her welfare and happiness.

You allude to an intimate acquaintance and friendship for several years which has ripened with time. It appears from her similar statements that you are better acquainted with each other than I feared was the case. Young people sometimes, but rarely after a long acquaintance, in the fervor of imagination, look upon each other as perfect, and after experiencing the realities of a married life, mutually feel disappointed in discovering in their partners for life some of the usual faults that all are prone to. Much better that they should know each other's frailties before the solemn vows are taken. I presume I need not remind you that Julia is not perfect. Her nervousness at times renders her sensitive to a fault, and you may find her at times somewhat willful, yet withal she has a kind and generous disposition and sincere in her friendship.

In consulting her happiness, as well as your own, recollect at all times her sanguine nervous temperament, and the more pleasant your mutual intercourse (even by an effort to that end, if necessary), as well as her friendly intercourse with others, the less you will see of it. I trust, with your mutual love for each other, you will each bear and forbear and live happily.

You each asseverate that your future happiness depends upon your union, and I shall not interfere, but freely give my consent to it.

Hoping that God in his mercy and providence will guide and prosper you through life, is the wish and prayer of

Yours truly,

—C. W. B. Allison.

NASHVILLE, TENN.
January 9, 1865.

DEAR "WIFE,"

It has been so long since I wrote to you that I fear you will be alarmed about my safety and well-being and stay awake at night, or grow thin. I think I have heard of such things. I answered your long letter some time since, or tried to, but fell far short of it. Hope all yours will be of that kind: I mean, long ones.

Yesterday was Sunday. I was out in the country five miles, and got my dinner at the only Union man's house in the vicinity in which he resided. Capt. Burke, Capt. Coslett, and Lieut. Young were with me. I furnished the horses, and we started from Camp early in the morning, crossed the river on the Bridge, and went out on the Buena Vista Pike.

The country was beautiful, though rather hilly, the road leading through groves of cedar, past plantations and farms fenced with stone, through forests and fields, until we came to Mr. Saddler's Plantation, where we halted, dismounted, and cleaned our boots. Were invited in very cordially by the Old Gent and Lady, and took seats around a large fire, where we were soon joined by a very pretty young lady (whom I had had an introduction to at a party some weeks since) and also quite a bevy of little (for once!) clean-faced children. A pleasant conversation immediately ensued, touching on all subjects, and the time passed until a *black girl* came and informed *Misses* "dat de dinner was all cooked and ready for de gemmen." The party then adjourned to dinner by mutual con-

sent, as it were, and oh! what a dinner! It made me
think of the old farmer-like meals I had sat down to at my
Uncle's in the country.[27]

I shall not attempt to describe all the good things there.
Only let me say that Capt. Burke ate until I was ashamed of
him. Capt. Coslett called me "Colonel" once or twice before
going to dinner, and you would laugh to see how the old Lady
heaped the dainties on the "Colonel's" plate. The young lady
understood the joke, and when the old man called me "Colonel," she would look at me and laugh. I, of course, remained
as dignified as a Brigadier.

We remained until eve, when we prepared to go. Mr. Saddler gave us a pressing invitation to repeat the visit, which we
promised in good faith to do. Our horses being ready, we all
mounted but Burke, who stayed for some time on the portico,
talking with Miss Saddler. While he was busy talking, his
horse, tied to the fence out in the lane, lay down and rolled
over in the mud, got up,—and such a looking saddle! all covered with mud! This was just what pleased us who were waiting, and we galloped off, leaving Burke and Saddler washing
the saddle in a creek. We had almost reached the ferry when
Cap overtook us, his horse wet with sweat. Of course, we
didn't laugh at him *much*. It was after dark when we reached
Camp, and we roused the guards. When our party appeared,
covered with mud, we resembled a company of Johnny cavalry.
Our pass from Gen. Miller proved to the contrary, however,
and we were admitted. So ended the day!

I have no doubt my little Julia passed the time more becoming than I did. Yes, far, far away in the old *civilized North,* I
imagine I see her tonight while it rains. I am glad to know she
has a shelter from the storm. My tent, though a new one, is
not proof against the pelting blast, and the water drops
through on my paper, looking like tears of deep sorrow for
some sad misfortune befallen. They are not tears, Julia. I am
too hard-hearted to cry for anything that could happen in
this world. No accident or mishap could bring tears from the
fountain long dried.

[27] Harris Hopkins, who lived on a farm two miles west of Lewistown, in
Logan County, Ohio.

I should like to know who Sue Braughton is? I never saw her, that I remember. What in the world does the girl know of me? You are a dear good girl for taking my part when wicked people slander me. I will send you a big kiss for it. Oh! I forgot that's a privilege you allow no one! You don't? Ah! I think I remember! All right, dearest, stick to that. No one has a right to kiss you but myself, and I will chastize any man who attempts to infringe upon my rights.

Isn't it strange how rumors will float? How do you suppose people ever took into their heads that Julia Allison was going to marry a Lieutenant in the Army? Did you ever see that Q.M. they talk so much about? What kind of a looking fellow is he? What's the reason he didn't come home? I should like to see such a fortunate man. He must be tall, noble and handsome, rich, brave as Napoleon! Have you heard his name? Johns Hopkins! What! you don't say! Is that so? Well, I declare!

But enough of this foolishness. Ask Mary if I shall show Capt. Burke her photo. He will be sure to fall in love with it. Give my "love" to Jack Wilson;[28] ask him if he remembers a conversation the night we landed at Vicksburg while on the route to White River from Morganza. He was on duty, and I was Sergeant of the Guard. I do, very distinctly.

Haven't received the papers you sent yet; perhaps they will be here tomorrow. I also look for a letter from you then, and one from home also. Last one from there said that, after they heard I couldn't get a furlough, Almon started for New York, to be gone all winter. Yourtee has also gone off onto the railroad again. Mother was about to start to see the two girls in Iowa, leaving the House deserted, as my Sister (Eliza) will stay with Al's wife until Ma returns. Ours is a scattered family at present, but I hope for the time when we may all meet again, when this cruel war is over.

I must close for tonight, for my eyes are heavy, and I fain would sleep. I hope you won't strangle tonight; it must be a disagreeable sensation indeed. I wish it were someone else than my Julia; I dread to hear of anything happening to her. Can't you arrange to sleep in a colder room? Of course, it's

[28] Andrew S. Wilson, Company K, Forty-second, O.V.I.

the close warm room that causes it. I am busy making out receipts and invoices for January, and hope to get them off in time to start home the first of February.

Love to all,
—YOUR JOHNS.

NASHVILLE, TENN.
January 12, 1865.

MY DEAR JULIA,

I received yours of the 6th. inst. this evening and I will answer without delay, as requested. Part of it I couldn't read, or can't by candle light, but perhaps can make it out in the morning. Your ink was very pale, and must have faded since writing. However, I can make out most of the questions.

Have been torn up considerably *at our house;* have had a detail of carpenters at work enlarging my office, and tonight am writing in the coziest little room back of the Office you ever saw. Carpet on the floor, a good stove, a warm, soft, comfortable bed, and everything to make a soldier happy, except . . . . Major West says I must be going to send for *my* wife, as I am enlarging so extensively. By the way, the Major has heard of you by some means. Oh, yes, in doing up the Head Quarters' mail, he saw a letter directed to you and knew it was my hand. Today, he attacked me about it while we were alone. Says he has seen your father at Columbus,[29] but isn't acquainted with him. He starts for Ohio on Monday. Says he will see your father and tell him what kind of a fellow I am, and what a wild son-in-law he is going to have. Says *he begins to see my object* in trying to get a leave of absence. Major is a splendid fellow, but too honest, easy, and slow dispositioned for a military man. Is Representative of Adams County. Will perhaps resign his commission, from what I hear him say.

I never received the gem sent from Oskaloosa; would have mentioned it. Yes, the carmine ink is very nice, especially for writing letters; looks well; wish you would write with it every time.

That would be hard to do: I couldn't give a definite answer

---

[29] C. W. B. Allison was the representative from Logan County in the State legislature.

whether I could be there or not in three weeks from last
Saturday. I will send my application next Monday, and by the
time I am ready to start, it will have gone through the
regular channel for approval.

The Regiment will be paid off for the first time next week.
Was mustered some days since. I was out in the rain all day
last Saturday week, and I have caught cold; haven't been well
since, and didn't sleep two hours last night. Woke up about
eleven o'clock, and lay awake while three reliefs were posted.
The Guard in front of Head Quarters on the second Relief
must have been a Christian man, as he sang and prayed all
night. He would first give out two lines, and then sing them in
regular old *Methodist style;* then he would go into the sentry-
box and pray. I was somewhat amused, though I was far from
being in the best of humor.

I have built barracks for the Regiment, and now am rigging
up Head Quarters' Building into a house for Colonel and his
lady. I waited until the men were made comfortable before I
gave the Colonel a board.

So you think I write quite a love-letter? Perhaps I do; perhaps may be silly and unbecoming at times, but I can't help
saying in all my letters: "I love you truly." Is there harm in it?
If so, pardon me. If you could only be here, you would think
the season changeable. Early in the morning, it may be bitter
cold; then, at noon, the sun comes out and it is pleasant. At
three o'clock, warm; at five o'clock, cloudy and threatens rain;
at eight o'clock, rain and sleet falling, changing to snow and
wind "tempestuous"; and again, in the morning, all the ink in
the office frozen up. Now what do you think of Nashville?

You like bashful men, do you? Must have taken a fancy to
me, then, before this. Adjutant Douglas was dishonorably
discharged from the service and is like me: would rather enter
the Rebel army than go home after disgracing, not only his
own character as a man, but that of all his relations. I saw him
yesterday downtown. Doesn't know what he intends to do. I
feel awful bad tonight; am sure I'm going to be sick. Head-
ache, bad cold, and bad feelings generally.

It is very easy to see why I admired you in preference to any
Lady I ever was acquainted with. I will tell you the reason

when I see you. Why can't you give me the advice *now?* I always like advice, and try to follow it when the advice is good and I respect the adviser. A *little angry,* were you? Do you ever get that way with your "little pet"? You can't make me angry; suppose you try it! You can make me feel a little serious at times, when you talk of being tired of waiting for me. Julia, I am more anxious than you for our speedy marriage. I will then have a perfect right to address you as "My Wife," whether you like that way of commencing a letter, or not. Can Claude compose as well as I? Guess not! I always take such pains in composition, don't I? It would seem so unnatural for me to put on the rhetoric while writing to my little darling Julia. I sent love to Sam's Norwalk girl *on a chip* the other evening, and tonight he sends his love to you in a basket; also sends comps. to Mary and Effie. He has five different photos of his Norwalk girl, and is shuffling them like cards on the table; has dealt them out a hand and wants to know if my Bellefontaine lady goes ahead of that.

Capt. Burke was in this evening about two hours. When he went out, said he was going to write five letters tonight. Of course, I gave him the messages. The Sutler just sent down some very nice ———— which I must help *put out of the way.* Lieut. Wood is detailed as A.A.C. and Inspector General of the 2nd. Brigade, 4th Division, 20th Corps: the same position which I was detailed for through mistake by Brigadier Mason.

Why do you call me *proud?* I am proud in some things, but I hope not detestably so, as I have known men to be. I sent you a copy of your father's letter in my last; tell me what you think of it. Isn't it most too late to back out? I am glad of it! I only fear your father will be disappointed in his son-in-law when I get there. My hair is turning gray, and isn't fit to send to a young lady, though I will send you a handful some day. Better wait until I come home, when you can cut it off yourself. Do you want a lock tied up with *red tape?* We Q.M's. are awful fellows for Red Tape. I am quite confident that you and Sister will make a *team,*—a wild one, too! I don't want to be in the same house when you two get started, especially if Yourtee is there to help. He and Sister can make more noise than I have made in the last three years, except with my musket. I want to know who said I was *wild?* They told the truth, but I wasn't aware that anyone knew it. I am wild only at times, and then I am as quiet as any one at others. I will try my best to be with you by the first of February; if I succeed, won't I be a happy youth!

My love to Carrie, Katie, Ma and all, and a soldier's regards to Lieut. Price. Tell the Lieutenant I am sorry to keep him waiting,[30] but he will understand my situation. Write soon to your

Friend,

O. J. HOPKINS

Lieut. 182nd. O.V.I. and Q.M.

P.S.—Sent in my application for a leave of absence. I sincerely hope it will be granted. Tell Lieut. and Carrie not to wait for me; I may not succeed. Everything is so uncertain.

NASHVILLE, TENN.

January 17, 1865.

MY DEAR JULIA,

I received a letter from you last evening, dated the 10th and mailed the 12th. It was the best letter I ever had from you, my little darling *wife.* I was *very* glad to hear from you, as I had felt lonesome and *bluish* all day. The life of a Q.M. is so monotonous when there is no variation from the same routine of business, among his abstracts, vouchers, invoices, receipts, and returns, and is one calculated to make one feel reserved and sour as an old Bachelor. It is well you send in your triweekly reports, Miss Julia, or *I* would become so.

The only variation I have had from the duties of my department was last Sunday. An order came from Brigade Head Quarters for a Grand Review and dress parade of the garrison. Our Adjutant, who is a little *raw* and at present not well, requested me to act in his place during the day, which I declined, until Col. Butler made a similar request, when I concluded to do it. Buckling on my sword and mounting my horse, I began to feel the soldier's pride returning as it did in the days of the old 42nd.

---

[30] A double wedding had been planned with Lieutenant Price and Carrie McClure.

We marched through the city to the tune of "The Girl I Left Behind Me," and proceeded out on the Charlotte Pike until we reached the place designated for the parade. A large common where the rest of the Brigade had already formed and were surrounded by thousands of citizens and spectators, civil and military. Our Battalion forming on the extreme right, the review commenced, the troops composing the command manoeuvering with more precision than I have heretofore ever witnessed in new troops. Everything passed off pleasantly, and altogether it was quite an interesting affair. I enjoyed it hugely, and could not help but wish I was where my knowledge of the tactics could be exercised, and in some capacity where I would be of more service to the country. However, I suppose someone must be Q.M., and why not Johns, as well as some one else?

Yes, my little one, I am *perfectly* satisfied you were only joking and in fun when you wrote that, though at first I didn't know what to think. It's all right now. I will know how to take you after this. So you like the Photograph, do you? I was afraid you wouldn't; the eyes were so poor. You would call me perfect, if you knew me better. I have a notion to tell you just what kind of a fellow I am. Am sorry you didn't get the Album. Perhaps it will turn up yet; if it doesn't, I will have to send you another one.

Tell Jennie [31] you are already the wife of "J.H."—all except the ceremony. She must try and be present when that comes off. You must be very careful not to take the ring off, —remember! Yes, you are very savage when once aroused. You really frighten me! I won't ask what you are angry at. I know very well. What are you going to do about it? I shouldn't have made the remark, but I was full of fun, as I had been laughing at the very serious look you both had in that gem. [32] Can't imagine how you two contrived to look so serious. Mary, especially. I am glad you are going to send me a sensible one. Send it in your next letter. I will take the best of care of it; indeed, I will.

[31] Jennie Seevers, of Oskaloosa, Iowa.
[32] The photograph of Julia and Mary that amused him so much and caused his remark about an "old Lady" in his letter of January 6, 1865.

I should think Jim Stanton could learn you to ride horse-back. Why doesn't he? I so admire a Lady who knows how to ride well. I will learn you the first thing I do. I have a splendid horse; would just suit you. No, Julia, you didn't wound my feelings in the least; more than frightened me a little—something a soldier should never suffer from (fright). But I acknowledge I was a little, just a little, surprised when you wrote that way. I will doubt you no more, and if the thought once entered my mind, recollect it was not for want of faith-fulness on my part. I see now the very thought wrongs my promised one, and I kneel at her feet for forgiveness.

I am sorry Carrie and Lieut. Price have to wait on me. Tell them I think they had better not wait, as it is so uncertain when I can come. I received a letter from Sister last night; she said Almon got hold of the letter I wrote to Mother tell-ing her all about it, and didn't have a single objection to find with my choice. Of course, how could he! Sis says she longs to see you, and wants me to get your Photo for her album. Can't you send me two: one for her and one for Johns? Yourtee is running between Cincinnati and the Indiana line.[33] I haven't had a letter from him lately. I do pity Effie; hope she is well by this time. Be sure and tell me if she is better. My *best* to her! I have some good news for you, but won't tell it now; will wait until a certain event transpires. *I won't always be a mere lieutenant.*[34]

The Major left early Monday morning for Columbus. Said he would tell Mr. Allison what a wild *chick* I was. Write and tell your father not to believe half he says. If we were only al-ready married, I would send for you to come down and stay all winter.

Sam is reading Artemus Ward and making more noise than a ten-pounder in action. Weather has been very pleasant for the past week, and the mud is all dried up. Believe I haven't told you yet that I have had a very sick spell, but am feeling better tonight; have had more bad health since coming to Nashville than I had in the whole three years' service.

[33] Yourtee was a Railroad Express messenger between Cincinnati and Con-nersville, Indiana.

[34] He may be hinting at a position in "a new organization" for which Colonel Butler recommended him to Adjutant General Cowen, February 16, 1865.

I must close, as it grows late. My love to *all* in every sense of the term, and as much as you want for your own dear self. Write soon to,

YOUR OWN JOHNS.

NASHVILLE, TENN.
January 22, 1865.
MY DEAR JULIA,

Contrary to expectation, I received no dear letter from you today, and so concluded to write one tonight. Have just returned from the country with the Adjutant and Lieutenants Young and Wood, where we had one of the best dinners imaginable at Mr. Drake's, two miles across the river. Went out early this morning and stayed until afternoon. The family consists of the old gent, his wife, and four girls, one of whom (sad to say!) is married. Two of the young ladies are very beautiful and entertaining, and the day passed off before we were aware of it.

We returned to camp in time for supper, at which I received a good scolding from Mrs. Chase for leaving on Sunday, when she had taken such pains to oversee the cook in preparing a splendid dinner. Colonel Mason, commanding the 2nd Brigade, was here and took dinner at "our house," and Mrs. Butler said they had as good as she generally had at home. I told her I couldn't help it; that I had to fill a previous engagement, which was the cause of my absence, and that I had a sumptuous repast in the country. She laughed and said she must inform my "Bellefontaine lady" of how I was going out into the country every Sabbath. I don't know how they know so much, but nevertheless several of the officers have it that I am going home next month to be married. Lieut. Wood asked me today if it was so. I told him I wished it *was so,* for the sake of the furlough. The evening I sent you the last letter, Col. Butler brought in my *application* disapproved, stating at the same time that he couldn't spare me until after I had made another issue of clothing to the Regiment, which will not be until the first of February. To send in my application then, I would be under the necessity of waiting two or three weeks before I could receive actual leave; consequently, it would be late in February before I would be ready to start, and so late in the season that I am almost discouraged from trying again.

Cousin Carrie and Price need not wait longer for me, but proceed with their arrangements with regard to their union. It would indeed be quite a pleasure to have a double marriage come off at the same time, but as it is, I must submit to circumstances, with the "comforting" assurance that I am the unwilling cause of it being otherwise.

Captains Whissen and Cooke came in just here, and I was obliged to lay aside the pen and entertain them. They remained until a late hour, and I am again talking to my sweet "promised wife," as the drums are beating the Tattoo and the rain is dashing on the roof of my "mansion." Sam is in the outer room composing a letter to his "distant" one in answer to one he received today. The Q.M. is writing in answer to one he *didn't* receive. I sent three last week and didn't receive any.

Mrs. Butler says I look very much like my brother. I told her I considered that highly complimentary for brother Al's personal appearance, and thanked her for Al's sake. I am going with my train across the river about five miles tomorrow on a foraging expedition. Will make sure of my dinner at some farmhouse, if nothing else, unless the Rebs get me. Guess I won't finish this now, but wait and see if there will not be a letter for me tomorrow evening, when I return.

Meanwhile, Guardian Angels watch over my precious wife in her slumbers tonight, and a thousand kisses and as many prayers from the depths of a soldier's and lover's heart for God's richest blessings to rest and abide with Julia, now and forever. Good night, my love.

—JOHNS.

(*January 23rd*)—No letter came today, and I resume my pen to finish the letter for the morning mail. Last night, a heavy snow fell, and this morning Lieut. Young and I went out rabbit hunting to pass away the time. I fired at one with my revolver, but it was running so fast I missed it. Young gave out before noon, and we returned to camp in time for dinner (without any rabbits, of course!). I didn't go out into the country today as I had intended, for the reason that the ferry was out of repair. Will go in the morning, if it isn't too cold.

Julia, why don't you write? Do you delay because you are waiting for one from me? I don't wait for answers, but write whenever the spirit moves me. I will not scold you; believe you write often, but I don't receive all of your letters. I am confident of this fact, judging from incidents mentioned in some recent letters referring to questions said to have been asked in former ones, and which I am satisfied I never received. What the cause is, I could never ascertain, unless we hold the mail agents responsible. Let the fault be where it may, it often subjects me to unpleasant apprehensions with regard to the health and safety of my dearest one, causing me to wonder whether or not she is in perfect enjoyment of health and happiness, and all the other blessings this world can afford. To reflect that either of these is witheld from her, or more particularly, good health, is a source of anxiety to him who loves her, soul and body. Even to read in her *last letter* that she was subject to spells of suffocation, is enough to cause the greatest anxiety for the *next*.

So, as you love me, Julia, write as often as you can make it possible without subjecting yourself to any inconvenience. And remember, while writing, what satisfaction it gives your "soldier-boy" down at Nashville to read the soul-stirring though oft-repeated assurance you hold him still in "fond remembrance," and love him yet with all the devotion of a woman's first love. Yes, recollect, Julia, that to read such marks of fidelity upon your part almost compels me to worship you in fact. I do *idolize* you (as you say), and that, too, with all the deep and passionate love of my nature. You, who changed the whole prospect of my life, the aim, the ambition of my existence.

Had it not been for you, Julia, where would I have been today? Entering the army—that worst of schools—at the age I did, exposed to all the vices and temptations incident to camp and field, I was on a fair way to become *wild* in every sense of the word, had it not been for the silent, though hopeless, love I retained for Her who I thought to be the most perfect of womankind. Thus was I restrained from the more excessive follies and habits of my surroundings. Always, when tempted to depart from the path of duty, the image of her I loved would come before me, and that, with the influence of a pious Mother's advice, kept me more on my guard than I would otherwise have been. And now, since I know that my hitherto silent love is reciprocal, I trust God will ever keep me from committing one act or deed which would in the least make me unworthy of your confidence, your esteem, your friendship, your love.

I must close this letter, which has already reached a tiresome length, by kindly requesting you to present my regards to all friends, and accept as usual all the love for Julia. Write very soon to your anxiously waiting

—JOHNS.

NASHVILLE, TENN.
February 2, 1865.

MY OWN DEAREST,

I send you, per Adams Express, the light of my frowning countenance, which I had taken some days since, but delayed sending until now. I have not received a line from you for dear knows how long! I am, in consequence, *very* uneasy. The only trouble with the picture, it makes me look too young, as all the professed judges tell me. However, that's a pardonable fault when you take into consideration my extreme youth: scarcely twenty-one! I am going down town this morning, and have not the leisure to write; will write this evening. Please write very soon. My regards to your father and also the rest of the family. And, as ever, the love of my heart and soul for Julia,

—JOHNS.

R.Q.M. OFFICE, 182ND. O.V.I.
NASHVILLE, TENN.
February 6, 1865.

JULIA,

You have often mentioned the brevity of my letters, and I have concluded to write one of which you will find no reason to complain, if you are still so disposed after my last one, sent this morning. You will readily see that long silence on your part has a tendency to improve me so far as frequency is concerned, but if you haven't marked the change, perhaps I have done wrong in telling you, for fear you will repeat the experiment. If no letter comes this week, prepare yourself for one of the *savagest* letters you ever received. I shall begin to believe that a few lines in one of my recent letters have made you *angry*. I hardly know what to think; whether it's the fault of carelessness on the part of post office clerks, or *something* I dread to name.

I am not happy, Julia, in the present state of affairs. The constant surmise of what may be the reason why I hear nothing from my promised bride, receive no more of those dear, long, interesting and comforting assurances of true affection. My heart is sad. Yet in all this, believe me, dearest, I have never doubted you for a single instant. No, I have implicit faith in you. Your eyes told me too truly the sincerity of your heart, when you promised to be the bride of him who loves you dearer by far than life . . . . God bless you, sweet one. How I should joy to look upon you tonight, with all the pride and devotion of my soul as it swells now when I think of you. To be with you and listen to your dear voice, gaze into those deep-speaking eyes,—so beautiful! Once you told me you imagined yourself the homeliest girl in Bellefontaine. Believe me, I think you are the prettiest, sweetest, dearest woman that I ever met. And, as I have often told you, the very ideal of all that man could wish: a *perfect* woman in form, features, complexion, hair, disposition, and temperament. You will— you must!—believe this, when you remember how I hate flattery.

Captain Coslett was looking over my shoulder slyly and read aloud: "Miss Julia Allison, Bellefontaine, Ohio." Our cook, who happened in just then, heard the name, and today at dinner he told Mrs. Chase what she had been trying to find out for some time. I had no peace during the entire meal. They all gave me *fits*. One thing, the cook forgot the last name and could only think of the word "Julia." Mrs. Chase said *there* was where that picture of mine went, instead of to my Mother. Colonel said I might as well confess *all,* as the women had found out the first name; but I didn't confess. He told me to hand in my papers and he would approve of them. If I do, Julia, I will give you due notice. Will go home first, and prepare things there.

I have been very busy in the past few days, and it is well that I have, or I would die of the blues. When not engaged, I am constantly walking the floor before I know it, and am as uneasy as a fish out of water. Sam and Ollie noticed it on me but too plainly, as I am led to believe by their sly glances and curious looks. However, I can't help it. I am invited *out* tomorrow evening, and if I can, will enjoy myself for the time being. Much of the writing formerly done by Ollie, I do myself lately, more to pass the time than for any reason I can give, but I believe I have told you sufficient to satisfy you that I will be a "gone up" Q.M., if I don't get a letter soon.

Did you ever tell Ez Allmon what I requested you to? So Capt. Hutch has gone into business in Bellefontaine? He must think more of that rusty old town than I do. I will never settle within one hundred miles of it. I didn't intend to finish this all in one day, and as it grows late, I will close the chapter. May write more tomorrow,—and may not. Have a notion never to send this unless I hear from you soon—but tomorrow, what may it bring forth?

Adieu, sweet Julia,

—Your Johns.

(*February 7th.*) And yet no letter from Bellefontaine! A heavy snow fell last night, and this morning it is four inches deep on the ground. The greater part of the regiment was out snow-balling. I kept closely to quarters for several reasons until evening, when Capt. Coslett and I rode over the river to fill an engagement at a friend's house, where we found several gents and ladies present. The gents were officers of the 176th Ohio Infantry. We had a *wild time,* and I forgot all about my troubles and cares until it was time to go. We have just returned to camp, and after warming my fingers, I am seated to write until I get tired.

I wish you could see Mrs. Butler on horseback. She is a splendid rider—so graceful! I accompanied her on one of her rides last Saturday afternoon. How I wished it was Julia at my side, instead! I wish you were here; I would soon learn you. One of my horses would just suit you: a large gray, high spirited, with a graceful curve of the neck, though perhaps too wild to trust with a new hand. He is continually seeing scarecrows, and is extremely shy of women (just like his master, in the last!) ; hates the looks of them. "Oh, yeth!" I hear you say. I have two private horses, besides two belonging to the government. The gray I brought from Columbus is a regular racer. You shall learn to ride before you are Mrs. Hopkins two weeks.

One battalion of darkies are encamped near us. Their behavior reflects great credit upon their very gentlemanly officers, and proves plainly that discipline *can* be enforced to better advantage among the black than in the white regiments, I am sorry to say. The majority of our regiment are men who have hitherto belonged to the Northern Peace party, and this class of individuals reluctantly acknowledges the efficiency of drill as attained by the 101st U.S. Colored Infantry, and the general good behavior of other colored regiments encamped near at hand.

Again it grows late, and again I lay aside the pen. Good night, my life's treasure,

YOUR OWN ANXIOUS JOHNS.

(*February 8th.*) I received a good long interesting letter from a little niece of mine in Ottumwa, Iowa.[35] The following is an extract of her letter:

"Your letter somewhat surprised me, and you ask what I think of it. I think *this:* that if you sincerely love Miss Julia, and she is your ideal of a *true woman,* as you say, and feel that apart from her you could have but half a life, and all your hopes and aspirations are connected with her, then take her, Johns, and your little niece's blessings go with you. But I believe, if I were you, that I would wait until out of the army. Still, you know your own heart best; decide for yourself. I hope you will get a *good wife,* a woman in every sense of the term, for you deserve one, my dear Uncle, and my prayer is that you both be happy, etc."

So you see, Julia, I have been telling tales out of school. She

[35] "Lide" Wilcox, daughter of Jemima (Hopkins) Wilcox.

is about the same age as myself; used to call me "Uncle," but I made her quit it. She now calls me plain "Johns." I wrote to her some time ago, telling her all about my dear little "pet" in Bellefontaine, but she was away from home visiting all winter, and had just arrived a few days before writing. Her father is Major of the 7th Iowa Veterans Cavalry. He has been in the Army ever since May 1861.

A large mail arrived for the regiment about one o'clock, and nearly everyone had a letter except the Q.M., who expected one from a lady in B——, but was disappointed. From all appearances, something has happened, for she hasn't written to him for *sixteen days*. The Q.M. declares he will not write again after sending a letter he is now writing, and I don't blame him! This is so, Julia; consider this my last. All I ask is for you to explain. How full of doubts, of sad thoughts! The dearest object of my life may at this time be ill; maybe . . . no! too cruel a thought!

What *must* I do? What shall I think, if I do not hear from you this week? If anything I have said or written in any of my former letters has made you angry, or has hurt your feelings in any way whatever, I beg pardon a thousand times. Do forgive me, won't you, Julia, if I have not done right? This, I think, makes the fifth letter to you, and no answer! Do you blame me, if I *am* uneasy? Can you censure me, if I make this my last letter until I hear from you, when others receive their mail regular, and I also get letters from others, and none from you? If unwell, have Carrie write three lines, at least, and let me know. I will come home, if I have to resign. This paper is nearly full, all to "writing round the edges," and I must close. My love to all. For my sake, Julia, write soon to your still trusting and devoted

—Johns.

R.Q.M. Office 182nd O.V.I.
Nashville, Feb. 8th, 1865

Captain:

I have the honor herewith to request that leave of absence be granted me for (20) Twenty days for the purpose of transacting business of importance at home.

After serving in the Army for a period of (3) Three years and six months, during which time I have never made application for leave of absence, I would respectfully request your favorable consideration of the above.

I am, Captain, Very Respectfully,

Your Ob't Sv't,

O. J. HOPKINS

Lieut. 182nd O.V.I., & R.Q.M.

To: *Captain Henry M. Cist,*

A.A.G., Dept. of Cumberland.

That same evening he handed his application to Colonel Butler, who immediately forwarded it with his approval through the proper channel. A week later Lieutenant Hopkins had his long wished for leave of absence, and lost no time in entraining for home.

TOLEDO, OHIO

February 19, 1865.

DEAR JULIA,

I arrived here last evening from Nashville, which place I left on Friday the 17th, with leave of absence for *20 days*. I long to see you, my sweet one, as my bride, and with that in view will hasten to Bellefontaine at the earliest possible moment. Look for me on Thursday next. I may come sooner, but I will designate Thursday at the farthest.

Took the family by surprise. They didn't expect me so soon. Yourtee is at Sandusky, but I look for him home tomorrow. Please answer soon and inform me of your plans. I shall consult your pleasure alone with regard to *day* and selection of *party*. Who shall I bring with me? I feel so strange when I reflect that the *day* of all others—the happiest of my life— is near at hand. And with impatience, I shall wait for it. I had a notion to stop at Sidney and take the train for Bellefontaine last night, but loss of sleep and proper rest since leaving the regiment put me *out* of the notion.

My brother and family, besides a number of friends, are downstairs, and I must return to them. Millions of kisses for my dear *wife,* and love to family, regards to friends, and comps. to Mary and Effie.

—Your devoted Johns.

Five days later, Lieutenant Hopkins and Julia Allison were married at the bride's home in Bellefontaine, Reverend J. Kalb of the First Presbyterian Church officiating. It was a quiet, family affair.

On St. Valentine's Day, in a tent on Lookout Mountain, a few miles from Chattanooga, a young officer in the United States Army wrote to Julia Allison what was to be, no doubt, a farewell letter, since it reached her on the eve of her wedding day. At some later time, Mrs. Hopkins fastened the letter inside the cover of her treasured autograph album, her father's gift at Christmas, 1859, when she had been at home on vacation from the Seminary at College Hill. There, the letter joined the penned sentiments and signatures of her girlhood friends and schoolmates. Claude K—— had loved and lost, but would be remembered.

To Miss Julia A——.

Fair Lady, how can pen portray
    The brilliancy of thy deep-dark eyes,
More soft and bright than sun-lit ray
    That bursts upon the morning skies?
They sweetly fall upon the heart,
And seem of life itself a part.

We meet thy glance, we see thy face,
    And madly bend before thy shrine;
Upon thy blushing cheek we trace
    Enchantment, beauty, so entwined—
Enraptured captives, we adore,
And are thy slaves forevermore.

But though thine eyes are starry-bright,
    Thy very lips like cherries red,
Thy step so graceful and so light,
    It seems almost an angel's tread,
These charms not like that witching smile
So love bewildering all the while.

Oh! lovely girl, could I but claim
  A heart like thine, so soft and pure,
I'd envy not the hero's fame;
  All ills of life I could endure,
And, living e'er in joys like this,
  Would never seek for greater bliss.

May roses by thy pathway twine,
  And flowers e'er blossom on thy way,
Bright hopes, like gems, forever shine
  Around your heart where'er you stray,
Encircling life with roseate hues,
  Fresh as the rose embalmed in dews.

Princess thou art, and hast thy throne
  In youthful hearts, that love the chain
That makes them all, all thine own;
  Though captured, they do not complain;
They love, and wish not to be free,
  And feel 'tis bliss to love but thee.

Thy voice, like music o'er the sea,
  Steals on our hearts, a thing divine;
Ah! n'er did courtly minstrelsy
  Breathe forth such softened strains as thine;
"So soft and low and sweet they fell,
  Like echoes of some fairy bell."

Bright child of hope and love and joy,
  Sweet are the blossoms of thy spring—
Sweet be thy dreams, without alloy,
  And, like some bird of heavenly wing,
May you spread pleasures where you go,
  Pure as the mountain's virgin snow.

Their honeymoon was short. Lieutenant Hopkins' leave of absence for "transacting business of importance" expired on the tenth of March. The bride's expense account shows that they were on their way back to Nashville on the seventh, but in no hurry (see Appendix D).

At the post, they occupied army quarters and usually ate at the Headquarters mess in the "Brick House." However,

Julia bought some "crockery ware," hung curtains at the windows, covered the rough board flooring with a carpet, draped the pine table with a gay red and black, flowered tablecloth, and had a charge account for groceries and supplies at the Regimental Sutler's store. Occasionally, the young couple rode horseback together—at least, we know that Mrs. Hopkins bought a riding skirt. They were enjoying the amenities of garrison life uninterrupted by wartime disturbances, according to letters they wrote to Lide Wilcox, in Eddyville, Iowa.

NASHVILLE, TENN.
April 2, 1865.

MY DEAR NIECE,

I have come to the conclusion to write you a few lines by way of inquiry as to why in the mischief you don't write! Certainly it can't be on account of my marriage with one of the sweetest women in the world, though I am half inclined to believe it, as you said in your last letter that married people were so different from single folk. Remember, I'm the same old "Johns," with all the propensities of my youth, and surely I have not lost a single item of the love I have always had for my little Lide.

I wish you could see my little Better Half, who is at this moment writing near me. I'm sure you would kiss her to death. We are living in real old-fashioned style in camp. Mrs. Butler and Mrs. Chase are here and will remain until we are mustered out. So will Julia, if she doesn't get tired of it. Our Camp is splendidly situated, with men engaged constantly improving its appearance with cedar trees and sod.

My own quarters stand on a square in which are planted beautiful green trees and graveled walks, with many other ornaments to add beauty to the view from my front window. In fact, I am as happy as a king and at times too light-hearted to look far into the future, where trials await everyone who expects to advance through the world.

I have much to do yet before starting into real life, and feel the importance of improving every moment of my present mode of life in order to fit myself for the changes to come. I hope you will not delay writing; hereafter, I will be more prompt, myself. Love to Mother and the rest, and a share for yourself.

> Your loving Uncle,
> —JOHNS.

> NASHVILLE, TENN.
> April 2, 1865.

MY DEAR NIECE,

Johns has requested me to write something. What it will be, I know not. As you know, whether you have ever tried it or not, it isn't the easiest thing in the world to write a person you have never met. Besides, I am most "played out," as I have written a sheet this size to a friend at home, half a one to Pa, and a quarter of one to Doc Thompson.

I like Camp life so much; it's splendid! Nothing in *my* life has equalled it. It may be the *company* I have now has something to do with it. Have no doubt it has, which you will find out some day, and Johns says: "At no distant period!" I can partly sympathize with you, as I expected my husband home the first of January. But he got home for the 24th of February, so I was a *little* better off than you.

I suppose Mother is out with you ere this. Johns received a letter from Yourt day before yesterday, in which he said she had started for the West. I was out to Iowa last fall, visiting at my Uncle's in Oskaloosa, Judge Seever's. Tell Mother she must go up to see them before she returns to Ohio. They won't like it, if she doesn't. Well, it is getting *very* late, and I suppose I must quit. My love to Mother and Sister and yourself. Tell Mother, *for my sake*, to go up to Oskaloosa. Well, good night; write soon.

> Your Aunt,
> —JULIA.

A week later, on the ninth of April, at the home of Mr. McLean in the village of Appomattox Court House, Virginia, a stubby bearded man in the stained and worn uniform of a private soldier with the shoulder straps of a lieutenant general sat down at a table in a room filled with Confederate and Union officers. Facing him stood General Lee, tall, dignified, in full dress uniform, a glittering ceremonial sword at his side.

The man at the table dipped his pen in an ink bottle and scrawled on a sheet of yellow paper a note that began: "General: In accordance with the substance of my letter to you of the 8th inst., I propose to receive the surrender of the Army of North Virginia on the following terms . . . ."

The long and terrible struggle between the States had come to an end.

When the news reached Nashville, the Mayor and General Thomas planned a victory procession and "illuminations" for the fifteenth of April, the day before Easter. But early Saturday morning, the "Nashville Union" issued a small, three-column flier, an "extra," with heavy black rules and headlines:

THE REBEL FIENDS AT WORK

President Lincoln Shot
Secretary Seward Stabbed
The President and Mr. Seward Both Dead
Grief of Mrs. Lincoln
Seward's Son and Attendants Attacked
Young Seward's Skull Fractured
Wilkes Booth the President's Assassin
Seward's Assassin Escaped
No Celebration in Nashville

There would be no parade. Wherever flags were out, they would be draped in black.

For Lieutenant Hopkins the day was doubly tragic. Less than forty-eight hours before, his commanding officer, Colonel Butler, had summoned him to Headquarters and informed him that he had been dismissed from the service of the United States, the dismissal to take effect immediately. The order, dated March 2, 1865, was signed by General Thomas. It stated that court-martial proceedings held at Nashville, December 7, 1864, had found Lieutenant Hopkins guilty of conduct, alleged to have been committed on the preceding thirtieth of November, "prejudicial to good order and military discipline" and "unbecoming an officer and a gentleman."

The action of the court came to him with the unexpectedness and stunning impact of an exploding shell.

It was no less unexpected by Colonel Butler, who had not known of the incident, trial, and sentence until receipt of the dismissal order. He immediately dispatched a letter to General Thomas.

HEADQUARTERS, 182ND O.V.I.
NASHVILLE, TENN., April 14, 1865.

GENERAL:

I am just in receipt of an order, dismissing Lieut. O. J. Hopkins, Quarter Master of my Regiment, from the Service of the United States. I am entirely unacquainted with the circumstances of the case, but I am free to state that the language, said to be used upon that occasion, is far from being characteristic of the man. At the time the offence was committed, he was a comparative stranger to me and I never saw the charges until today. This offence took place in the fore part of November last, since which time he has served honorably and faithfully, and in all respects conducted himself as a gentleman, and from what I know of his character before and his conduct since, I am led to believe that great injustice has been done a good man. He had served three (3) years a noncommissioned officer in the 42nd. Ohio Vol. Inf., and had been discharged only four days before he was commissioned Quarter Master of my Regiment.

Very Respectfully,
Your Ob't Servant,
—LOUIS BUTLER
Col. com'd'g Reg.

Major General Thomas.

Mrs. Hopkins had already sent a letter to her father, who was in Columbus attending the session of the State legislature, telling him of the disaster that had befallen them and the great concern she had for the grave condition of her husband. Mr. Allison had returned to Bellefontaine, and there was a week's delay before she received his reply.

BELLEFONTAINE, OHIO
April 19, 1865.

MY DEAR DAUGHTER,

Yours of the 13th inst. is at hand, forwarded to me from Columbus. The Legislature adjourned on the 13th.

It would be useless for me to conceal my chagrin upon the receipt of your letter informing me of the dismissal of my son-in-law whom I much respect. I am really sorry, however, that his mind has been shaken by it in the manner you describe. Some disgrace attaches, of course, to a dismissal from service, and therefore I would not have been pleased to hear that he received the sentence with indifference.

The cause of his dismissal, as you give it, does not attach much dishonor to it, particularly to an officer so young. Let him bear it like a man and sternly resolve that, instead of being kept down despondingly, that by honesty, integrity, and industry he will secure the respect of mankind, as well as a competency for himself and family, notwithstanding the dismissal. The world is open to him. His friends will not leave him through a mere boyish indiscretion.

It will be perhaps the means of making him a more valuable man to his community. I hope he will rise above the despondency manifested at the date of your letter, and immediately return and get into some honest business. There are plenty of opportunities, I have no doubt, which will offer success by care and attention.

My advice would be to leave Nashville immediately and return to his friends, and endeavor to get into some kind of business as soon as possible. Do not remain at Nashville in the hope of getting reinstated. That is uncertain, at best, but in any event it would be perhaps months before anything would be heard from an application. It has taken months to hear of his dismissal; a reinstatement will be slower still. Capt. Alex Stanton, when he returned here dismissed, had many kind assurances from friends and associate officers that he would be reinstated. An application has now been pending two or three months, but nothing can be heard from it.

My family at home are all enjoying their usual health. I

will be pleased to see you and Johns at any and all times, and hope you will both return immediately

Your affectionate Father,

C. W. B. ALLISON.

MY DEAR SON,

I have heard of your dismissal. You have honor and the respect of friends left to you, and more than all, a loving wife. With these, you can yet easily succeed by industry and perseverance in gaining a respectable position in a community. Resolve to do so. If you can get some certificates from your associate officers, do so, but I would not place much reliance in getting your sentence revoked. Do not delay a day in Nashville for such purpose. You are young and a world of business is before you. If I am not deceived, God has endowed you with a talent for business, and you have but to make proper use of yourself to insure success. No man should, nor has he a right to give way to despondency. Life has two sides; misfortunes are allotted to us all. All are at times sorely tried, and true manhood is made the better and brighter thereby. In this your hour of adversity, arouse and show yourself a man.

I hope to see you soon. I am truly

Yours affectionately,

C. W. B. ALLISON.

The incident that led to the court-martial, and the subsequent actions taken in regard to its findings, are correctly and succinctly set forth in a service record prepared years later for official purposes by Lieutenant Colonel Hopkins of the Ohio National Guard. A pertinent extract is given here, together with certain letters and orders having a special bearing on the case.

. . . One morning I was ordered by Colonel Butler, the commanding officer of the regiment, to ride to the city on an important errand, and to make all haste possible on the trip. I was hardly in condition to mount my horse, but nevertheless started to Nashville. When about half way to the city, I was passing through a dense growth of hazel bushes, when a sentinel suddenly sprang into the path and cried: "Halt!"

My horse, being on a rapid trot, could not be checked up suddenly, and crossed the line. Then, an officer, one Lieut. Drumheller of the 176th O.V.I., appeared out of the bushes and roughly seized my bridle rein, with an oath in broken German, demanding why I did not stop when halted by the guard. He was so uncivil and overbearing that I was irritated beyond measure, and words followed between us until both became very angry. I told him I had a standing pass to go through the lines at all times, but had that day left it in my overcoat pocket in camp, and asked him to let me ride on, and I would secure a duplicate pass in the city and show it to him on my return. This he refused to do, and roughly backed my horse, using oaths and vile language, until, losing my head in anger, I spurred my animal, which, being a high spirited one, sprang away, and I galloped to the city.

After cooling off, I began to realize what I had done: namely, committed a serious breach of discipline by failing to respect a guard, and I reported the fact to General Mason, the Commandant of the Post, who said he was sorry it had occurred, and that I might have trouble from the act, but that he would give me a pass back to camp, which he did, and transacting my affairs in the city, I hastened back to camp.

Lieutenant Drumheller, in due time, preferred charges against me. These were served while I lay on a sick bed, and my friends in the regiment succeeded in having the trial postponed until I was well enough to attend. Finally, when the Court assembled, I was convalescing from a long spell of illness, and I was neither mentally nor physically in condition to make a proper defense, but let matters drift as they would,[36] hardly realizing the dangers of such a course, and so, when the verdict of dismissal was rendered, it was a severe shock to me and to my regiment, as well as to all my friends, who immediately joined in a petition to have the findings of the Court set aside. This was signed by every officer in the regiment, and also by many of the officers of my old regiment,

[36] ". . . Owing to the repeated assurances of the Judge Advocate at the time of my trial that my case was not a serious one, I brought but very little evidence to bear in my own defense, though I was offered it by numerous officers of the command."—O. J. H. [An excerpt from a statement submitted to the Adjutant General, in Columbus, when application was made for a review of his case.]

the 42nd O.V.I., the latter accompanying their petitions with letters stating my former service in the army and earnestly requesting my reinstatement.

This was in March, 1865, and the end of the war was near at hand, and it took time to get the papers before the proper authorities, but finally the authorities at Washington issued an order removing disability, but inasmuch as the vacancy of Quarter Master of the regiment had been filled, it was out of the question to secure reinstatement in my old position, but Governor Brough issued me a new commission as First Lieutenant in the same regiment, and with this I hastened back to Nashville, only to find that the regiment were under orders to go to Columbus for muster-out. I accompanied it home, with my whole life embittered over my experience.

I was young, and perhaps not of sufficiently mature years or judgement to have placed on my shoulders the rank and responsibilities of the position to which I had been elevated, and from which I had been so cruelly removed. I will, at this late date, while the memory of the whole unfortunate affair still rankles in my mind, admit that I lacked the judgement I should have exercised at the time, and that my offense was a serious one in the eyes of military men.

There was but the evidence of this half-drunken German lieutenant to substantiate the specifications to the charges, and many of them were false as sworn to by him, particularly as to my language toward him. I say "drunken officer" because I was aware that he had been drinking, and was then half intoxicated. His guard was stationed much nearer our camp than it had been the day before, when I had passed the same point without challenge, it being customary for all commissioned officers to pass a camp guard at that point without question. . . .

NASHVILLE, TENN.
April 24, 1865.

Lieut. O. J. Hopkins,
DEAR SIR,
In accordance to my promise, I hereby transmit to you our private tribute to your known worth. Pleace accept on my

part, the condolence of a friend, whose sympathy for your case is most heartfelt and sincere.

Yours Respectfully,

—A. A. WHISSEN

Major, 182nd O.V.I.

Having learned that you bid us farewell tomorrow, we could not let the occasion pass without making known to you our high appreciation of you as an officer and a gentleman, during your sojourn amongst us. Efficient, competent, and faithful, you have shown yourself on every duty you have been called on to perform, and entering the Service at the beginning of the war, we consider this a small tribute to one who has served his country as faithfully as we know you to have done. Rest assured, comrade, that you carry with you to your home the earnest wish of every officer of this command for your future success and welfare in whatever sphere of usefulness your life may be cast. Long may you live to enjoy the friendship of the remainder of the little band that started at their country's first call and have so often met around the camp fires to while away the hours in social intercourse.

Again, comrade, we bid you farewell.

A. A. WHISSEN

Major, 182nd O.V.I.

Signed:

LOUIS BUTLER, *Colonel*

J. A. CHASE, *Lieut.-Col.*

GEORGE CASSADY, *Surgeon*

WILL H. WOOD, *1st. Lieut., Co. K*

A. H. HER, *1st. Asst. Surgeon*

THOS. J. THOMPSON, *2nd. Asst. Surgeon*

WM. H. SHRIVER, *Capt. Co. A*

E. D. LEEDOM, *1st. Lieut. and Adjutant*

W. W. COOKE, *Capt. Co. D*

J. K. POLLARD, *2nd. Lieut. Co. I*

J. N. SMITH, *2nd. Lieut. Co. D*

I. A. NOBLE, *Capt. Co. C*

JOHN SHELTON, *Capt. Co. H*

I. G. STOLL, *1st. Lieut. Co. E*

D. A. TERRY, *Capt. Co. E*

L. L. CONNER, *2nd. Lieut. Co. G*

JOHN J. SAVER, *1st. Lieut. Co. B*

LAWRENCE WAMSLEY, *Lieut. and Act. R.Q.M.*

GEO. M. YOUNG, *1st. Lieut. Co. D*

ERNEST F. LOPEZ, *1st. Lieut. Co. I*

THOMAS MITCHELL, *Lieut. Co. G*

A. F. STONER, *1st. Lieut. Co. F*

H. B. O'HARRA, *2nd. Lieut. Co. E*

R. R. TURITIN, *Lieut. Co. F*

A. M. LANG, *Capt. Co. G*

JAMES L. DEPUTY, *Lieut. Co. A*

HENRY PENCE, *1st. Lieut. Co. H*

CHAS. A. WRIGHT, *Capt. Co. K*

G. W. B. ETTINGHAM, *2nd. Lieut. Co. H*

WM. H. BROOKER, *2nd. Lieut. Co. C*

In placing our names to this, we only acknowledge the worth of a true soldier and Gentleman.

SAMUEL GODEAU, *Sutler, 182nd O.V.I. and late Lieut., 27th Illinois V.I.*

DR. W. H. DAUGHERTY, *Asst. Sutler, 182nd O.V.I.*

Following Mr. Allison's advice, Lieutenant and Mrs. Hopkins left Nashville, on the twenty-fifth of April, for Bellefontaine. They then went on to Toledo, where they set up housekeeping while they waited for action in Washington on the petitions. The mills ground slowly, indeed. It was two months before the Adjutant General of Ohio, acting on an order from the Governor, filed some of the necessary papers.

The following letter was sent to the Adjutant General at the War Department.

ADJUTANT GENERAL'S OFFICE
COLUMBUS, OHIO. May 12, 1865

Respectfully referred to Col. Thomas M. Vincent, A.A.G., for investigation:

By the accompanying papers it will be seen that there was an understanding that Lieutenant Hopkins might pass the Grand Guard without a *pass.*

The offense, with the explanations which accompany the papers, is almost entirely explained away. Prior to this occurrence, Hopkins bore an excellent character. He was a soldier for Three years in the 42nd Regiment, and discharged every duty faithfully and was appointed Quartermaster of the 182nd Regiment last fall for merit alone. Lieut. Hopkins is an officer worth saving, and it is hoped a review of his case may be had at once, and he be reinstated, at least honorably acquitted of the serious charge preferred against him, and his disability removed that he may be recommissioned.

By Order of the Governor,
—B. R. COWEN
Adj't Gen., Ohio.

Hopkins' father-in-law reported on the progress of his case in Washington.

BELLEFONTAINE, OHIO
June 15, 1865

DEAR SON,

I see in the papers yesterday that Gen. Steadman is in Cincinnati, and presume he was in Toledo upon his return from Washington. Do you know whether he did anything for you? Mr. Stanton was in Washington a week after Gen. Steadman arrived there, and was surprised when informed at the proper office that no application had been made for your reinstatement, either by Gen. Steadman or any other person. Mr. Stanton then presented the papers from the Adj.-Gen'l's office of this state, with the Governor's recommendation, of which I sent you a copy, and was interceding for you when he was informed that a written application for your reinstatement must first be filed, which, with any other papers or proofs relied upon, must be filed and must first be examined and passed upon by the Judge Advocate General, Judge Holt, who was then busily engaged in the assassination trials.

Mr. Stanton, thereupon, filed an application for your reinstatement and the other papers, with a memorandum that some of them were copies, the originals of which were in the hands of Major-General Steadman. That was all he could do at that time. Steadman remained there for some time afterwards. Unless there is some person there occasionally to keep it moving, it will be a long time before it is heard from. Steadman is now with Gen. Thomas, and if he would get the latter's recommendation for a reinstatement, there would be no doubt of our success. I am not acquainted with Steadman, or I would write him. Your friends in Toledo can manage him. Mr. Stanton will be in Washington again in a few weeks, when I will have him again stir the matter up, if not heard from before.

His application for his son's [37] reinstatement had been pending for months, and had been passed upon by Judge Holt, but when he went there, the papers had been lost, and nothing further would ever have been heard from it, if he had not gone there himself. He procured copies from Judge Holt's office, where they had been recorded, and saw the Secretary of War. He succeeded in getting the Secretary's order to have him recommissioned as a Captain in the Regulars. He could not be reinstated, as his vacancy had been filled. He was assured the appointment would be forwarded in a few days, but it has not yet arrived.

My family are all enjoying usual health. Love to Julia.

Yours affectionately,

—C. W. B. ALLISON.

However, in a week, the long-awaited decision arrived.

WAR DEPARTMENT
ADJUTANT GENERAL'S OFFICE
WASHINGTON, June 23, 1865

Mr. Owen J. Hopkins
late 1st Lieutenant 182nd Ohio Vol. Infty.
Care B. Stanton, Esq., Washington, D.C.

SIR,

I am instructed to inform you that the disability resulting from your dismissal by sentence of General Court Martial Orders No. 11, March 2, 1865, Head Quarters, Department of the Cumberland, has been removed by letter of this date to His Excellency the Governor of Ohio.

---

[37] Benjamin Stanton's son Alex had been released from Libby Prison in an exchange of prisoners.

You are, therefore, authorized to re-enter the service as a Commissioned Officer, provided you are recommissioned.

I am, Sir, Very Respectfully,

Your Obt. servant,

—THOMAS M. VINCENT

Asst. Adj't Gen'l.

The re-appointment followed immediately.

IN THE NAME AND BY THE AUTHORITY OF THE STATE OF OHIO

To all whom these presents shall come, greeting:

Know ye, That reposing special trust and confidence in the patriotism, valor, fidelity and abilities of—OWEN J. HOP-KINS—, by virtue of the authority vested in me by the laws of the United States and the State of Ohio, I, JOHN BROUGH, Governor and Commander-in-Chief of said State, do hereby appoint and Commission him First Lieutenant in the One Hundred and Eighty-Second (182) Regiment of Ohio Volunteer Infantry, raised under the authority of the President and Congress of the United States of America, for One year, with rank as such from the Thirtieth (30) day of June, 1865. He is, therefore, carefully and diligently to discharge the duties of said office according to law and the regulations governing the Armies of the United States.

In testimony thereof, I have hereunto set my hand and caused the Great Seal of the State to be affixed at the City of Columbus, this thirtieth (30) day of June in the year of our Lord, one thousand eight hundred and sixty-five, and in the eighty-ninth year of the Independence of the United States of America.

JNO. BROUGH

By the Governor

WM. HENRY SMITH

Secretary of State

Adjutant General's Office
B. R. Cowen
Adjutant General of Ohio

*The ordeal was over at last. Lieutenant Hopkins, rein-
stated in his regiment, his honor vindicated, returned to Nashville at once. But the War of the Rebellion had ended, and
the One Hundred Eighty-second had been mustered out. He
returned with the regiment to Columbus. While he was away
from home, he wrote to his wife in Toledo the last of his wartime letters.*

COLUMBUS, OHIO
July 5, 1865

MY DEAR WIFE,

I arrived here at 3:35 this morning, and had the desired
change made on my papers. Could get my pay,[38] if the Paymaster, Major Williams, was here, but he is absent from the
city and will not return until tomorrow. I will have no difficulty getting it at Cincinnati or Louisville.

Am well, but sleepy. Saw Capt. Gardner this morning.
Carrie is staying at home. I learn that Alex Stanton has been
commissioned in Hancock's Veterans Corps,[39] instead of the
regular army. The weather is very warm. Saw several of the
old 42nd boys last night. Write immediately, if not sooner.

YOUR AFFECTIONATE BETTER HALF, O. J. H.

CINCINNATI, OHIO.
July 5, 1865.

MY OWN DEAR WIFE,

I reached here O.K. this evening, at sundown, covered with
dust. Tried to sleep, but before I go to bed I will send you a
few lines. Am at the "Spencer House," and will leave for
Louisville on steamer *General Lytle* in the morning. I think I
will have time to get my pay before I go. Don't think I ever
suffered so with dust and heat as I have today; my eyes, nose,
mouth, ears, and pockets are filled with dust, and I will have
to lie and soak in some river before it will come off.

Before yesterday and today, I never had an idea of what it

---

[38] He was unable to collect his pay for his service between March 2, 1865,
and the actual date of severance, April 15, until 1868, despite the combined
efforts of friends and attorneys in Washington.

[39] General Winfield Scott Hancock, who commanded the Second Army Corps
in the campaign of the Army of the Potomac, 1864–65.

was to be away from you. How I would like to have just one kiss before I go to sleep tonight. But I hope you will enjoy yourself before I come back. It grows late, and I must go to bed. A daily increasing love of mine for you, and Good Night,

YOUR OWN JOHNS.

NASHVILLE, TENN.
July 8, 1865.

MY DEAR WIFE,

I arrived here last night and found the Regiment mustered out of service, with orders to report to Camp Chase for final payment. We leave here some time this evening on the train for Louisville, thence to Columbus. I am very glad of it, as I am sick of Nashville. We will be home sometime next week. Mrs. Chase and the Colonel are sick and look like skeletons. She is as yellow as a lemon.

I got here just in time, and will be satisfied to return with the Regiment. Things have changed very much here since last winter, and "times" are dull. I was over to see the Regiment, and they nearly ate me up alive. Haven't seen Doc yet, as he was down town. They are in barracks over near Fort Negley, though Colonel's Head Quarters are where they formerly were.

You can't imagine how lonesome I am without you, and I don't see how men can stay in the army three or four years, who have wives and a family at home.

Will you promise not to scold, if I tell you I danced on the Boat coming down from Cincinnati? We had a gay time. More ladies than men. I won't do it any more. Look for us about the last of next week. I will be paid off at Columbus with the regiment. Meanwhile, I remain as ever,

Your own, dear, true, faithful Husband,
O. J. H.

COLUMBUS, OHIO.
July 10, 1865.

MY OWN DEAR WIFE,

We left Nashville on the 8th., and arrived here about two hours ago, and the Regiment marched down to Camp Chase to await final payment. It is now ten o'clock P.M. Had a very pleasant trip, but I was sick nearly all the way with something very like the flux.

Indeed, am not well yet, though much better tonight. I wish you could see how Colonel Chase served his wife. It has been the subject of general conversation amongst all of us since we left Nashville. The train from Nashville to Louisville was composed of box cars, with one emigrant car for officers which was not cushioned but had rough seats made of cast iron and lumber. Chase, instead of taking her on the regular passenger train, took her into our car with him, when she was too sick to hold her head up. There was no chance to sleep, and the poor woman had to worry it through. At Cincinnati, she had to walk a mile to the Hotel, he being too stingy to take a carriage. She looks like death. Suppose she is in Toledo by this time, as she left Cincinnati this morning on the D. & M.R.R. for that place.

Don't know when we will be home, but think by Friday next, at least. Doc is down at the Soldier's Home, near the Depot, with all the sick, the other doctors taking care of "No. 1." Col. Butler told Col. Chase tonight that Thompson was better than all the other doctors put together to look after things and take care of men.

Chase, Butler, and myself are at the "American" tonight. I am writing with both of your pictures on the table before me. I look at them so much that I can hardly write. When night comes, it does me good to know that you are loving me still, and perhaps thinking of me at the same moment. By the way, I have two awful dirty shirts which will make somebody sweat to wash; also, one or two black white handkerchiefs. I haven't been able to draw any money yet, but think I can get it tomorrow, if the paymaster is in town. My greatest fears are that, in my absence, my poor lonely little wife will want for something and have no money to get it with. I thought about it last night, and couldn't sleep for fear that, in these dark moments of our early married life, you would lose confidence in me, and come to the conclusion that you had married a shiftless man, and that your future life is to be spent in a log cabin. But, Julia, I beg of you to have faith in your own true Johns a while longer, and all will be well. At times, I am on the eve of total discouragement; then I think of you, my dear wife, of what I have to live for—feeling that I have a wife who is in every way calculated to make me happy —and I hope that brighter days may come, that the sun of prosperity will suddenly dawn after these few hours of apparent darkness.

I showed your picture to every one I got acquainted with going down to Nashville, and they all said it was splendid, but didn't believe I was married, as I looked so young. Must close, as it grows late. With a thousand kisses for my little idol, I remain,

—YOUR LOVING JOHNS.

V

EPILOGUE

1865—1902

The era of the Great Rebellion ended in three tragic events which took place within as many weeks in the spring of 1865: General Lee surrendered at Appomattox, General Johnston capitulated at Durham's Station, and President Lincoln was assassinated.

Suddenly, unexpectedly, thousands of volunteer soldiers like Lieutenant Hopkins found themselves civilians again, found themselves faced with the hardships and anxieties common in the aftermath of war, and obliged to adjust their ways of life to a changed society and to restore painfully and laboriously what had been destroyed.

The brash youth who was Private Hopkins in June, 1861, emerged from the service in July, 1865, a matured veteran of twenty-one—married, and sobered by the immediate necessity of finding a job, choosing a career, and establishing a home of his own. The choice of an occupation was not an easy one to make. He had an untrained talent for drawing and designing, some skill as an engineer (an ability he had revealed during the planning and building of the fortifications at Plaquemine and Morganza), and an aptitude for accounting (which had proved valuable during his service as army quartermaster). In addition, he had a deeply rooted interest in military tactics. Moreover, he was a man dedicated to the service of his country and his fellow man. It was this dedication that led to his greatest accomplishment in the years to come.

In the last months of 1865, following his marriage to Julia Allison and his discharge from the army, he worked for his brother Almon as bookkeeper in the office of Hopkins and Griffith, grain and produce commission merchants in Toledo.

Almon had promised him a partnership in the firm, but when this did not materialize, Owen resigned. In February, 1866, against the advice of his father-in-law, who urged him to seek a business career rather than a political appointment, he entered government employ as a mail agent on the Cincinnati, Dayton, and Toledo Railroad between Toledo and Cincinnati.

In April of that year, their first child was born,[1] and the long absences from his family in Maumee City that were necessitated by his job became distasteful to him. The following October he quit railroading and returned to bookkeeping, this time as a clerk in the Toledo freight office of the Cleveland and Toledo Railroad. Three years later, he transferred to the grain office of the Lake Shore and Michigan Southern Railroad.

His wages as an accountant were two dollars a day. The position held no allure and little promise for an imaginative young man with a growing family. From childhood he had been plagued by an urge to draw; and while he was in service, he had often made sketches for his own amusement between marches and battles. Therefore, after the financial crash of 1867, in which his brother Almon had lost his commission business and a sizeable fortune, and also the army pay that Owen had sent to him during the war as an investment, he considered using his artistic talents as a means of earning a livelihood. He had, in fact, for some time been supplementing his wages by drawing and engraving at night in his home. His younger brother Yourtee, whose cartoons were appearing in Winchell and Small's *Wild Oats,* Monro's *Fireside Companion,* and other seaboard journals,[2] had been sending drawings to him for engraving from New York, and he was receiving commissions from Strong[3] and Kellogg[4] in Chicago. Conse-

[1] Annie Allison Hopkins.
[2] Later, Yourtee contributed cartoons to *Scribner's,* the *Graphic, St. Nicholas,* the *Comic Almanac,* and various newspapers.
[3] C. E. Strong founded the Chicago Newspaper Union in 1870; and following the Great Fire of 1871, he helped the burned-out publishers of the *Republican, Post, Union,* and *Staats Zeitung* to maintain their circulation. The Union became a powerful influence in the Middle West press through its "auxiliary sheets" services.
[4] Ansel N. Kellogg, founder of the famous "Kellogg Lists," supplied country papers with literary material, cuts, advertisements, articles, and so on. He initiated the use of such ready-printed material as early as 1864-65.

quently, in May, 1872, he decided to leave the grain office and set himself up in the engraving business. His wife and children [5] were in Oskaloosa, visiting the Seevers, when he wrote to her:

> Today I notified Mr. Wheeler that I would resign on the first of June and requested him to have a man ready to take the books by that time . . . . I promised to stay until the sixth, although I will doubtless be at work in my own office part of the time after the first. I have found a room in Scott's Block, corner of Summit and Perry Streets, just back of the officer formerly occupied by the *Democrat:* terms $8.00 per month, so the clerk told me, but thought I could get it for $6.00 . . . . I have been up to the store and have ordered a table and some cheap office chairs. The table will be six or seven dollars, the chairs seventy-five cents apiece. I have much work on hand for Chicago, and no time here to do it. My eyes are so affected that I had to quit working by gaslight. By keeping good office hours, I will doubtless be able to do my engraving by daylight hereafter, and have my evenings at home with my little family . . . .
>
> I have received the following letter from Chicago: "O. J. Hopkins, Engr. Dear Sir, We should like to make some arrangement with you to get up some sketches of Chicago celebrities for the *Sun,* if you are disposed to do something for us in that line on reasonable terms. We think of putting a series of cuts in the *Sun,* accompanied by local sketches, etc. It may be necessary for you to come here and see the parties to be sketched. Please answer immediately. Yours, etc. R. E. Hoyt, Editor *Chicago Sun*."
>
> To this I replied: "Send photographs of your celebrities and a written outline of what you want, and I can doubtless 'fix you out' satisfactorily, both as to terms and quality of work. Your patronage is respectfully solicited." Adding also that my arrangements would preclude the idea of going to Chicago and making sketches from life. The *Sun* is a big institution issuing three editions daily, and I can probably secure in them another good patron.[6]
>
> The two cuts I send you are part of a series of four, all portraits, for which I am to get $45 (instead of $40 as I wrote you) for their first use. They illustrate a short story, *Love Without*

---

[5] The Hopkinses then had three children: Annie, born in 1866, Oliver Perry, in 1868, and Frederick, in 1870.

[6] It is not known whether the *Sun* complied with his request.

Nonsense.[7] I cut out these two in one day; how is that for making money? . . .

I wrote Kellogg to return the *House Cleaning* cuts to me if he didn't want them for $30, and he replied: "The electros of *Cleaning Day* were ready to send to you when, although my views as to using them are unchanged, I felt that our pleasant relations would be better represented by a cheque for the amount you named as a midway sum. So I send you the money ($30) and put the cuts away for the Spring of 1873. Always subject to your convenience, Yours faithfully, A. N. Kellogg.[8]

During the next six months, his commissions from Strong, Kellogg, and others increased and a bright future for the aspiring young cartoonist seemed assured. H. S. Knapp, for whose *History of the Maumee Valley* (Toledo: Blade Publishing House, 1872) he had drawn and engraved the frontispiece,[9] hailed him as "an artist of rare merit and cleverness," whose productions as a caricaturist were published "in the illustrated papers of the Atlantic and other cities." And in a letter to his vacationing wife, he wrote with pardonable pride: "Yourt says he saw a flattering notice for me in a New Hampshire paper not long since. Give me time and I will make my mark, as the man said who couldn't write."[10]

In spite of his success, however, friends persuaded him to run for the office of police commissioner; and he was elected for the term 1873–74; but at the end of the year, he declined renomination,[11] and returned to his drawing table and wood blocks.

His letter-head of 1874 carried a cut of the old four-story brick and stone Myers Building, where he had his office in Room No. 4, and the legend, "Office of O. J. Hopkins, De-

---

[7] He states later that the story was "a prose article burlesqueing the modern style of novels." Mr. Kellogg eventually paid him $35.

[8] He had received the poem for illustration on April 16, but did not finish the engraving until May 8; spring had waned.

[9] The caption for the frontispiece read: "Landing of the Old Continental First Regiment of Infantry at Fort Industry." Hopkins confessed that the drawing was based on his imagination.

[10] For Kellogg he illustrated "Bully Bly," "Insurance Agent," "Song of the Shears," "The Old Man in the Stylish Church," "The Engineer," "The Fat Man's Story" (by Ralph Keeler, in *Appleton's*), and so on.

[11] In 1890, a Zanesville paper stated that "he served acceptably . . . and introduced many needed reforms in the police department of the city."

signer and Engraver on Wood. Real Estate Plats. Book Illustrations. Posters. Views of Buildings, etc." During the next seven years, while he was at this address, he produced hundreds of drawings and cuts, ranging from advertisements for wheelbarrows, pumps, downspouts, raincoats, furniture, and wagon wheels, to labels in two or three colors for beer, coffee, bluing, soap, and tobacco; from drawings of business establishments, hotels, fish hatcheries, and real estate plats, to designs for badges, insignia, center-heads for newspapers, and membership and insurance certificates.

He had accounts with the *Toledo Sunday Journal,* the *North Ohio Democrat,* the *Bowling Green News,* the *Perrysburg Journal,* the *Grange,* the *Railway Guide,* the *Railroader,* the *Toledo Bee,* and the *Toledo Blade,* furnishing political cartoons, special block type, autographs, ornaments, portraits, and news illustrations. D. R. Locke and the *Blade* were his best clients.

Between November 14, 1878, and August 14, 1879, the *Blade* ran in serial form John McElroy's [12] *Andersonville: A Story of Rebel Military Prisons,* which Locke later published in book form. It became a classic in Civil War literature, reappearing in the G.A.R. *National Tribune* years afterward. Ninety-eight of the one hundred and thirty illustrations were drawn and engraved by Hopkins. These and a few drawings for D. R. Locke's works of "Petroleum B. Nasby" mark the close of his career as a professional artist and engraver.[13] In later years, he took up painting, but solely for the enjoyment of members of his family. For the majority of his canvases, he chose his own war memories as subjects. The titles of some of them are "Thompson's Hill," "Siege of Vicksburg," "Artillery in Action," "The Bugler," "On Picket Duty," and "Tramp on the Rails."

In the ten years between 1871 and 1881 that he had devoted to an artistic career, either as a side line or as a main source of income, he had made his mark, though not too indelibly.

[12] John McElroy was a member of Company L, Sixteenth Illinois Cavalry, and had been imprisoned in Andersonville, Richmond, Savannah, Blackshear, and other Southern camps.

[13] He engraved Yourtee's *Nasby, The Robbery,* and his own poster and six cuts for *Nasby's Dream.*

In 1902, the Bellefontaine *Examiner* had this to say about him: "O. J. Hopkins was widely known some thirty years ago as a newspaper artist. He made woodcut illustrations of great merit, of humourous character, and was connected with a Toledo newspaper several years. He was a talented man in many respects and he first came into prominence as an illustrator of Bret Harte's poetry . . . ."[14]

His work had not been very remunerative. He seldom received as much as ten dollars for a cut. Often he had to take payment in kind: coal, shoes, clothing, cigars, furniture, or his own advertising. Payments were slow, adjustments common. It was difficult to maintain a family budget on such an uncertain and scanty income. Besides, his connections with the National Guard had become more exacting of his time and attention, for he had become captain of the Fourth Battery of Light Artillery. Therefore, toward the close of 1881, he turned in his key to No. 4 Myers Block, and took down his sign.

Again he thought of public service. A group of eighty-six prominent Toledoans, learning of an approaching change in the office of railroad commissioner, petitioned Governor Foster to appoint Hopkins to that position. Their attempt was unsuccessful. As William Lawrence, First Comptroller of the Treasury, explained to Mrs. Hopkins: "I know and esteem your husband as a friend very much. I would cheerfully do him any favor in my power. But before the receipt of your letter, I had promised to recommend another person . . . ." However, Lawrence was no doubt instrumental in procuring for Hopkins an appointment as assistant superintendent of construction for the new U. S. Custom House and Post Office. He served in that capacity from 1881 to 1888, when the building was completed; then he returned to auditing in the employ of the Northwestern Gas Company.

Twenty-five years had passed since he was mustered out of the army at Camp Chase. He had tried railroading, bookkeeping, auditing, art, and public office—all had proved to be

---

[14] For examples of his illustrations, see Harte's "Dow's Flats," in *Corn City's Compliments* (Toledo: George Smith and Nathaniel Dyer), IV (June, 1874), 1-2.

bread-and-butter jobs. His real and abiding interest was in the military.

In 1866, he had joined a group of veterans from Battery H, First Ohio Volunteer Light Artillery, which had fought on the Potomac and in the Gettysburg campaign. In July, 1867, it applied to the adjutant general for a grant of ordnance,[15] and the following year, as the officially organized Toledo Light Artillery, it received two bronze six-pounders. It was renamed the First Ohio Independent Battery in 1872, and retained that title until it was attached to the National Guard as the Fourth Battery Light Artillery, with First Lieutenant O. J. Hopkins commanding, on November 7, 1877.[16] Three days later, Lieutenant Hopkins was elected captain.

He was recommissioned captain in 1882 and again in 1887. In 1890, he was appointed major of the First Regiment Light Artillery, O.N.G., and was recommissioned in 1895. The following year, he was made lieutenant colonel. The regiment comprised eight batteries with a total complement of 550 men.

While he was captain of the battery he compiled and published a tactical manual for the Gatling gun,[17] which, because of its clarity, completeness, and accuracy, was officially recommended for use by the United States Army and was adopted by the National Guard organizations of many states.[18] A revised and illustrated edition was in use as late as 1900.

At the outset of the Spanish-American War, the Governor called up all but three batteries of the Regiment, converted them to infantry, and attached them to the Tenth Ohio Infantry Regiment. The fourth, Battery D, was not called up—an act of political intrigue that deeply hurt Colonel Hopkins. At the close of the war, by order of the Governor, the artillery regiment was disbanded.[19] As a retired officer, Lieutenant Colonel Hopkins was given a clerkship in the Financial Divi-

[15] Letter from Adjutant General B. R. Cowan to C. A. Hall of Toledo, July 8, 1867.
[16] Cf. Special Order No. 239 by Adjutant General C. W. Karr, November 7, 1877 (Battery Order Book, p. 52).
[17] *Gatling Gun Tactics* (Toledo: Montgomery and Vrooman, 1886; Columbus: H. C. Lilley & Co., 1887).
[18] The *Zanesville Courier*, June 25, 1895, states that the Army and Navy Co., New York, published the manual in French, Spanish, and German translations.
[19] See the *Toledo Blade*, February 11, 1905, for an illustrated article on the First Regiment, and many encomiums for its Lieutenant Colonel.

sion of the Adjutant General's office in Columbus. Ironically enough, he was back again at auditing.

For ten years he had been on the regimental staff, and in that time "he probably did more to perfect the National Guard Service in Ohio than any other man in the state." [20] His was a commanding figure and a directing mind in all of the Guard's activities—serving on committees; [21] attending state conventions, encampments, and commemorations; marching in parades; participating in field practice and armory routines; and serving on special assignments. He was in command of his battery when it was called out for the protection of Toledo during the Great Railroad Strike of 1877, the plot of the "Dynamiters" at the Paulding Reservoir in May, 1887, and the mining riots of 1894. His erect, imposing figure, clothed in the colorful uniform of the Guard, seated on his favorite white horse, and riding at the head of a procession as its grand marshal, was for Toledoans an emblem of national security and civic pride. He enjoyed this esteem and affection to the end of his life.

The *Zanesville Courier,* reporting on the unanimous renomination of Major Hopkins at the state convention of the First Regiment Light Artillery in January, 1895, said of him:

> The popularity of Major Hopkins rendered opposition impossible . . . . He is one of the most picturesque figures in Ohio soldiery and is a recognized authority on matters military to which he has devoted nearly a quarter of a century . . . and is the ranking officer of the state in point of service in the Guard. His magnificent physique and soldierly bearing is complemented by a happy disposition, and his geniality and readiness to extend sympathy and assistance to his fellow-soldiers have endeared him to the Guard of Ohio . . . . He possesses brilliant military and social attainments . . . .

To this the *Times Recorder* added: ". . . He is a most thorough and accomplished gentleman. There is perhaps no one in the service more revered than he."

[20] Cf. C. S. Van Tassel, *Men of Northwestern Ohio* (Toledo: C. S. Van Tassel, 1898), p. 95.

[21] In 1883 and 1884, he served on the State Committee on Permanent Organization of the National Guard, and in 1901, on the editorial advisory board of the *Cleveland Plain Dealer* for the preparation of a history of the Ohio National Guard.

Almost simultaneously, the editor of the Glouster *Valley Gazette,* on the occasion of the arrival there of Major Hopkins with a carload of clothing and provisions that he and his men had obtained in Toledo for the relief of those who suffered the effects of the mining riots of the preceding month, remarked in the editorial column:

> We found the major to be a most genial and consistent gentleman . . . . The genial, warm-hearted major is just the kind of a gentleman whom we always love to clasp by the hand. In every utterance during his conversation with us, his sympathy went out in deep earnestness for the distressed people of this valley . . . .

This comment must have pleased the Major even more than the commendatory letter from President McKinley for "the spirit of kindness manifested by the Guard" and for his comprehensive report on the conditions found in the mining communities of the Valley.

Hopkins rarely talked about his personal experiences in the war; but at times, like many another veteran, he paused to look back and to hold things in remembrance, as in a letter addressed to Captain Pardee at the time of the annual reunion of the old Forty-second Regiment, at Akron, in 1882.

FOURTH BATTERY, O.N.G.
LIGHT ARTILLERY, TOLEDO, OHIO
Captain George K. Pardee,

DEAR COMRADE,

I am in receipt of your kind invitation to be present at the eighteenth annual reunion of our regiment at Akron, Ohio, 30th inst., and I thank you for remembering me. I am, however, compelled by business engagements to forego the pleasure of meeting with you this year. I shall, however, upon that day think of my old comrades in arms and recall some of the incidents of the days long gone; of the marches by day and by night; the hardships as well as the pleasures of our army life; the glorious deeds of the Forty-second, its wild yell and rush (for rations, when hungry), the gallant charges made (against the defiant bees' nest) in the Big Sandy Valley, where honey was wanted to flavor the ancient hardtack, and how we followed Tom (Hutchins) through the darkness to where the savory hen sat on her midnight roost; how, at Vicksburg, we, on the 22nd of May, '63, started to go into the city by a short-cut, and some fellows behind a big pile of dirt shot in our direction, and—and—we came away, and waited for formal invitation to visit the city in due form.

These scenes and a thousand others flash across my memory as I think of the approaching reunion; and whilst I think of it, let us not forget the services of those patient, long-suffering patriots whose wearied cry at early dawn betokened, alas! too often for them, a breakfast of cypress rails seasoned only with meagre strips of wagon-covers, or perhaps only a cold lunch of wagon-tongue and hoop-iron, too often their only diet. I say, as you gather in fraternal meeting again, drop a tear for the army mule, without whose faithful work the Union would have been lost, and the rebel flag floating over this country.

The next to claim our sympathy is the private soldier, and if by chance one turns up at the reunion, speak to him kindly and assure him that, *next to the army mule,* he is foremost in the hearts of his countrymen; that he *did* have some hand in suppressing treason, and that his name will be inscribed high upon the roll of fame (at some Soldier's Home), and when all the Generals, the Colonels, and the Captains are provided for at Washington, he may aspire to preferment, either as assessor or constable, or some such lucrative office, and "may the Lord have mercy on his soul" as his hair silvers with gray, and he treads down the hill of life (with a hand-organ), playing "The Girl I Left Behind Me."

Convey my old love to the boys who remember me, and trusting you may have the usual good time, I am,

Fraternally yours,
O. J. HOPKINS
Late of Co. K, 42nd O.V.I.

Five years later, another reunion invitation brought the following response.

TOLEDO, OHIO
August 25, 1887

Captain P. H. Foskett,
Medina, Ohio
MY DEAR FRIEND AND COMRADE,

I am in receipt of yours of recent date (as the prize-fighter said when his adversary struck him below the belt), and I hasten to return the fire.

Let me say now, since you mention it, there was once upon a time a war between the South and the North, and in that war there were a few regiments from Ohio, one of which sailed into the vortex, so to speak, with the number 42 upon its battle-flag, and 40 rounds of ammunition in its cartridge boxes, and the receipt of your letter reminds me that in the first three years of that war I affectionately ate the wormy crackers and hunted the festive grayback with the afflicted heros of that regiment.

Nearly a quarter of a century has slipped away since then, and my memory cannot be trusted in the light of truth to undertake any rehearsal of the events of that experience of mine in the army, yet, with the garrulous proclivity common to the veterans of that war, I still keep on tap a goodly stock of old chestnuts to crack upon the rising generation. Chestnuts so often cracked perhaps, that, like all lies often told and well stuck to, they become veritable truths in the mind of the author of them.

But to return to my text. Have you not in later years, Captain, learned with some chagrin and disappointment that our Regiment did not, alone and single-handed, put down the rebellion, that we actually had some assistance in that work?

If you have not thought of this, then I ask you to read *The National Tribune* wherein thousands are now individually claiming to have cleaned out Jeff. Davis and his Confederates without any assistance from outsiders. No, Foskett, my old friend and fellow *tramp,* my share and yours of this great achievement are so insignificant that they are hardly worth the mention.

We had *help;* there is no use denying that fact. For instance, when your ethereal form sank waist deep in the mire of

Chickasaw Bayou in that attempt of yours to enter Vicksburg without a formal invitation, there were several others
around you, although you may not have known it at the time,
but you certainly do remember the helping hand I gave you to
pull you out of the mud. And there was Lieut. Pardee with a
bundle of love-letters, a daguerreotype, a telephone directory,
the latest baseball score, and several certificates of Natural
Gas Stock in his pocket to stop the bullet aimed at his vitals.
There were Hutchins, Gid. Kinninger, Hubble, the Kreider
twins, the writer, and several other brilliant Brigadiers, following in your wake as a moral support in the charge you
made. That you failed in your attempt to seize the Rebel
stronghold then and there, was no fault of yours, and history
must record that, owing to the bad roads and the lateness of
the season, Vicksburg could not be so taken, and that the
honor of finally capturing that City a few months later, remained for the writer, with the able assistance of General
Grant.

Perhaps, Captain, my memory is a little defective on the
minor details of your campaigns, but of one thing I am certain: no Southern hen ever found a roosting-place too high for
the soldiers from Medina County. No meek and lowly porcine
wallower in the dismal swamps of Louisiana, or long-legged,
single-breasted rooter after acorns on the slopes of the Cumberland range, ever escaped the eagle eyes and swift vengeance
of the Men of Ashland, nor did the sting of the festive mountain bee deter Tom Hutchins and the Bellefontaine Boys from
sipping sweet nectar from the busy hive.

All these eccentricities of genius as displayed by the 42nd,
crowd upon the memory, but of all our glorious achievements,
none shine more radiantly than the charge we made on that
vast array of provender spread by the good citizens of Wheel-
ersburgh on our return from Cumberland Gap. No experience
of the war more indelibly impressed itself upon my memory
than the terrible pangs of colic incident to that feast. There,
foundations were laid for future pensions and unmarked soldiers' graves.

How and in what manner we managed to *back out* of that
patriotic little town in broad daylight without paying our

board bills, will at least be remembered by the oldest inhabitants and the girls now grown to womanhood. To me, in my then undudelike attire, the recollection brings to my damask cheek a blush of modest shame. However, we left no cards, and the incidents of our visit may (who knows?) now be forgotten. (N.B.—I have bought an entire new suit of clothes since then.)

But seriously, Captain, I would like to meet the boys again and swap romances a few hours with them in this coming reunion. Having but just recently returned from an encampment of my regiment of Ohio National Guards at Delaware, and finding my business affairs needing my undivided attention for the next thirty days, I shall be obliged to forego the pleasure this year. To say that I regret this, is to faintly express my disappointment, and I must be content to send through you, instead, my regrets and a soldier's love and greeting to all my old comrades.

Trusting to hear from you after the reunion, and that the boys will have had a good time, I am as ever,

Yours in fond recollection,

O. J. HOPKINS, *late Serg't, Co. K.*

In the spring, twenty-eight years after Appomattox, Hopkins, accompanied by his wife and young son Benjamin, visited some of the battlefields, camps, and towns that he had known as a soldier. From Middlesborough, Kentucky, Mrs. Hopkins wrote a motherly letter home to her daughter Cordelia, in Toledo.

MIDDLESBOROUGH, KY.
May 6th, 1893.

MY DEAR DELIA,

We went up into the Gap this morning. Two horses and a surrey. You never saw such roads or such climbers as the horses! Part of the time, we were hanging downwards; part of the time, expecting to go head-first forward. However, we got along nicely. Had good quiet horses, and a good driver, "who was a slave during the war." Papa was just wild! We found lots of places he could remember. Saw the stone he used to sit on, that marks the corner of the three states, Kentucky, Tennessee, and Virginia.[22] It is a large square stone of white granite. Has 1859 in large letters and the names of the three Governors of each state at that time. It is a wonder the soldiers didn't hack it to pieces.

Trees have grown up, but the breastworks and rifle pits are still there. We were in the rifle pits of one fort called "Lyons," and there, behind the works, in a trench, were lots of bones of human beings, all bleached and all in pieces. I have a stone I picked up there for you. I also picked up one at the foot of the stone that marks the three states, and one up at the Pinnacle. That is at the top, and it is a precipice on the Tennessee side. It is where our boys hurled the spiked cannon from, when they evacuated. It is 2,000 feet high.

I send some flowers picked from the spot where your father's tent was; at least, as near as he could locate it. He thought it was the exact spot. At that time, they had little tents. Afterwards, not any. The yellow is for you; the violets, for baby; the white, for Annie; and the pink locust, for Perry.[23] The tree was growing right in the middle.

Papa is about wild! He is down on the front veranda (*of the hotel*) sketching the mountains on that side and talking to an ex-rebel Captain. He was at the siege, but on the other side. He seems like a very nice man; is fifty-five, now. Was in a Kentucky regiment. They are having a very nice time. Ben is with them; he is real nice, but I can see he thinks his side was a little bit better. I left and came up stairs.

They have a parrot here, who roams at will. She is now out in the hall by my door, calling at the top of her voice: "Polly? Here, Polly, Polly? You, Polly!" She makes me nervous. She speaks as plain as a person . . . .

Well, Polly has gone upstairs to bed, she said. I went out into the hall, and the housekeeper came and took her. Polly said: "Come on, Mammy, take me to bed. Polly sleepy." She took her on her finger and Polly shut her eyes, and as they started upstairs, she called "Good-bye!" Bennie had come upstairs, and he haw-hawed; so did Polly. The housekeeper says

---

[22] See page 31. The road they followed was probably the one which at that time was called "Forest," or "Harlan," Road.

[23] They had five children: Annie, Oliver Perry, Cordelia, Benjamin, and Julia.

the first thing in the morning, when Polly gets awake, she will ask: "Get me a cup of coffee, Mammy." She will call for it and cry until she gets it. You should have heard Polly laugh while she was telling it! She said Polly knew the difference between good and bad coffee, and that she wanted it sweet like molasses.

We go to Cumberland Gap Monday evening. There is a train from here at five in the morning and seven in the evening; as it only takes one half an hour, we prefer sunset to sunrise. Think now we will leave Cumberland Gap Wednesday morning for Knoxville.

I found a piece of a lock, like from a camp chest, right where Company B, 42nd. O.V.I. had their Head Quarters. I happened to step on it. It was all grown over, and flowers were growing in the keyhole. Papa found half of a Union canteen among the bones I told you of, and Bennie found a piece from a Rebel's further down. In Fort Lyons, he also found a piece of a camp kettle hook. This is a lovely place. Well, goodbye, and write soon.

Lovingly,
MAMMA.

The next day, at the Gap, Bennie and his father went up into the cavern that Hopkins had explored during the Cumberland Campaign (see pages 29–30). Because the day was rainy and muggy, Mrs. Hopkins stayed behind in their room.

At Knoxville, she was delighted to see the house of Parson Brownlow, the fearless "Fighting Parson," and wished that she might have met him. During their stay, his widow gave her an engraved portrait of her husband. They then hurried on to Chattanooga, and Jackson, Mississippi. On their way back, they visited Nashville and the old camp ground. Before he left the city, Mr. Hopkins wrote his last letter to be dated from Nashville, not to a young lady in Bellefontaine, but to a young daughter in Toledo.

NASHVILLE, TENN.
May 14, 1893.

DEAR DAUGHTER,

We left Chattanooga yesterday at 2 P.M., arriving here at 7:30 P.M. Passed through a corner of Alabama and Georgia, up through Bridgeport, Tullahoma, Murfreesboro, and other noted scenes of strife in the War. This morning, we hired a *gentle* horse and dray, and drove out to our old camp ground near Fort Butler.

The ground is all in cultivation, except the fort itself, which only shows a series of high mounds, overgrown with briars and rank weeds and young shrubbery. This fort was built by our Regiment in 1864–5, and is about the only land-mark from which I could take my bearings, except the old brick house,[24] the headquarters of our regiment, where your Ma and I lived (or rather, fed) when stationed here. It has changed hands many times since the war, and is now occupied by a young Scotch farmer and his family. The house is just as it was then, and your Ma sends flowers gathered in the yard in front.

Just back of this old house, we found an old plantation darkie who lived on the place when our camp was pitched on the slopes to the right of his little cabin. He remembered Colonel Butler and us, and was often around when our offi-cers' mess were at dinner in the old brick building. He was as glad to see us as though we were old friends, and told us many anecdotes of the old days. He picked us a quart of cher-ries from trees growing on the site of the old camp. Said he had plowed up an old musket barrel, and used it for a long time for a fire poker, but one day he left it with the wrong end laying in the fireplace, and it *went off* like a cannon. He could not believe that he wasn't shot for some time after, turned a sommersault, and ran out of the cabin, etc. The story was very comical. Said he would hunt up the old gun barrel and send it to me.

Nashville has changed so much that I can hardly find my way around it. This afternoon, we will take a car and go out to Fort Negley. We have nice accomodations at this hotel [the "Nicholson"], but just at present it is filled full of Bap-tist preachers and their families here, attending a conference, convention, or pow-wow of some kind. Don't know if they are of the hard- or soft-shell species.

Flowers in this country are in full bloom and are very plen-

[24] He drew a sketch of it in ink at the head of the letter.

tiful; also strawberries and other early fruits and vegetables. We will leave here for St. Louis, via Evansville, some time tomorrow. Am having a good time, and are in good health. Look for us home when you see us. Take good care of baby,[25] and see that the doors and windows are *locked up* every night.

With love to all,
YOUR FATHER.

When the travelers arrived home in Toledo, Major Hopkins found a letter on his desk from G. B. Cockrell, a resident of Cumberland Gap and a trustee of the "Monumental Association," who was interested in identifying the location of certain landmarks of the battleground; his son had accompanied Major Hopkins from the cavern to the "old well by the Commissary," and had reported to his father the information he had gathered. Mr. Cockrell's queries must have gone unanswered, however, for the next year he wrote another, more detailed letter.

CUMBERLAND GAP, TENN.
Nov. 26, 1894

Major O. J. Hopkins,
Toledo, Ohio.

DEAR SIR,

Since your visit to this place on May 9, 1893, I became very much interested in opening pits, well, etc. in which Gen. Morgan's army deposited such things as would hamper their retreat, and buried them to prevent them from falling into the hands of the enemy. I had some success in one, finding 10,000 lbs. of lead, a thousand screwdrivers, 6,000 lbs. of cannon balls, and many other things. I have also been prospecting for what my son calls the "Hopkins Well" in the bottom or slope of the Kentucky side. He was with you from the Cave to where you showed him as being near the spot, but he now lives in Lexington, Ky., and as I desire more particularities, I write to you for them. I enclose you a rough sketch of the Gap; will you kindly point out to the best of your recollec-

[25] Their youngest child, Julia.

tion and return to me, and if I should be so lucky as to find
it, I will notify you at once, and whatever may be found you
shall have whatever and as much as you desire from it.

Yours truly,

G. B. COCKRELL.

*Major Hopkins answered promptly, marking on the dia-
gram the probable locations of certain sites. Mr. Cockrell's
next letter described further developments in the search for
caches.*

CUMBERLAND GAP, TENN.
Dec. 10, 1894.

Major O. J. Hopkins,
Toledo, Ohio.

MY DEAR SIR,

Your very welcome letter was received more than a week
ago, and would have answered sooner, but had hoped to have
the pleasure of reporting to you before this the finding of the
well. I have had hands at work the whole week passed, but
at this writing have made no discovery. I began at the old
chimney and dug S.E. 20 feet, 6 feet deep, then from beginning S.W. 20 feet, then a line between the two about in this
shape [a diagram appeared here].

You have no conception of how many opinions we have
heard expressed by various old soldiers while exploring. An
old gentleman now here that belonged to the Nineteenth Kentucky, named Price, says that he camped just above the old
Warehouse toward the Gap and not more than 100 feet from
the old log hut with chimney, and that there never was a
well there, but was one one-half mile out on the Harlan Road.
He however came back the next morning and said that during the night he had studied the matter over very carefully
and he remembered very well there was one, and he could
plainly see in his mind two large rocks on either side of the
well some distance down, but could not locate it.

There are at all times parties here that was in the 1862
campaign with Morgan, and are hunting for those things
they hid then, expecting some day to return and get them.

Some are successful; others are not. Some hunting for cannon; others, guns, lead, etc. And a party has just left hunting
for the murdered Paymaster's money, done in the spring of
1863. From what I have seen and heard in the last month, I
am pursuaded that he was murdered by two or more U.S.
soldiers in camp here, and the money securely hid, expecting
to hereafter get it. The parties that have been looking for it
are sons of old soldiers. Well, if I should continue in this
strain, you would really brand me as a crank. I am not, but
while I have a great number of relics, I would like to make
it attractive as possible and to divide with my friends.

I enclose you an article from the *Century Magazine*[26] that
may remind you somewhat of old times, but before I forget
it, do you know anything of the pit below the well that has
been opened, and the Magazine that was on the side of the
hill above where I am now digging? Members of the First
Tennessee say that a pit was dug by Col. Patterson of the
Engineer Corps about 20 feet square and 25 feet deep in between the two, but they differ so widely that I have wasted
no time on it. By the by, young Patterson is living down on
the Little Tennessee River.

Mr. Bales—J. H. Bales—is the name of the gentleman
with whom you stopped while at the Gap. He sends compliments in return also to the Madam and Son. Thanking you
for your kind letter, and hoping to see and know of you, and
that I may have the pleasure soon of going over the ground
with you, I am,

Yours Truly,
G. B. COCKRELL.

P.S.—I have located and intend to placard "Hopkins'
Rock." Am also under obligations for the likeness.

*The following spring, having made little progress in locat-
ing "Hopkins' Well" and "Col. Patterson's Pit" after long
and laborious search, Mr. Cockrell wrote again to Major
Hopkins.*

---

[26] David Dudley Warner, "Southern Lands" (December, 1890). The article
was written from "The Pinnacle," Middlesborough, Kentucky.

CUMBERLAND GAP, TENN.
May 26, 1895.

Major O. J. Hopkins,
Toledo, Ohio

DEAR SIR,

Since writing you in October, I have had considerable trouble with claimants for the war relics that I had unearthed here. That has, with the cold and wet weather, prevented the continuance of work, but with a setback to claimants and the return of good weather, and the sanction of the Treasury Department, I propose to spend some little time and money trying to uncover what we now call the "Hopkins Well" and the "Col. Patterson Pit," in which (when General Morgan re-equipped most of his men with new and improved guns) the major part were thrown. I feel assured that you will pardon me for again bothering you with questions, etc., but there is no other way for me to obtain the desired information but to enlist the aid of those that were here at that time.

Charlie Patterson has a map made by his father. I have seen it and know of a fact that it is not perfectly correct. The principal magazine that was in the mountain side S.W. from Hopkins well was, according to his map, almost north from the pit that he had dug. I have examined very carefully for it with much labor, and am almost certain that it is not there. He perhaps made his map in after years when reflecting upon the scenes that transpired in and around the Gap.

Mr. Williams, who belonged to a Tennessee regiment and who also lives here, now says that on the evening before the evacuation, his regiment and one other that was on the south side of the mountain were marched up to the head of the gulch that leads down to where your well is, and in going up the gulch as they marched in double column were ordered, when opposite Patterson's pit, to throw in their arms, which they did, going perhaps (as he thinks) 200 feet further to a long building standing just on the brink of what is now known as "Headquarters," and about 75 feet, as shown on the little plat sent you, from where I opened the well, they drew new guns.

It is strange to say, that out of the many that come here, they can locate the building from which they drew their guns, but no two can agree where the pit was where they dumped the old ones. Do you remember anything about this pit? Do you remember anything about where Morgan hid any of his cannon? There are five pieces here that he said had not been found. There are two men within ten miles of this place that assisted in burying two brass pieces, that have said to me that they would locate them for $25, and if not found, would pay the cost incurred. I shall give them the opportunity.

I dug fifteen pits, not less than six feet deep, with an X-trench, in search of your well, and want to go at it again soon, but felt that it would be advisable to write to you again, thinking perhaps after reflecting over the matter, you might say something that would lead me on to it, the first attempt. I have just been conning your letter of more than six months ago, and think I see something between the lines that had been overlooked before. That was [that] the water seemed to trickle in between the rocks and that the well was only from 12 to 15 feet deep. There is no rock at that depth near the spot marked, nor has it filled in anywhere around the base of the slope more than six inches since the war, for I find grape-shot bullets, pieces of chain, etc. at that depth. After due reflection, my opinion was that it must be near the base of the hill. I propose not to quit until I find the Hopkins well, and if you can think of either a rock, log, or tree, by which you can further assist, it will be highly appreciated, and I hope also that when I write you again, that I may be able to report its discovery and contents, and also to know what you desire most of the find. Mr. Bales, with whom you stopped at the Gap, and my son send kind regards.

Yours Truly,
G. B. COCKRELL.

Major Hopkins replied at once and inquired about hotel rates; he intended to visit the Gap again shortly, but for some unknown reason was unable to go. It must have been imperative, for no other memory of his war years was more vivid, more personal, than his part in the gallant defense of the Gap and Morgan's dramatic withdrawal from his encircled stronghold.

In June of the next year, Mr. Cockrell's hopes of finding the well and the pit had risen again. He reported the statement of Captain Angel of the Forty-ninth Regiment, Indiana V.I. that the pit was south of the fort in the gulch; and that

the first thing thrown in was a thousand picks and shovels . . . followed by everything from the large quartermaster's tent nearby, and that late in the evening various regiments and companies were marched up and threw in their guns—mostly Springfield rifles, cartridge-boxes, and bayonets—and drew from the same tent the Belgian guns;[27] and that the reason for that was because each regiment was ordered to carry 80 rounds of ammunition, and there was not 20 rounds to the man for the Springfields.

Mr. Cockrell added that he would continue the search, and would give Major Hopkins his choice of any relics he found. He suggested again that they should look for "Hopkins Well" together. But it was too late; Hopkins affairs had become too complicated, and he could not get away for a visit.

Time had already blurred the once sharp outlines of land and memory. The War of the Rebellion had receded into the haze of history.

On November 18, 1902, Colonel Hopkins left his desk in the Adjutant General's office in Columbus to join his wife for dinner at the home of a friend, Colonel H. M. Taylor. He never reached his destination. Alighting from a northbound streetcar on High Street, he waited for the passing of a southbound car, only to be struck by another following too closely and too fast behind the first one. The force of the impact killed him almost instantly.

The news of his death made headlines throughout the state and in other parts of the nation. Columbus, Toledo, Cincinnati, and Cleveland papers, in particular, were filled with personal and official tributes to the man and the soldier, detailing his war record, his accomplishments with the National Guard, his civic services, and his personal attributes.

[27] These long, heavy rifles, manufactured in Belgium, were used early in the war; they were of great range and accuracy, but, as Grant said, were "almost as dangerous to the person firing them, as to the one aimed at."

"A gentleman in all that the word implies," wrote the *Ohio State Journal,* "a fine soldier and of the most sunny disposition, he numbered his friends by the hundreds . . . ." A Toledo paper printed the following statement:

> Colonel Hopkins was a brave soldier, an honorable gentleman, but he was also one of the most modest of men, and stories of his valor in the War had always to be told by other tongues than his. And to a valiant soul and modest demeanor he added the grace of a gentle, cheerful heart, a steadfast loyalty that endeared him to his family and friends and rendered his death the greater bereavement . . . .

One of the largest newspapers in the state, the *Columbus Dispatch,* made the following comment:

> Colonel Hopkins was beloved by them all [in the Adjutant-General's office]. His quiet love of humor made him a participant . . . of all the little amenities that go on in such a department. Of innocent fun he was a great lover, but nothing coarse or brutal received his encouragement. Endowed with splendid health, he carried at the age of almost sixty the hearty relish for the pleasures of life that young men in their "teens" are supposed to have a monopoly on.

The National Guard and the Grand Army of the Republic accorded him full military honors. In Columbus, the cortege was escorted to the railroad station by the local cavalry troop, a battery of artillery, and a detachment of the Fourth Ohio Infantry. The following day, in Toledo, the members of Battery D, First Artillery, O.N.G.—his favorite organization —escorted the flag-draped casket to Memorial Hall where the body lay in state for three hours, flanked by an Honor Guard from the Battery. It was almost submerged in a mass of floral tributes from survivors of the old Toledo Cadets, the Toledo Artillery Veterans' Association, and local G.A.R. posts in the state; the Adjutant-General's Office, Battery A of Cleveland, Battery B of Cincinnati, and officers in Marion; and innumerable groups, neighbors, and friends. Long before the hour set for the ceremony, carriages lined the route of the cortege, and crowds gathered in and about Memorial Hall for the services.

In a moving eulogy, Reverend F. D. Kelsey, pastor of the Central Congregational Church, spoke of him as one who, "when wanted, was always in his place, a faithful citizen on whom all could depend . . . so quiet in his life that men failed to realize how grand a citizen we had among us." His life "was peculiarly centered around the flag of our country, . . . never did social occasion meet in his house, but the central decorations were the loved flag for which he had fought and suffered . . . . His was a home that held high the standard of patriotism and self-denial for the land of liberty and freedom . . . ." The listeners were deeply moved, not only by the eloquence of the speaker, but by the realization of their own personal loss in the death of their fellow citizen.

The G.A.R. ritual followed the eulogy. At the head of the cortege was the stand of colors that had been presented forty years before by Governor Dennison to Colonel Garfield's Forty-second Regiment, O.V.I., at Camp Chase on the eve of its departure for the front. Behind the colors came the caisson, and then, in military formation, the field and staff officers of the First Brigade Sixth Infantry, members of G.A.R. posts and the Toledo Artillery Veterans' Association, and Battery D, Light Artillery, O.N.G.

At the grave, a detail of artillerymen fired a salute, and a bugle sounded taps under the bleak autumn sky. Owen Johnston Hopkins, former Sergeant in Company K of the old Forty-second, O.V.I., had mustered out for the last time.

And what of the sweetheart "wife" of his wartime letters? Julia Hopkins died February 16, 1907, having never fully recovered from the shock of her husband's death. Her unswerving loyalty to her country, her interest in the perpetuation of patriotic principles, and her well-trained mind and boundless energy had long made her a leader in city and state. She enthusiastically participated in the activities of the Women's Relief Corps, and committees for the Xenia Orphan's Home and the Soldier's Home. She was a member of the Daughters of the American Revolution, a charter member of the National Society U.S. Daughters of 1812; and a member of the Hermitage Association of Nashville, the Lucas County

Pioneer and Historical Society, the Lucas County Memorial Association, and the Progress Club of Toledo. Yet she found time to be a devoted wife and mother and a generous friend.

At her funeral, the Women's Relief Corps of the G.A.R. took charge of the service. She was buried in a shroud of the American flag at the side of her husband.

MUSTER ROLL OF COMPANY K, FORTY-SECOND REGIMENT, O.V.I.

Captain Andrew Gardner, Jr. Bellefontaine. Commissioned at Camp Chase, Ohio, September 9, 1861. Resigned, January 28, 1863.

First Lieutenant Thomas L. Hutchins. Bellefontaine. Appointed Captain, January 28, 1863, *vice* Gardner, resigned. Wounded at Port Arkansas.

Second Lieutenant Porter H. Foskett. Medina. Appointed Captain, Company D, after serving as First Lieutenant, Company B. Resigned, left service.

First Sergeant Calvin C. Marquis. Bellefontaine. Reduced to ranks at own request; afterwards deserted at Portland, Ohio, December 19, 1862.

Second Sergeant Robert W. Southard. Logan County. Reduced to ranks, May 4, 1863.

Third Sergeant George G. Douglass. Bellefontaine. Promoted to First Sergeant to fill vacancy occasioned by promotion of A. B. Hubbell, January 28, 1863.

Fourth Sergeant William H. Leister. Bellefontaine.

Fifth Sergeant Martin McAllister. Hinckley. Detailed on detached duty at Plaquemine, Louisiana. Sent to Ohio, remaining until his term expired.

First Corporal Hiram W. Allmon. Bellefontaine. Promoted to Sergeant, December 16, 1862. Died in Hospital at New Orleans, August 25, 1863.

Second Corporal Isaac Thompson. Bellefontaine. Killed in Battle of Thompson's Hill, May 1, 1863.

Third Corporal Thomas Armstrong. Bellefontaine. Reduced to ranks at his own request, June 4, 1862.

Fourth Corporal Job S. Goff. Bellefontaine. Reduced to ranks, May 4, 1862. Discharged at Memphis, Tennessee.

Fifth Corporal Andrew J. Smith. Bellefontaine. Discharged at Memphis, Tennessee.

Sixth Corporal William C. Wilgus. Logan County. Reduced to ranks, May 1, 1862. (Van Voorhis promoted.)

Seventh Corporal Walter M. Crandall. Medina County. Reduced to ranks, January 3, 1863. (Hopkins promoted.) Wounded at Chickasaw Bayou, and discharged from service.

Eighth Corporal Orville N. McClintock. Medina. Reduced to ranks, May 23, 1862. Discharged from service, July 20, 1863.

Privates

Adams, William M. Cincinnati. Deserted the service at Cincinnati, November 5, 1862, while en route to Louisville, Kentucky.

Andrews, Joseph. Hinckley. Wounded at Thompson's Hill; arm amputated. Discharged, July 23, 1863.

Allmon, Ezra J. Bellefontaine. Promoted to Corporal, June, 1863.

Atkinson, William C. Logan County. Discharged, October 25, 1862.

Alden, Sidney S. Medina. Promoted to Corporal, May 23, 1862; to Sergeant, May 4, 1863.

Batch, Franklin O. Bellefontaine.

Beal, Calvin. Bellefontaine.

Baldwin, Alsinas. Logan County. Mortally wounded in assault on Vicksburg, May 22, 1863. Died, May 25, 1863, in Hospital.

Beales, Norval V. Logan County.

Ballinger, Samuel. Logan County. Discharged at Gallipolis, October, 1862.

Britton, Warren. Lunaville, Ohio. Discharged from service.

Batch, Joshua S. Bellefontaine. Died in Hospital at Ashland, Kentucky, of disease of the heart.

Buell, Samuel A. Hinckley. Served on detached duty in Fourth Wisconsin battery one year. Returned to company, August, 1864.

Bowman, Albert L. Medina. Promoted to Sergeant Major, May 23, 1862; to Second Lieutenant, March 3, 1863; to First Lieutenant, December 15, 1863. Wounded at Jackson, Mississippi.

Brandenburg, John. Logan County. Deserted at Louisville, Kentucky, April 12, 1862.

Ballinger, Isaac. Bellefontaine. Wounded accidentally in thumb, which was later amputated. (Portland recruit.)

Brown, Franklin A. Chatham Centre. Joined company at Portland, Ohio, October 26, 1862. On detached duty at Morganza.

Barnard, James W. Chatham Centre. (Portland recruit.) Served seventeen months in Fourth Wisconsin battery.

Bauer, Valentine. Medina County. (Portland recruit.)

Caskey, Jacob. Bellefontaine.

Callahan, John. Logan County.

Crandall, Lysander E. Medina. Sent to Hospital at Paducah, Kentucky, where he procured a discharge.

Clapp, George T. Medina. (Portland recruit.)

Clapp, Anson L. Medina. (Portland recruit.) Acting Wagon Master.

Drake, William H. Logan County. Discharged from service on account of consumption, August 24, 1863.

Dellman, Adam. Limaville.

Downes, Benjamin F. Zanesfield. Died in Hospital, Vicksburg, Mississippi, date unknown.

Elliott, William. Logan County. Discharged from service, March 13, 1863.

Fawcett, Asa. Logan County.

Gardner, George W. Bellefontaine.

Hubbell, A. B. Newburg. Promoted to Sergeant, May 23, 1862; to Second Lieutenant, January 28, 1863.

Hunt, Thomas C. Logan County.

Hoge, Andrew J. Logan County. Deserted at Memphis, December 19, 1862.

Hopkins, Owen J. Bellefontaine. Promoted to Corporal at Chickasaw Bayou, January 3, 1863; to Sergeant, August 31, 1863; to Quartermaster Sergeant, September 14, 1864.

Hartzler, Levi. Logan County.

Hickman, Franklin. Logan County.

Hobart, Milo A. Medina. Died at Paintsville, Kentucky, February 27, 1862, of typhoid fever.

Harris, George G. Medina. Killed in battle of Thompson's Hill, May 1, 1863.

Kauffman, Franklin (S.) Bellefontaine. Discharged from service, at Memphis, Tennessee, 1863.

Kreider, Jacob. Medina. Captured by the Rebels at Opelousas; afterward exchanged.

Kreider, Abraham. Medina. Served in regimental band as fifer.

Kinney, John. Logan County.

Marmon, Richmon(d). Zanesfield. Promoted to Corporal, June 4, 1862. Mortally wounded at Thompson's Hill, May 16, 1863; died May 18, 1863, at Grand Gulf.

Marmon, Henry R. Union County. Died at Piketon, Kentucky, March 23, 1863, of consumption.

Murdock, Oliver. Logan County. Died at Piketon, Kentucky, of chronic diarrhea.

Mitchell, Leonard H. Logan County. Died at Paintsville, Kentucky, February 7, 1862, of consumption.

Messick, William H. Logan County. Discharged from service at Hospital in New Orleans, January 26, 1864.

Myers, Benjamin F. Bellefontaine.

McFarland, William. Medina. Deserted at Cumberland Gap, September 17, 1862.

May, Franklin C. Medina. Discharged from service, January 6, 1863, on account of old age.

Morse, M. Vanburen. Limaville. Died at home (Limaville, Ohio), May 5, 1862.

Moore, Edward L. Bellefontaine. Discharged to be commissioned in Colored Regiment, May, 1863.

Mantz, Franklin R. Chatham Centre. (Portland recruit.) Promoted to Corporal, April, 1863.

McDonald, William. Medina County. Drafted for nine months. Discharged, July 15, 1863.

Osgood, J. S. Newburg. Discharged from service, October 6, 1862.

Oatman, Simon. Medina. Promoted to Corporal at Milliken's Bend, April, 1863.

Plummer, James. Bellefontaine. Discharged from service, October 27, 1862; general debility.

Perkins, Amos B. Logan County. Discharged from Regiment; transferred to Invalid Corps.

Pardee, George K. Medina. (Portland recruit.) Promoted to Second Lieutenant, July 25, 1862; to First Lieutenant, and then Captain, of Company D.

Rapp, Henry B. Logan County. Bass drummer in Regimental Band, and Leader.

Riddle, Alfred U. Hospital steward. Discharged from service, May 10, 1862.

Rossell, Jasper. Limaville. Died of intermittent fever, date unknown.

Runyan, Sanford T. Zanesfield. Wounded at Thompson's Hill, May 1, 1863.

Reese, William I. Medina. Discharged from service, October 26, 1862.

Richards, Fletcher G. Chatham Centre. (Portland recruit.)

Rickard, Cyrus A. Chatham Centre. (Portland recruit.) Promoted to Commissary Sergeant, September 14, 1864.

Ripley, Theodore F. Chatham Centre. Discharged from service at Vicksburg, Mississippi, August 9, 1862.

Rice, Daniel H. Chatham Centre. Died at Young's Point, Louisiana, February 13, 1863, of chronic diarrhea. Buried with the honors of war.

Stoll, Jacob. Logan County. Died at Plaquemine, Louisiana, March 29, 1864, of dropsy.

Southard, Leonard A. Logan County. Died at Cumberland Gap, September 5, 1862, of typhoid fever.

Southard, Sylvester E. Logan County. Promoted to Corporal, August 31, 1863.

Southard, Milton. Logan County. Discharged from service, April 30, 1862.

Southard, Joseph. Logan County. Died in service, March 3, 1864.

Smith, Robert W. Logan County.

Supler, Thomas C. Logan County. Died in Hospital at New Orleans, of chronic diarrhea, October 4, 1864.

Saunders, Mortimer E. Logan County. Discharged from service, October 16, 1862.

Saunders, Amos F. Logan County. Discharged from service, date not given.

Shauf, Henry. Limaville. Promoted to Corporal, April 30, 1863. Wounded at siege of Vicksburg.

Shaw, William. Medina County. Died of consumption at his home in Medina County, Ohio.

Sawtell, William. Medina. Discharged, April 10, 1863, by reason of wound received at Battle of Chickasaw Bluffs, December 29, 1862.

Styre, Samuel. River Styx, Ohio. (Portland recruit.)

Sickman, Samuel. River Styx, Ohio. (Portland recruit.) Captured by enemy near Opelousas, and afterward exchanged.

Turner, Quincy A. Medina. Discharged from service, March 3, 1863, at Milliken's Bend, Louisiana.

Tilley, Robert S. Medina. (Portland recruit.) Discharged from service, March 23, 1863.

Underwood, Elias. Limaville. Deserted at Louisville, Kentucky, in company with John Brandenburg, April 12, 1862.

Underwood, Hugh. Limaville.

Van Voorhis, Calvin C. Logan County. Promoted to Corporal, May 1, 1862. Killed at Vicksburg, May 22, 1863.

Vanvoorhis, Clark A. Logan County. Promoted to Corporal; to Sergeant, September 14, 1864.

Vandeuren, Don C. Hinckley. Wounded and right arm amputated, by reason of which he was discharged, September 29, 1863.

Wallis, David P. East Liberty, Ohio. Promoted to Corporal at Milliken's Bend. Wounded severely at Jackson, Mississippi, and discharged from service.

Winner, William H. Logan County. Discharged from service at Plaquemine, Louisiana, March 4, 1864, and afterward died.

Whitsell, James R. Limaville. Promoted to Corporal, June 18, 1863.

Ward, George H. Limaville. Deserted at Portland, Ohio, October 11, 1862. (Idiotic.)

Wallis, George M. Logan County. Discharged for general "profligacy."

Wallace, William. Medina. Discharged from service, and died soon after of disease contracted in the army.

Wilson, Andrew S. Bellefontaine.

Willard, Franklin B. Medina. Died April 25, 1862, of typhoid fever.

NOTE.—In a letter dated August 3, 1868, Captain Hutchins wrote the following to Lieutenant Hopkins: "Enclosed the History of Co. K, kept by you, hoping this will answer your purpose. I have one Copy of the Muster-out Roll. I am very careful to take good care of everything appertaining to the old Company, thinking it may be of benefit some day. I have all the Books, Muster and Pay Rolls, filed and put away in Company Desk and set in my Bed room. I often look at the old desk, and it brings to my mind many things that have passed . . . ."

Lieutenant Hopkins prefaced the copy of the Muster Roll in his 1869 manuscript with a note: "This was copied from the Rolls of the Company about the time of the Regiment's muster-out, and will be found correct. Some remarks are added by the writer from memory, but are reliable."—D(MS).

SERVICE RECORD OF OWEN J. HOPKINS

Enlisted as Private, Company K, Forty-second Regiment, Ohio Volunteer Infantry, Colonel James A. Garfield commanding, September 27, 1861. Took part in the campaign against General Humphrey Marshall in the Big Sandy River Valley, Eastern Kentucky, terminating in the battles of Middle Creek, or Prestonburg, January 10, 1862, and Pound Gap, March 15, 1862.

Returned with the regiment to Louisville, Kentucky and Lexington in the spring of 1862, when the Forty-second was assigned to the Third Brigade, Colonel John De Courcy commanding, of the Seventh Division of the Army of the Ohio under the command of General George W. Morgan. Was with that army in all its operations resulting in the capture of Cumberland Gap, Tennessee, participating in the engagements at Powell's Valley, June 13, 1862; Roger's Gap, June 18, 1862; Tazewell, August 6, 1862; and Big Springs, August 11, 1862. Took part in the celebrated retreat from Cumberland Gap to the Ohio River, in September, 1862.

Accompanied the regiment in the march to Charleston, West Virginia, up the Kanawha Valley, including a number of engagements with the enemy while on the march.

The regiment was then ordered to Memphis, where the Third Brigade, General Osterhaus commanding, joined the Third Division, Army of the Mississippi, Thirteenth Army Corps, General Sherman in command. Was in the battle of Chickasaw Bluffs and Chickasaw Bayou, Mississippi, December 26, 1862, to January 1, 1863. Promoted to Corporal, January 2, 1863.

Fought in the battle of Fort Hindman, or Arkansas Post, January 11, 1863, and in all the subsequent operations of the army under General Grant, including the battles of Grand Gulf, Mississippi, April 29, 1863; Port Gibson, April 30, 1863; Thompson's Hill, May 1, 1863; Champion Hill, May 16, 1863; Big Black River Bridge and Edward's Station, May 17, 1863; the siege and capture of Vicksburg, May 18 to July 4, 1863; and after the fall of Vicksburg, the three days fighting at Jackson, Mississippi, July 10 to 13, 1863.

August 11, 1863, was detailed to report to Camp Chase, Columbus, Ohio, to take charge of drafted men and escort them to the regiment, which had been ordered to New Orleans to support General Banks.

Promoted to Sergeant, August 31, 1863. Rejoined his regiment in New Orleans, October 28, 1863, and participated in the action at Brashear City and on the Teche River, returning to Plaquemine, Louisiana, in December, 1863.

Transported to Baton Rouge and engaged the enemy at Clinch River, May 3, 1864. Afterwards, joined Banks expedition at Simmsport on the Red River, May 18, 1864, and from Morganza, Louisiana, patrolled the rivers against guerrillas until expiration of service. Promoted to Quartermaster Sergeant, September 14, 1864. Mustered out with the non-commissioned staff, October 14, 1864.

Re-enlisted at Toledo, October 15, 1864, for one year, and commissioned First Lieutenant and Regimental Quartermaster, One Hundred Eighty-second, O.V.I., Colonel Lewis Butler commanding, October 21, 1864. Assigned to Army of the Tennessee, General Thomas in command, and stationed at Nashville until discharged, March 2, 1865. Recommissioned First Lieutenant, same regiment, June 6, 1865. Mustered out at Nashville, July 8, 1865.

LIST OF ARTICLES RECEIVED FROM CAPTAIN IRVIN BY OWEN J. HOPKINS, REGIMENTAL QUARTERMASTER, ONE HUNDRED EIGHTY-SECOND, O.V.I., NASHVILLE, TENNESSEE

November 18, 1864.

24	Mules	6	Water Buckets
6	Government Wagons	6	Feed Boxes
36	Government Wagon Bows	12	Single Set Wheel Mule Harness
6	Government Wagon Covers		ness
6	Double Trees	12	Single Set Lead Mule Harness
24	Single Trees		ness
6	Spreaders	6	Wagon Whips
6	Ridge Poles	24	Neck Straps
6	Tar Pots	24	Halter Chains

November 19, 1864.

1	Two Horse Ambulance	6	Horse Brushes
2	Mules	6	Bearing Chains
2	Sets of Mule Harness	6	Jockey Sticks
1	Water Bucket	6	Saddle Blankets
1	Wagon Whip		

November 25, 1864.

18	Mules	12	Single Set Lead Mule Harness
3	Government Log Wagons		ness
3	Double Trees	3	Wagon Whips
18	Single Trees	1	Curry Comb
3	Spreaders	8	Wagon Saddles
3	Tar Pots	3	Fifth Chains
3	Water Buckets	18	Neck Straps
3	Feed Boxes	3	Bearing Chains
12	Linch Pins, extra	18	Halter Chains
6	Single Set Wheel Mule Harness	3	Jockey Sticks
	ness	3	Saddle Blankets

A PRIVATE EXPENSE ACCOUNT,[1]
MARCH THROUGH JULY, 1865

March

7th	R.R. Fare, Bellefontaine to Indianapolis . .	$10.20
	Hack at Indianapolis	1.50
8th	Hotel Bill, Indianapolis	4.50
	R.R. Fare, Indianapolis to Jeffersonville . .	9.00
	1 pair Gaiters	4.00
	Lunch	.20
	Omnibus Fare, Louisville	1.30
	Contribution to a Blind Man	.50
9th	Hotel Bill, Louisville	6.25
10th	Hotel Bill, Nashville	7.00
	Hack Fare & Eatables	4.00
	1 pkge. Envelopes	.30
11th	Crockery Ware	2.70
12th	Spool of Thread, Coats No. 60	.20
15th	3 Lemons	.25
	Stays	.50
16th	Washing	.60
17th	Mess fund	5.00
18th	1 coarse Comb	.75
20th	1 Box Collars	.50
	Mess Fund	5.00
	Telegram	1.25
	Lunch	.60
25th	Table Cover (red & black checked woolen) .	4.50
	Window Curtain	1.00
26th	Carpet	6.75
29th	Bottle of Pomade	.50

[1] Like a true quartermaster's wife, Julia Hopkins kept a daily expense account in one of her husband's government ledgers during the first five months of their married life, March through July, 1865. The account covers the period between their arrival in Nashville after their wedding and Lieutenant Hopkins' mustering out, a period during which they lived for a time in Nashville and then in Toledo. Obviously, not all of their expenses found their way into the list, but enough of them, perhaps, to be of interest to readers a hundred years later.

April

1st	½ pint Camphor	$ .75
	1 bottle Turpentine	.40
	8 Postage Stamps	.25
4th	Pickles	.25
	Cincinnati *Gazette*	.50
5th	Washing	.40
	1 lb. Nails	.15
8th	Gingerbread	.30
	Candy	.75
	Riding Skirt	12.25
14th	Washing	2.00
16th	Postage Stamps	.18
19th	Paper, Cincinnati *Gazette*	1.60
20th	Washing	1.00
24th	3 Lemons	.25
25th	Socks	.40
	Portfolio	2.60
	Box of Collars	.50
	Lemonade	.50
26th	Cheese	.40
	Cake	.55
	Sutler, previous debts	25.00
27th	Fare to Louisville	15.00
	Oranges	.25
	Fare to Cinti	8.50
	Fare at Louisville	2.30
28th	Fare at Cinti	9.00
	Oranges	.60
	Fare to Bellefontaine from Cinti	8.40

May

1st	Bellefontaine to Toledo, fare	8.50
2nd	Bureau	30.00
	Hat	2.50
	Fan	4.50
	6 Oranges	.40
	Gingerbread	.40
3rd	Oranges	.15
	Cigar	.10
4th	Cooking Stove & Utensils	10.00
	Edgeing	.40
	Hooks & Eyes	.05
	Buttons	.23
	3 Spools Thread	.30
	Collar	.15

	Socks	$ 1.20
	Lamp Chimney	.25
6th	2 bus. Potatoes	2.00
	5 lbs. Steak	1.00
	1 Box Collars	.50
8th	2 cans Pine Apples	1.20
	Calico Dress	3.45
	Silk Sack	19.00
	Cologne	1.75
11th	Cocoa Oil	1.00
	Coal Oil	1.00
11th	pkg. of Envelopes	.20
	Ribbon	.60
	Neck tie	2.00
	Neck tie for Johns	.30
13th	Cocoa nut	.15
	Candy	.25
	Cash to Mother Hopkins	1.00
15th	Ginger	.10
	Molasses	.45
16th	2 yds. Lace	2.00
	Green Hair Ribbon	.30
17th	Beef	.75
	Onions	.15
	Radishes	.15
18th	Housewife	1.30
	Buttons for dress	.40
	Cream Pitcher	.40
	Eggs, Sugar & Butter	1.85
	Beef	.34
23rd	5½ lbs. Butter @30¢	1.65
	1 lb. Raisins	.30
	Saleratus	.05
	Bonnet	8.50
24th	Beef	.41
	Bread	.20
25th	Tacks	.10
26th	Sheeting & Pillow Ticks	5.50
	Dining room Table	7.00
27th	Sugar	1.00
	Tea	1.00
	Onions	.10
	Lettuce	.10
29th	Onions	.10
	Lettuce	.10
30th	Beef	.75
	Strawberries	.75

	1 Box Collars	$ .50
	Confectionary	.40

June

5th	Hat	5.25
	Dress	10.12
	Belt	.75
	Kid Gloves	2.00
	Gaiters	2.50
	Corset Stays	.25
3rd	Beef	1.00
	Indigo (blueing)	.50
	Starch	.15
12th	Beef	.40
13th	Wood	3.00

July

7th	Matches	.05
4th	Johns' Fare to Columbus	3.25
	Supper	.50
5th	Breakfast	.75
	Collars	1.00
	Fare to Cincinnati	2.50
	Bill, "Spencer House"	3.00
	Fare to Louisville	2.00
6th	Fare to Nashville	3.80
15th	Butter	1.00
	Meat	1.00
	Chicken for Mother Hopkins	.30
	Ginger	.20
18th	Gingerbread	.25
19th	Boots fixed	2.50
20th	Meat	.50
22nd	Meat	.59
	Onions	.05
	Bread	.10